OXFORD PALAEOGRAPHICAL HANDBOOKS

General Editors
R. W. HUNT   C. H. ROBERTS

GREEK LITERARY HANDS

A.D. 400–1600

BY

RUTH BARBOUR

formerly Fellow of St Cross College, Oxford

CLARENDON PRESS · OXFORD
1981

Oxford University Press, Walton Street, Oxford OX2 6DP
GLASGOW NEW YORK TORONTO MELBOURNE WELLINGTON
CAPE TOWN NAIROBI DAR ES SALAAM
DELHI BOMBAY CALCUTTA MADRAS KARACHI
KUALA LUMPUR SINGAPORE HONG KONG TOKYO

ISBN O 19 818229 5

Published in the United States
by Oxford University Press, New York

Typeset by Fotron SA, Athens, Greece
Printed in Great Britain
at the University Press, Oxford
by Eric Buckley
Printer to the University

TO

A. P. H.-T.-C.-B.

CONTENTS

PREFACE ix
ACKNOWLEDGEMENTS xiii
INTRODUCTION xv
BIBLIOGRAPHY xxxi
NOTES ON PLATES, DESCRIPTIONS, AND TRANSCRIPTIONS xxxv
PLATES 1-110, WITH DESCRIPTIONS 1
TRANSCRIPTIONS 31
INDEXES
I. MANUSCRIPTS ILLUSTRATED OR MENTIONED 45
II. DATES 48
III. PLACES CONNECTED WITH SCRIBES OR PATRONS 49
IV. SCRIBES 50
V. CONTENTS 51

PREFACE

There is much to be said for a ban on general surveys of Greek palaeography, and *a fortiori* on compressed summaries such as this. In the first place, they presuppose a solid basis of established facts about every feature of the physical appearance of vast numbers of manuscripts, which does not yet exist. Many more collections of facsimiles and studies of special categories of dated and placed manuscripts are needed first; though when all has been done, it seems unlikely that the data will ever yield a neat or clear-cut classification of Greek manuscripts. Secondly, the characteristics of a manuscript are difficult to describe or illustrate; in learning to judge dates or places of origin, books are no substitute for the personal inspection of large numbers of manuscripts or at least of facsimiles. Since the feature of a manuscript's make-up that is easiest to illustrate is the writing, any attempt at a survey is best made by giving the largest possible number of specimens of this. I therefore confine my attention to the writing to the exclusion of all other aspects of book production, and sacrifice the advantage of showing the layout of whole pages, as well as the extra space for comment on writing styles, in favour of the widest possible range of examples. The disadvantage of small illustrations I have tried to offset by referring to other published facsimiles.

To illustrate the development of Greek literary hands from 400 to 1600 within even the extended compass of 110 facsimiles requires that the examples be chosen on the most rigorously austere principles. My selection has been determined by the following considerations, usually in this order: (1) that every manuscript must be explicitly dated or fairly closely and certainly datable; (2) that there should be at least one good example of every major style of writing, and where necessary several, as widespread in time and space as possible; (3) that the place of writing or the identity of a known copyist should be explicit and not merely deduced; (4) that the manuscript should be of some intrinsic importance; (5) that it has not already been often reproduced. (1) and (2) cannot always both be attained to an equal degree: many of the most interesting individual and scholarly hands are undated.[1] The extreme difficulty of (3), in so far as place is concerned, needs stressing. Numerous pitfalls beset any attempt to deduce the scribal traditions of a particular place from place-names appearing in subscriptions, and so many hopeful deductions of this kind have been

[1] For the need to omit these I am now consoled by the excellent reproductions of many of the most interesting hands in Oxford manuscripts in Wilson, *Mediaeval Greek Bookhands*.

disseminated as facts that the point needs to be laboured by enumerating some of the possible ambiguities: mention of a scribe's place of origin suggests that he is not writing there, though he may have learned to write there; a patron's place of origin is likewise not necessarily the place of copying; even a manuscript said to have been copied in a place may be (and sometimes explicitly is) by a scribe from elsewhere, and which then is the 'centre of copying'? It should not be necessary to point out the fallacy of assuming the present home of a manuscript to be its place of origin without supporting evidence. Much work done on the localization of Greek manuscripts has not allowed for these uncertainties and is based on subjective judgements; the conclusions are not necessarily wide of the mark, but are not sufficiently well founded to use here. The paramount importance of (1), (2), and (3) and the difficulty of finding manuscripts that satisfy them all give (4) and (5) little chance to operate; this regrettably excludes some important manuscripts, particularly of classical authors (though some of these would be excluded by (5) and have sometimes been reproduced in full). In an attempt to help classicists, I have, with some diffidence, added references to classical manuscripts whose style of writing I think comparable to that of manuscripts illustrated here.

I have included what may seem a disproportionately large number of conventional hands from the middle period, because here there is least clear demarcation in styles and writing habits, and problems of dating and placing are correspondingly more difficult. If each style is not illustrated by several manuscripts of different dates and places, a misleading impression is created that the characteristics of one example are typical of that time and place alone and of no others, which is rarely the case. The far more numerous and interesting manuscripts that survive from the thirteenth and fourteenth centuries are being exhaustively and magnificently dealt with by Professor Turyn, and Renaissance scribes need equally large-scale treatment illustrating the hands of large numbers of scribes; my selection of both these categories is purely *exempli gratia*.

All possible ways of arranging illustrations that are not on loose sheets or at least each on a separate page have serious disadvantages: by shelf-mark is unthinkable; purely by date obscures the lines of development of different types of script that a history of writing should try to illuminate; by place is impossible owing to the ambiguity of the evidence. To arrange by styles of writing (a) involves subjective judgements which no two people — nor even one person at different times — will make alike; (b) has to find places equally for hands that have affinities with several groups and with none (to include only manuscripts easily classifiable in obvious styles would give a false impression of tidy development); (c) faces the final impossibility of herding the manuscripts into neat threes and fours to fill each page of plates without separating members of distinguishable groups or uniting incongruous bedfellows. I have nevertheless chosen this last arrangement because it does illuminate some strands in the development of different styles, and on the whole produces fewer meaningless combinations of images on one plate than any other. Since the purpose of this book is to trace what pattern there is in the development of Greek writing, such pattern as can be found should show in the plates; if it is sometimes difficult to follow, this faithfully reflects, to some extent at least, the fluid lines of that development.

Christmas 1973 *R.B.*

Postscripta

(1) Exceptional delays in printing have made it impossible to take account of any but one or two fundamental works published since 1973.

(2) Readers accustomed to the high standards of accuracy and presentation that distinguish Clarendon Press work will not fail to recognise that this volume has had to be prepared without the help of their expert printers and the vigilant scrutiny of their readers, who would have eliminated the myriad mistakes, a proportion of which will inevitably have escaped the author's untrained eye.

ACKNOWLEDGEMENTS

I should like to express my warm thanks for much help and kindness in many ways, to M. Charles Astruc, Professor Robert Browning, Mgr. Paul Canart, Père Jean Darrouzès A.A., Père François Halkin S.J., Professor Jean Irigoin, Professor Elpidio Mioni, and M. l'abbé Marcel Richard.

The work would not have been conceived nor the major part accomplished without all the advantages I enjoyed while I was on the staff of the Bodleian Library; it certainly would never have been finished without the exceptional kindness and efficiency of the staff (especially Miss Joan Gibbs) of the University of London Library, whose generous hospitality alone makes scholarly work possible in London. I have also enjoyed special privileges and consideration at the Bibliothèque Nationale in Paris, the Vatican Library, and the Biblioteca Marciana in Venice.

All attempts to obtain photographs of manuscripts located in Greece having failed, I am particularly grateful to Professor Kurt Weitzmann for his generosity in giving me prints from his negatives of Meteora MS. 591, and must also thank the American Academy of Arts and Sciences for permission to reproduce nos. 17, 34, 46, and 53 from K. and S. Lake, *Dated Greek minuscule manuscripts to the year 1200*. I am very grateful also to the Revd. Canon Edward Every for the care he took in procuring photographs from the Patriarchal Library in Jerusalem.

For photographs of other manuscripts and permission to publish them I am indebted to

Berlin, Staatliche Museen
Escorial, Real Biblioteca
Florence, Biblioteca Laurenziana
Grottaferrata, Badia Greca
Jerusalem, Patriarchal Library
Leningrad, Gosudarstvennaya Publichnaya Biblioteka
London, British Museum
Milan, Biblioteca Ambrosiana
Moscow, Gosudarstvennii Istoricheskii Muzei
  Nauchnaya Biblioteka im Gor'kogo Gosudarstvennogo Universiteta
New York, Metropolitan Museum of Art
Oxford, Bodleian Library
  Christ Church
  Corpus Christi College
  Lincoln College
  New College

Paris, Bibliothèque Nationale
  Musée du Louvre
Vatican, Biblioteca Apostolica Vaticana
Venice, Biblioteca Marciana
Vienna, Österreichische Nationalbibliothek.

INTRODUCTION

There are probably more than 3,000 extant dated or datable Greek manuscripts written between A.D. 400 and 1600, and well over 1,000 that contain some indication of provenance. Such a profusion of fixed points ought to make it easy to map the development of Greek writing both in time and space; but two unrelated obstacles stand in the way: on the one hand, the fixed points are very unevenly spread over the whole field; on the other, changes in style and habits of writing are never spectacular or sudden, with sharply defined boundaries. (1) The great majority of dated manuscripts falls into two groups: formally written sacred texts of *c.*950 to *c.*1200, and manuscripts of all types written between 1300 and 1600. Outside these there is virtually a famine of datable manuscripts, in particular of uncial before 800, of classical texts before 1200, and of any manuscripts between 1200 and 1260. The small number of all surviving uncial manuscripts and of manuscripts copied during the Latin occupation of Constantinople from 1204 to 1261, sufficently explains the scarcity of datable ones in these categories; but no satisfactory reason has been suggested to show why so few early classical texts were signed and dated. (2) The second great obstacle is the lack of sharp stylistic distinctions according to the time or place of writing. The causes of this are fundamental, being one manifestation of the remarkable uniformity of Byzantine culture. In strong contrast to the fragmentation of the Western empire after the fifth century and the consequent emergence of distinct national entities, each expressing its developing personality in new and individual ways — of writing as well as of more exciting forms of expression — the survival for so long of a single Eastern empire reduced the possibility of regional divergencies of all kinds. These were further diminished by the loss to the Arabs of the more distant provinces by the end of the eighth century. Moreover, defending this empire for eleven centuries against a steadily encroaching sea of enemies, the Byzantines perhaps came to prize more highly the traditions they felt to be at stake, and to feel drawn together in a closer unity, than they might otherwise have done. The result, in our small field, is that it is rarely possible to distinguish a different style of writing originating in a particular part of the empire, and certainly never one differing in the radical ways that Latin national scripts differed from each other. Nor is there ever a sharp break in style between one age and another; characteristics which may fairly be considered typical of a particular period will almost always be seen making a gradual appearance for some time before, and disappearing (if they ever do) equally gradually; to date a hand solely by the presence or absence of a single characteristic is extremely rash.

In so far as these limitations allow, the lines of development of Greek writing can be traced most clearly by distinguishing two different types of change which moved along parallel lines but cannot be bounded within the same periods. On the one hand there are the main obvious changes in the general style of writing; on the other there are changes in the minutiae of scribal habits (e.g. in the use of certain forms of letters or ligatures, and in the shape of accents and breathings) which only occasionally affect the general appearance of the writing. Each provides some criteria for dating, but as the rough periods into which they can each be divided do not always coincide, it is convenient to deal with them separately, and to take changes in the general style of writing first.

Styles of writing

Uncial, 400-1200

The word 'uncial' is not very aptly used, especially of the later styles that developed from biblical uncial; but, since the precise meaning of the word has never been established nor any satisfactory alternative suggested, it remains the most convenient term to describe writing that is not minuscule and yet not entirely capitals. The exact course of development of uncial is exceedingly difficult to plot. Not a single uncial manuscript is explicitly dated before 800, and very few after that date; a few only can be dated by external evidence — some more, some less reliably. Two periods can be distinguished and, running through both of them, three fairly distinct types of writing.

(1) From the fifth until some time in the eighth century, when minuscule came into use, uncial was the regular script which was necessarily used for literary texts, and therefore kept to a certain degree a plain functional character. Two distinct types of hand that had developed side by side since the second century continued into this period, each for a different purpose.
1 (a) 'Biblical' uncial,[1] the most formal of all, is found mainly in *de luxe* productions for presentation, often illustrated. After its finest flowering in the fourth and fifth centuries this style became heavier and stiffer, with exaggerated contrast between thick and thin strokes; but it was still even, and the letters solid, of uniform size, and square in area.
4 (b) The plain sloping hand, the least formal type, is represented by fewer extant examples, and those usually of a private or documentary nature; but it seems likely that it was widely used at the time for working copies of

[1] For a discussion and very full illustration of this script see Cavallo.

literary texts few of which survived because they were sooner replaced and
destroyed than grander copies. This style changed little from its earlier
days, as one would expect of a working hand, and remained a plain, clear,
rather angular script, with only light contrast between strokes, although
slightly more deliberate and less flowing than before. (c) At some time 8
within our period, probably not before the mid-fifth century, there began
to evolve out of 'biblical' uncial a third type of writing which developed into
the so-called Coptic-type uncial.[2] This very distinctive style, which had
some of the formality of 'biblical' uncial, was at the same time more
mannered, with a conspicuously curly appearance, and more current, with
a tendency to join certain letters together. It was used both as a chancery
hand in the patriarchate of Alexandria (from which come the only two
dated examples) and for literary texts during the sixth to eighth centuries.
There is a gap in our datable evidence of literary texts during the seventh
and eighth centuries, probably due partly to a decline in production (at
least of *de luxe* editions with greater chances of survival) during the
exceptionally disturbed times of the Heraclian dynasty and the iconoclastic
struggle, and partly to the Arab conquest of Egypt where alone papyrus
was produced and could survive.

(2) The second period in the development of uncial therefore opens
suddenly, as it were, in the ninth century when minuscule was already
established and its use spreading. The whole function of uncial then
changed; from the normal hand in which literary texts were necessarily
written, it became a specialized hand used only for certain purposes to give
particular dignity or elegance to copies for presentation or for the imperial
library, for liturgical books where the large letters could be more easily
read in dimly lit churches , and as an auxiliary script in manuscripts written
mainly in minuscule. (a) 'Biblical' uncial, still an elegant formal script 2
at the beginning of this period, is recognizably the parent of the hands
found in lectionaries from the tenth to as late as the twelfth century: a 3
completely ossified style, heavily ornamented, artificial to the last degree,
with wide variations between the widths of different letters. (b) In the 5
absence of evidence from the seventh and eighth centuries, it is impossible
to see whether the plain sloping style grew, like 'biblical' uncial, stiffer and
more artificial until it reached the same degree of formality, or whether
'biblical' uncial itself fathered this style also; but, whatever its origins, there
was already established at the beginning of this second period a sloping
hand of monumental character which differed from the liturgical style by its
uniform angularity and compression. This lighter, more elegant style is
found in a number of striking classical and patristic volumes, imperial and

[2] For a discussion of this script and a list of extant manuscripts see Irigoin, 'L'onciale grecque de type copte'.

presentation copies, produced during the ninth century in Constantinople.[3]
9 (c) The Coptic-type uncial seems not to have been used in this period for
the main text of books, but it persists from the mid-tenth to at least the
mid-twelfth century as a favourite ornamental style for headings, lists of
contents, and such adjuncts to minuscule manuscripts, particularly in
10 Constantinople. (d) A more formal type of ornamental capitals was also in
common use for headings, etc., during the tenth to twelfth centuries and
6 occasionally as late as the fourteenth century. (e) Uncial survived into the
minuscule period in one other form of auxiliary script: a very small plain
type of writing, which may have been a survival of the earlier plain sloping
style, was used for marginal scholia both by professional scribes and by
scholars such as Arethas. In some of the earliest minuscule manuscripts
scholia were written in small minuscule; soon uncial came into regular use
for them (both are found in the earliest dated minuscule manuscript of
7 835); but in the second half of the tenth century (rather later in S. Italy)
minuscule again began to be used, and by the eleventh century scholia in
uncial were a rarity.

Beginning of minuscule, seventh to eighth centuries

The conditions that produced a dark age in the seventh and eighth
centuries, from which few manuscripts have survived, probably also
brought the need for a new type of book-hand which should be more
compact and space-saving than uncial, more easily and quickly written, and
yet clear and even enough to take its place for formal use. Constantinople
and the north-western provinces were cut off in the mid-seventh century by
the Arabs from their supplies of papyrus, the main cheap writing material,
while the constant incursions of Arabs, Slavs, and Bulgars during the whole
of that century led to increased poverty and the search for a more
economical use of the more expensive parchment. In the 8th century the
polemics of the iconoclast controversy demanded a speedy, informal type
of writing, while persecution drove many monks to seek refuge beyond the
jurisdiction of the Byzantine emperor, some of whom may have seen the
beginnings of Latin minuscule in the West. The first experiments in
developing a current, compact, but clear hand may have been made in the
seventh, and must at latest have occurred in the eighth century, since the
13 first dated evidence, of 835, shows a well-established, fluent hand.
Unfortunately the absence of any datable examples of any kind of
minuscule book-hand before then leaves darkness covering this interesting
stage in the history of writing. It is likely that the experimental period lasted
some time, and that various attempts were made, perhaps in different parts

[3] A group of these manuscripts is discussed and illustrated by W. Jaeger.

of the empire, perhaps based on different types of documentary hands, which failed to produce practical styles. One of these abortive minuscules, which had no descendants presumably because it conspicuously lacked clarity, is known only from a few undated examples.[4]

The minuscule hand that finally satisfied all the conditions seems to have
been based on what was already the clearest of the documentary styles: that
used in the late seventh and early eighth centuries, mainly for accounts and **11**
for certain official letters and proclamations. The process of development is
hidden from us; a few marginalia in uncial manuscripts may represent an
intermediate stage, but none is dated, and the earliest complete manuscript
shows a fully developed minuscule. The likelihood is that this was evolved **13**
in Constantinople, probably at the monastery of the Stoudion, where the
earliest dated minuscule manuscript was certainly written, but the
supposition is based on a number of individually inconclusive arguments.[5]

Early minuscule, 800-950

This first period, lasting from the beginnings of minuscule to the peak of the
renaissance of learning under the Amorian and Macedonian em-
perors, was characterized by a number of distinctive styles of writing of
marked individuality. The styles illustrated may to some extent (but the
evidence is slender) be related to the purpose for which, and the type of
scribe by whom, particular manuscripts were produced; (1) several stiff **14-17**
angular styles, perhaps originating in the Stoudion, may be typical of
monastic production in general; (2) an elegant curly style was used for **20**
manuscripts for the imperial family or other presentation copies; (3)
several more individual styles, perhaps characteristic of secular **18, 26, 37,**
professional scribes, are found in texts copied for scholars such as Arethas, **61, 97**
and seem in some respects to foreshadow later styles in a way that (1) and
(2) do not. One characteristic common to all these styles is the regularity of
the writing, in that letters are of uniform size and joined to each other or not
according to fixed rules; another, which sharply divides them from those of
the next period, is a crisp, fresh, idiosyncratic quality which makes these
hands in some ways akin to later individual hands.

Formal minuscule, 950-1600

From about the middle of the tenth century formal hands seem to lose their individuality and become characterless; distinctions between styles are blurred and the strands of their development difficult to disentangle. It is more apt now to speak of different varieties of the same basic formal style

[4] e.g. Vat. gr. 2200 containing the *Doctrina patrum*, written on paper perhaps in Syria or some other eastern province under Arab rule. Facsimiles in Pal. Soc. II. 126 and Cavalieri and Lietzmann, tab. 5.

[5] See Allen, 'The origin'.

which is marked by great regularity and a somewhat mechanical, lifeless
appearance. Although not always clearly distinguished from one another,
these varieties continued in one form or another throughout this period.
The following are a few of the most easily distinguishable types of hand: (1)
49-52 an easy, plain, round type which varied little in essentials from the
mid-tenth to the mid-twelfth century and is found in both eastern and
53-6 western provinces; (2) a plain, solid, rounded type, aptly named
'Perlschrift' from the effect it gives of round beads strung together, found in
enormous numbers of standard copies of patristic works[6]; this can be
viewed both as a solidified, set version of (1) and as the basic model from
which evolved all the formal styles used up to the time of the Renaissance
62, 63 and beyond; (3) a heavy, thick type used almost exclusively for liturgical
64, 66 books throughout the eleventh century; (4) a distinctive type evolved
specially for use in liturgical texts with music, abnormally flat and
disjointed in order to accommodate itself to the flourishes of the musical
notation above it; this is found mainly in the twelfth and thirteenth
41-4 centuries; (5) a less distinctive type, lighter and looser than the others,
which became common in the twelfth century when there was a general
tendency for hands to become less compact.

Although the same varieties of style persisted in their fluid fashion, the
last half of this period, from the twelfth century onwards, is marked by
some obvious changes which resulted from the seeping into formal hands of
certain modifications which had already begun to be noticeable in, and
were later to be the main characteristic of, personal hands. The most
conspicuous change is that the size of individual letters, which had up to
now been substantially uniform, began to be varied by enlarging some and
reducing the size of others; but formal hands always kept the size of those
letters and parts of letters that fall between two notional inner lines far
more uniform than did personal hands, and in particular eschewed extreme
reductions in the size of letters. Other less noticeable changes introduced
20 from personal hands (changes in letter forms or in minor scribal habits) can
be seen in formal manuscripts almost as soon as they appear in the others,
but they tend to be rare and scattered and their detection is chancy. With no
distinctive styles emerging, hands are distinguished only by being more or
57, 58, 62, 63 less addicted to enlarged or flourished letters. In general, these tendencies
24, 34, 45-48, increase from hardly discernible beginnings as far back as the mid-eleventh
59, 67-70 century, to exaggerated proportions in the twelfth to fourteenth centuries,
60 then decrease in the more restrained hands of a number of
fifteenth-century scribes (many of them from Crete) who copied
prodigious numbers of manuscripts of all kinds mainly for Italian patrons.
But these characteristics also vary from scribe to scribe and with the

[6] For a description and examples of this script see Hunger, *Studien*.

purpose or patron for whom the book was written; as usual, most of the roughest examples are provincial products, but so too are some of sober conventionality.

Provincial hands, 950-1500

It is extremely difficult to be certain that a manuscript was copied in a particular centre unless this is explicitly stated in an unambiguous subscription. Features that can be regarded with reasonable certainty as peculiar to provincial manuscripts alone are very few, if evidence is admitted only from unquestionably authenticated manuscripts — far fewer than have sometimes been assumed in studies which were based partly on manuscripts judged to be provincial on subjective grounds. Even when the evidence of authenticated manuscripts alone is relied on, the frequent use in an unsigned manuscript of a particular form of letter or ligature, abbreviation or tachygraphy, cannot point with certainty to the centre or region in question, so long as we know practically nothing of the models which provincial centres had before them (in most cases, it is fair to assume, from Constantinople). It is inherently likely that often features which originated in the main centres, where their use may later have died out, might afterwards have become popular in one or more provincial centres; the date of a manuscript is thus crucial to a judgement of its origin. **17, 46**

Although the formal hands discussed in the last section rarely betray their places of origin, there are nevertheless certain types of hand that can be assigned to provincial centres. In the first place, there are certain general features that mark provincial products in any civilization and age: rough **29, 32, 33, 35,**
irregular hands, inferior materials (e.g. the use of palimpsests), crude **51, 52, 68**
decoration, etc. But an examination of specifically dated and placed manuscripts shows that judgement must never be made on the basis of one only of these features; no single one by itself is proof of provincial origin; only a combination, producing an impression of the manuscript as a whole, is a safe guide. In particular, the script of some authenticated provincial manuscripts is sometimes, considered by itself, indistinguishable from **42, 45, 47,**
known products of Constantinople (more often so in the products of **54, 56, 63,**
eastern than of western provinces). Therefore, while a rough, uneven hand **69, 70**
can with some probability be assigned to a provincial centre (though rarely to any particular one), many manuscripts which may in fact have been written in the provinces will escape detection.

In the case of manuscripts copied in southern Italy and Sicily, two fairly distinct styles of writing did evolve in the course of this period. (1) S. Neilos, **38**
who led his monks as they were driven further and further northward by Arab attacks, to settle finally in his foundation of Grottaferrata in 1004, was famous as a calligrapher and had an individual style of writing which

influenced that of his followers. It was small and neat and close-set and
made use of a system of shorthand which has not so far been found
elsewhere, although in its ordinary abbreviations and other scribal habits it
25 differed not at all from Constantinopolitan usage. (2) During the twelfth
century there flourished an even more distinctive style, elegant and
delicately curly; all examples of the fully developed style where the place of
copying is explicit originated in S. Italy or Sicily, but the possibility that
their models came from centres nearer the capital is suggested by some
early examples in which inferential evidence, most noticeably the
ornament, points to Constantinople. For the rest, S. Italian and Sicilian
hands are either distinguishable from other provincial hands only by the
39 use of a western-type pen (i.e. one cut to give contrasting thick and thin
strokes) or not at all except by features other than the writing, in particular
the use of western styles of decoration.

Personal hands, tenth to fifteenth centuries

After the middle of the tenth century, when the earlier, more individual
styles of formal writing gave way to characterless uniformity, there were
some professional scribes whose style of writing had more in common with
75, 78, 79, 86 scholarly hands, and later were indistinguishable from them; some are
85 known secular scribes, some are unknown, others are monks, some copying
74, 76, 80, 83, the typika of their monsteries. They can be found at any time and almost
89, 99, 105 any place, and cannot be grouped into particular styles for they were simply
81, 84, 90 personal variations of the formal writing of the time.

The hands of scholars are much more rarely seen before the last half of
the twelfth century, but from the beginning of minuscule there had always
been an occasional scholar who copied, or more often annotated, his own
6 manuscripts. Arethas, although all his marginalia are in small uncials,
showed even in them a marked individuality which distinguishes his hand
from those of professional scribes copying notes in the same style. Much
wider is the difference between scholars and professionals writing
minuscule. Perhaps the earliest dated example of a whole book written in a
98 hand of scholarly type is a collection of philosophical works copied by
73 Ioannes γραμματικός in 925; another example is the copy of commentaries
on Gregory of Nazianzus of 986, the style of which has much in common
with the hands of some early classical manuscripts. But examples are
71, 72 comparatively few until, in the last half of the twelfth century, some really
77 distinctive personal styles usher in the new age of individually identifiable
scholars' hands. From this time on it became gradually more common for
scholars to copy manuscripts for themselves instead of commissioning them
from professional scribes, not only from economic pressure in the harder
times under the Angeli and Palaeologi, but also because scholars like

Triklinios prepared their own 'editions' of classical authors by copying 94
from several sources instead of having a single manuscript copied for them and adding variants from others in the margin as earlier scholars had usually done. From now on it is not so much a question of recognizing different styles of writing as of identifying individual copyists.

There were, however, still certain fashions in style with very wide influence; only a few of the most obvious can be mentioned here. During
the tenth century the habit of enlarging some letters, which had from 97
Roman times been a convention of documentary hands, began to invade personal hands and break up their original evenness; once the enlargement and flourishing of some letters became common, the practice grew until it reached a crescendo of exaggeration. Throughout the thirteenth century a
very distinctive, ebullient style was used in which some letters were blown 83, 90
up to an absurd size and others reduced to microscopic proportions, giving the writing a chaotic uncontrolled appearance. By the end of the century the wildest exuberance was dying down and a more sober style began to prevail; the evenness of earlier times never returned, but the difference between the sizes of different letters became less disproportionate. The
transition to a plainer style is seen in the hands successively of Maximos 93
Planudes and Demetrios Triklinios, and the tendency continued in the 94
writing of scholars well into the fifteenth century, for example in the hands
of Pletho, Scholarios, and Bessarion. Besides this severe style, there was 91, 95
also in the fourteenth and early fifteenth centuries one more curly and 104, 105
mannered. But now the varieties of style are numerous and overlapping, and there is no clear distinction between styles thought suitable for copying Biblical and patristic texts and those for secular manuscripts; still less are there any differences according to where in the by now shrunken Byzantine empire a manuscript was written.

The Renaissance

The transplanting of Greek culture to Italy between the mid-fourteenth and mid-fifteenth centuries brought about a multiplication and cross-fertilization of styles of writing as the Greek immigrants introduced their already wide variety of styles and taught their Italian pupils to write Greek. The first generation of Greek scholars to come from
Constantinople and give public teaching — for example Manuel 87
Chrysoloras (*c.* 1350-1415) and Theodore of Gaza (*c.* 1400-1475) — had particularly clear round hands, perhaps deliberately made as plain as possible for the benefit of their pupils, who then copied them. The hands of
most of the early humanists — e.g. Aurispa, Guarino, Palla Strozzi, 88
Leonardo Bruni — have an almost child-like clarity, which may have been influenced also by the humanist Latin styles; but one or two, like the

106 self-taught Ciriaco, and Filelfo, have highly idiosyncratic hands. After the
Council of Florence, from about 1440 onwards when Greek scholars and
scribes established themselves in Italy in large numbers, the whole variety
of Greek writing styles was let loose there and imitated in most cases with a
distinctively Italian flavour. Here it is possible to mention only a few of the
most widely diffused styles. A mannered flourished hand was affected by
96 John Argyropoulos, teaching at Padua from 1441, and later by Janus
102 Lascaris, Lorenzo de Medici's agent in collecting manuscripts, and this
103 clearly influenced the Greek writing of Politian, working mainly in
Florence between 1472 and 1491. In striking contrast to this was a plain
sloping current hand used in the last half of the century by, for example,
Constantine Lascaris writing in Milan 1460-8 and in Messina 1470-1501,
George Hermonymos of Sparta writing mainly in Paris, John Serbopoulos
92 of Constantinople copying manuscripts in Reading Abbey in 1494-1500,
and Giorgio Valla. One of the commonest styles at the end of the fifteenth
and beginning of the sixteenth century was a rather mannered, neat,
compressed type of writing used equally by Greeks and by their Italian
imitators, which was taken as a model by the early printers of Greek, who,
ignoring one of the main points of the new invention, took over all the
ligatures and variety in letter forms from their handwritten models. The
remarkable way in which printed and manuscript books persisted side by
107 side for more than a century is illustrated by the activities of Zacharias
Callierges, who himself copied in this style of hand and organized the
copying of manuscripts in Venice and Rome between 1499 and 1524, and
also printed Greek books in a similar style in both places in 1499-1509 and
1515-23. Another common style, that spread in the course of the sixteenth
century from Crete to France, was bolder, rounder, and more current than
the last, and culminated in the elegant mannered hands of Angelus
108 Vergecius and Nicolas de la Torre, the former of whom used his own
writing as model in designing the 'grecs du roi' types cut by Garamond for
Robert Estienne in 1542, the ancestor of nearly all Greek types for more
109 than two centuries. A rather shapeless version of this style continued in use
in Greek lands up to the nineteenth century, and was used at the beginning
110 of the seventeenth century by John Sanctamauras, scriptor at the Vatican
and the last of the Greek scribes in the West. By then manuscripts were
rarely copied except for scholars wanting to collate them for editions; they
were the equivalent of modern microfilms, not of modern books.

Changes in minor writing habits

These, unlike the gradual changes in general appearance that have just been described, might seem to lend themselves more easily to statistical treatment which would yield precise criteria for dating. But this is not yet, and may never be, the case. Up to now the obstacle has been the obvious impossibility of scrutinizing every letter, breathing, etc. in every extant dated manuscript; but even if computers were taught to read Greek manuscripts and provide us with completely comprehensive data, it is doubtful whether the greater accuracy of the picture would permit more precise dating. The nature of the material is against it. In the first place, surviving manuscripts are not necessarily a fair sample of all those originally produced, and extant dated ones are certainly not a fair sample of all surviving manuscripts. But, more fundamentally, the production of thousands of individuals, influenced by such imponderables as age, nationality, the nature of the book, or the patron, does not lend itself to statistical analysis; such limited results as we have show this. The kind of picture that emerges is that, for example, of a new form whose first few isolated appearances are scattered over at least a century before it is found in regular use, which takes several centuries to supplant the old form completely (if it ever does), and which may even give way again later to the old form used with deliberate archaism. It seems likely that more accurate and comprehensive data will reveal no more precise lines of demarcation than exist already, but merely illuminate the lack of precision. It would be carrying pedantic scruples too far, however, to refuse for this reason to give any outline of these changes in minor scribal habits. The following summary deliberately avoids the false precision of giving exact dates of earliest-so-far-noticed instances, in favour of a rough indication of the time when a certain habit was well established.

Letter forms in minuscule manuscripts

The earliest extant minuscule is a pure minuscule, in which every letter which has a form distinct from the uncial form (i.e. all except ϑ,ι, ο,ϱ,τ,φ,χ) is invariably written in that form. Very early, however, uncial forms of certain letters were reintroduced and began to be used alongside the minuscule ones (they never completely replaced them); and since some uncial forms appear before others, and nearly a century elapsed before uncial forms of all seventeen letters were in common use, the presence or absence of particular ones during this time may provide a very rough guide to the date of a manuscript. The order in which each uncial form came into regular use between about 890 and 980 (after which any of them may be found) is roughly as follows: λ,ξ,ϰ (all found before 900); ζ,γ,ν,π,σ (by 915); α,ε,δ,η (by 945); ψ (by 960); β,μ (by 970); finally ω and υ. (This ignores the use of occasional uncial forms — in particular α and σ — at line ends, a habit found in otherwise pure minuscule manuscripts from earliest

times.)[7] But the counting of relative frequencies of each form, though it may occasionally help to distinguish between different scribes or different stages in the development of one scribe, is not an infallible guide in dating a manuscript, for factors such as the degree of formality of the manuscript, or pure choice, or the age or nationality of the scribe play an unpredictable part in his use of uncial letters. The last factor is of prime importance, particularly in dating a manuscript written in pure minuscule. The last dated pure minuscule manuscript so far known was copied in 965; but since
(a) it has a markedly rough provincial appearance, (b) the next latest
17 known was copied in Reggio Calabria in 941, and (c) all other known dated
ones lie between 835 and 899, it is reasonable to suppose that after about 900 pure minuscule was used only in provincial centres.

After the assimilation of uncial forms into minuscule, no major changes took place in the basic shapes of letters until certain late forms, in many cases approximating to modern ones, began to appear. None of these was in general use in literary texts before the thirteenth century, but nearly all of them can be found in an occasional manuscript long before then. Most came in from documentary hands, and therefore it is no surprise to find
isolated examples of them at almost any date. The clearest examples of
20 completely new shapes are: small-bowed ϛ found occasionally from the
75 mid-tenth century; η with neither or sometimes with both strokes
prolonged — n or h — found occasionally from the eleventh century;
86 broken-backed ε and the modern ν on rare occasions in the twelfth century;
93 ς with an embryonic tail only at the end of the thirteenth century, by which
time all the new shapes are in common use. As with other changes, old and new forms continued in use side by side, and in the most formal hands the old forms predominated to the end.

Ligatures, joining of letters, word division

Ligatures, in the sense of two letters joined together by having one stroke in common, were sometimes used in uncial as a space-saving device for keeping the ends of lines even or the number of letters in a line constant. In minuscule, the object was different: to decrease the number of separate strokes needed even beyond what could be done by simply joining the letters. From the beginning, minuscule took over from cursive a certain number of standard ligatures, simple forms which for the most part did not distort the shape of either letter. At first the use of the appropriate ligature seems to have been considered almost obligatory whenever the two or

[7] The divergencies between this list and the latest data published in E. Follieri, 'La reintroduzione', are due mainly to differences in the manuscripts used and the amounts of each examined, and also in the letters chosen for study; they well illustrate the relativity of the results of such studies.

three letters in question occurred in succession, even at the end of one and the beginning of the next word; likewise the ordinary joining of such letters as might be joined together under the very rigid rules that forbade the joining (for example) of ι with the following letter. In consequence, early minuscule gives an impression of word division which is illusory; the divisions are caused by the gaps between letters that are not allowed to be joined, and occur as often in mid-word as between words, which may sometimes be joined by ligature. The tendency to join wherever permissible gradually slackened as pure minuscule gave way before the infiltration of uncial forms unsuited to joining; but the same ligatures continued in common use, at the choice of the scribe. There was little change in their basic shape, only in the tendency to flourish them which grew as writing became more florid in personal hands in the course of the twelfth century. At the same time some of them were reduced to the barest
minimum indication of their shape, for example ꝗ (ει). Finally the whole **75, 86**
range of ligatures was taken over, with extraordinary illogicality, by the early printers of Greek, and perpetuated in their most sophisticated and varied forms in printed Greek until the eighteenth century.

The ambiguity over word division remained for nearly the whole of our period. It is never clear cut as in Latin, and such as it is it was never universally practised even in the Renaissance. The presence of breathings and accents both increased the appearance of there being some division and decreased the need for it as an aid to reading.

Breathings and accents

In the early part of our period breathings and accents were not considered necessary except to remove particular ambiguities or to elucidate difficult texts. It is not possible to observe the exact time when their use became general without personal examination of all the manuscripts concerned, for in early manuscripts they have often been added by later hands which is not always obvious in photographs. Their general use was certainly not an integral part of the first stages of minuscule, but it became more common in the course of the ninth century and by about 900 it was almost invariable in both uncial and minuscule manuscripts.

The slow evolution of the shape of breathings well illustrates the difficulties of trying to establish precise dating criteria from these minutiae. At first all were square, either the original ⊢ and ⊣ shapes or ⌊ and ⌋ The rounded forms c and ɔ , used along with square ones, are first found
in 862, but thereafter apparently not until the second quarter of the tenth **14**
century; this mixed use is found in the majority of manuscripts from the last quarter of that century until the beginning of the twelfth century when it gradually, during the next fifty years, dies out. The use of square breathings

alone, however, though it decreases rapidly all this time, yet persists just into the twelfth century. Meanwhile manuscripts in which only round breathings are used, which first appear soon after the middle of the tenth century, remain in a minority until the beginning of the twelfth century, after which they rapidly become the only ones, with the exception of a few consciously pedantic revivals of square breathings by individual scholars. Therefore there is a period of nearly 150 years (between about 950 and 1100) when any shape of breathing may be found, used exclusively or mixed.

Apart from this specific change in shape, a rather more noticeable change came over the way of writing accents and breathings when the flourishes of documentary hands began to infect personal styles. Individual signs, from being small, neat, and separate, gradually became sprawling and ultimately joined to each other. The earliest change is in the circumflex accent when used over the same vowel as a breathing: at first placed side by side, during the last half of the tenth century the circumflex is found more and more often above the breathing, becoming enlarged first in that position only and later wherever it occurs; by the mid-eleventh century it commonly spreads over large parts of the word, and in the twelfth century other accents begin gradually to spread in the same way. In the middle of the eleventh century, accents began to be occasionally joined to abbreviation marks (ῶν became ∼) and finally, not until towards the end of the twelfth century, to breathings (῎ became ᵛ) and to the letters to which they belonged (ά became α/). By the thirteenth century all these habits were well established as one aspect of the flowing individual hands of the time. They are much more rarely found in formal hands.

Abbreviations, diaeresis, mute ι

Abbreviations are of three kinds: (1) *nomina sacra*, the only Greek abbreviations by contraction, in which the middle of the word is omitted and the whole is surmounted by a line or wavy stroke, were constantly used in all types of manuscript both before and throughout our period. At first an accent was hardly ever placed over the contracted word, but from the middle of the eleventh century (earlier on compounds such as φιλανθρωπία) it became customary to add the accent appropriate to the unabbreviated word. (2) Plain suspension of the last few letters of a word was also in use before this period, the missing letters being replaced either by one of them (usually the last) suprascript, or by suprascript — or \ or by / added to the foot of the last letter present. In the early part of our period, in both uncial and minuscule manuscripts, this method was limited to indicating the omission at line ends of ν by — and more rarely of α by \ , and to writing ϗ for καὶ in any position in the text; but in the current

styles of writing adopted from the twelfth century onwards, this type of arbitrary abbreviation became more and more widely used for any syllables and even for the major parts of words, especially for technical terms. (3) Certain conventional signs, each representing either a single syllable (mainly case endings) or a preposition or part of the verb 'to be', are found already standardized in earliest minuscule. In formal manuscripts at any date they were not often used in the main body of text, except at line ends, but commonly in marginalia. Indeed, until the twelfth century they were used regularly throughout the text in only a few manuscripts (written
perhaps for a scholar's own personal use?), the earliest dated one being of 98
925; later, they may be found thus used in any scholarly or personal copy. The general shape of abbreviation signs developed along the same lines as that of breathings and accents; at the beginning they were neat and for the most part angular; but from the middle of the eleventh century they began to get larger, more flourished, and curved (e.g. ✓ for ας, \ for ου, ч for ως became ✓, ⌝, and ч), and also to be joined to accents and eventually to letters. By the thirteenth century this was normal in personal hands, and it is found occasionally in formal manuscripts.

The diaeresis had been used from early times over ι and υ in three ways: to mark one of two consecutive vowels not forming a diphthong, in foreign (particularly Hebrew) names, and when either of these letters stood at the beginning of a word. These uses continued (never obligatory, merely at the choice of individual scribes), but there also crept in a more liberal use of the sign, on any ι or υ even between two consonants in mid-word, still as a matter of individual choice. There are isolated instances of this wider use from the beginning, but it only became common in the second half of the twelfth century.

Mute ι was, throughout our period, often omitted; it was used more often in classical than in biblical or theological texts. Until the twelfth century it was always adscript; then there was a tendency to drop it slightly below the general level of the letters, still keeping it at the side; only in the thirteenth century did the completely subscript position become regular.

Position of writing and ruled lines

In Greek manuscripts, except where there was direct Western influence, lines to guide the writing were always ruled with a dry point. Uncial was invariably written standing on the lines, and not until the late liturgical uncial were two lines drawn to contain the writing. The first minuscule, likewise, stood on the lines, but from the time of the earliest examples we have, there are also many instances of the lines being used merely as a guide passing through the middle of the writing, or above or below it indiscriminately. These two methods were in use until at least the end of the tenth century, but from the second quarter of that century the habit of making the writing hang from the lines began, and by the beginning of the eleventh century was all but universal. There was always the odd manuscript in which no lines (or occasionally only alternate lines) were ruled for the writing, or only a framework of bounding lines was provided; but it was not until well after the introduction of paper in the late eleventh century that this practice became general. Presumably the just-visible chain- and wire-marks of paper at first made ruling seem unnecessary; but the habit of not ruling spread to parchment also, and except in formal or *de luxe* manuscripts became common practice from the thirteenth century.

BIBLIOGRAPHY

This is not exhaustive, merely introductory, and is concerned only with writing. It includes all works referred to in abbreviated form throughout the book, and a few more of the most useful studies of particular problems and types of writing. Full bibliographies (and references to earlier ones) are in J. Irigoin, 'Les manuscrits grecs 1931-1960', *Lustrum,* 7 (1962), 5-93, and in the annual 'Bulletin codicologique', *Scriptorium,* 13- (1959-).

The standard general works on Greek palaeography are of historical rather than practical value; they are listed in R. Devreesse, *Introduction à l'étude des manuscrits grecs* (Paris, 1954) pp. V-VII. To them should be added two useful summaries:

E. E. Granstrem, 'K voprosu o Vizantiiskom minuskule', *Vizantiiskii Vremennik,* 13 (1958), 222-45.

H. Hunger, 'Griechische Paläographie' in *Geschichte der Textüberlieferung der antiken und mittelalterlichen Literatur* (Zurich, 1961-4) I. 72-107.

COLLECTIONS OF FACSIMILES

(There is a list of dated Greek manuscripts of which published facsimiles then existed in Devreesse, *Introduction,* pp. 286-320.)

N. A. Bees, *Τὰ χειρόγραφα τῶν Μετεώρων* (Athens, 1967-).

V. Beneshevich, *Monumenta Sinaitica,* II (St. Petersburg, 1912).

J. Bick, *Die Schreiber der Wiener griechischen Handschriften* (Museion Abhandlungen, I) (Vienna, 1920).

P. F. De' Cavalieri and J. Lietzmann, *Specimina codicum Graecorum Vaticanorum,* ed. 2 (Berlin and Leipzig, 1929).

F. Dölger, *Aus den Schatzkammern des heiligen Berges* (Munich, 1948).

— *Facsimiles byzantinischer Kaiserurkunden* (Munich, 1931).

—and J. Karayannopulos, *Byzantinische Urkundenlehre* (Handbuch der Altertumswissenschaft, XII. 3.1.1.) (Munich, 1968).

E. Follieri, *Codices Graeci Bibliothecae Vaticanae selecti temporum locorumque ordine digesti...* (Exempla scripturarum... IV) (Vatican, 1969).

C. Graux and A. Martin, *Fac-similés de manuscrits grecs d'Espagne* (Paris, 1891).

Greek manuscripts in the Bodleian Library. An exhibition held in connection with the XIIIth International Congress of Byzantine Studies (Oxford, 1966).

D. Harlfinger, *Specimina griechischer Kopisten der Renaissance* (Berlin, 1974-).

A. D. Komines, *Πίνακες χρονολογημένων Πατμιακῶν κωδίκων* (Athens, 1968).

K. and S. LAKE, *Dated Greek minuscule manuscripts to the year 1200* (Monumenta Palaeographica Vetera, series 1) (Boston, Mass., 1934-45).

L. T. LEFORT and J. COCHEZ, *Palaeographisch Album* (Louvain, 1932-4).

E. MAUNDE THOMPSON, *An introduction to Greek and Latin palaeography (Oxford, 1912).*

R. MERKELBACH and H. VAN THIEL, *Griechisches Leseheft* (Studienhefte zur Altertumswissenschaft, 10) (Göttingen, 1965).

New Palaeographical Society, *Facsimiles of ancient manuscripts, etc.*, ed. E. M. Thompson and others, Series I and II (London, 1903-32).

H. OMONT, *Fac-similés des manuscrits grecs datés de la Bibliothèque nationale du IXe au XIVe siècle* (Paris, 1891).

—*Fac-similés de manuscrits grecs des XVe et XVIe siècles... de la Bibliothèque nationale* (Paris, 1887).

—*Fac-similés des plus anciens manuscrits grecs en onciale et en minuscule de la Bibliothèque nationale du IVe au XIIe siècle* (Paris, 1892).

Palaeographical Society, *Facsimiles of manuscripts and inscriptions,* ed. E.A. Bond, E. M. Thompson, G. F. Warner, Series I and II (London, 1873-1901).

A. SOBOLEVSKI and G. TSERETELI, *Exempla codicum Graecorum litteris uncialibus scriptorum* (St. Petersburg, 1913).

F. STEFFENS, *Proben aus griechischen Handschriften und Urkunden* (Trier, 1912).

O. STRUNK, *Specimina notationum antiquiorum* (Monumenta musicae Byzantinae, VII) (Copenhagen, 1966).

L. TARDO, *L'antica melurgia bizantina* (Collezione meridionale, III. Il mezzogiorno artistico) (Grottaferrata, 1938).

J.-B. THIBAUT, *Monuments de la notation ecphonétique et hagiopolite de l'église grecque* (St. Petersburg, 1913).

G. TSERETELI and S. SOBOLEVSKI, *Exempla codicum Graecorum litteris minusculis scriptorum...* I: Codices Mosquenses, II: Codices Petropolitani (Moscow, 1911-13).

A. TURYN, *Codices Graeci Vaticani saeculis XIII et XIV scripti annorumque notis instructi* (Vatican, 1964).

—*Dated Greek manuscripts of the thirteenth and fourteenth centuries in the libraries of Italy* (Urbana etc., 1972).

G. VITELLI and C. PAOLI, *Collezione fiorentina di facsimili paleografici greci e latini* (Florence, 1884-97).

W. WATTENBACH, *Scripturae Graecae specimina,* ed. 3 (Berlin, 1897).

— and A. VON VELSEN, *Exempla codicum Graecorum litteris minusculis scriptorum* (Heidelberg, 1878).

N. G. WILSON, *Mediaeval Greek bookhands* (Mediaeval Academy of America, Publication no. 81) (Cambridge, Mass., 1973).

M. WITTEK, *Album de paléographie grecque: spécimens d'écritures livresques du IIIe siècle avant J.C. au XVIIIe siècle, conservés dans des collections belges* (Ghent, 1967).

LISTS OF SCRIBES

M. VOGEL and V. GARDTHAUSEN, *Die griechischen Schreiber des Mittelalters und der Renaissance* (Zentralblatt für Bibliothekswesen, Beiheft 33) (Leipzig, 1909).

C. G. PATRINELES, '"Ἕλληνες κωδικογράφοι τῶν χρόνων τῆς ἀναγεννήσεως', *Ἐπετηρὶς τοῦ Μεσαιωνικοῦ Ἀρχείου,* 8/9 (1958/9), 63-125.

P. CANART, 'Scribes grecs de la Renaissance', *Scriptorium,* 17 (1963), 56-82.

K. A. DE MEYIER, 'Scribes grecs de la Renaissance', *Scriptorium,* 18 (1964), 258-66.

B. L. FONKICH, 'Grecheskie pistsi epochi vozrozhdeniya', *Vizantiiskii Vremennik,* 26 (1965), 266-71, 28 (1968), 283-5.

D. HARLFINGER, *Die Textgeschichte der pseudo-Aristotelischen Schrift περὶ ἀτόμων γραμμῶν* (Amsterdam, 1971) pp. 405-20, Taf. 1-26. Anhang: Neuidentifizierte Kopisten griechischer Aristoteles-Handschriften der Renaissance.

J. WIESNER and U. VICTOR, 'Griechische Schreiber der Renaissance', *Rivista di studi bizantini e neoellenici,* N.S. 8-9 (1971-2), 51-66.

OTHER WORKS

T. W. ALLEN, 'A group of ninth-century Greek manuscripts', *Journal of Philology,* 21 (1893), 48-55.

—*Notes on abbreviations in Greek manuscripts* (Oxford, 1889).

—'The origin of the Greek minuscule hand', *Journal of Hellenic Studies,* 40 (1920), 1-12.

BHG: Bibliotheca Hagiographica Graeca, ed. 3, and *Auctarium,* ed. F. Halkin (Subsidia hagiographica 8a and 47) (Brussels, 1957-69).

P. CANART, 'Le problème du style d'écriture dit "en as de pique" dans les manuscrits italo-grecs', *Atti del quarto Congresso storico calabrese* (Naples, 1969) pp. 55-69.

G. CAVALLO, *Ricerche sulla maiuscola biblica* (Florence, 1967).

E. C. COLWELL, *The four gospels of Karahissar,* I (Chicago, 1936) pp. 111-18, 225-41 [statistics of uncial letters in minuscule New Testament manuscripts].

M.-L. CONCASTY, 'Manuscrits grecs originaires de l'Italie méridionale conservés à Paris', *Studi bizantini e neoellenici,* 7 (1953) (Atti dello VIII Congresso internazionale di studi bizantini, I), 22-34.

J. DARROUZÈS, 'Manuscrits originaires de Chypre à la Bibliothèque nationale' and 'Autres manuscrits originaires de Chypre', *Revue des études byzantines,* 8 (1950), 162-96, 15 (1957), 131-68.

R. DEVREESSE, *Les manuscrits grecs de l'Italie méridionale* (Studi e Testi, 183) (Vatican, 1955).

N. X. ELEOPOULOS, Ἡ βιβλιοθήκη καὶ τὸ βιβλιογραφικὸν ἐργαστήριον τῆς μονῆς τῶν Στουδίου (Athens, 1967).

E. FOLLIERI, 'La reintroduzione di lettere semionciali nei più antichi manoscritti greci in minuscola', *Bullettino dell' 'Archivio paleografico italiano'*, 3rd Ser. 1 (1962), 15-36.

F. HALKIN, 'Manuscrits galésiotes', *Scriptorium*, 15 (1961), 221-7.

H. HUNGER, *Studien zur griechischen Paläographie* (Biblos-Schriften, 5) (Vienna, 1954).

J. IRIGOIN, 'L' Aristote de Vienne', *Jahrbuch der österreichischen byzantinischen Gesellschaft*, 6 (1957), 5-10.

—'L'onciale grecque de type copte', *Jahrbuch der österreichischen byzantinischen Gesellschaft*, 8 (1959), 29-51.

—'Structure et évolution des écritures livresques de l'époque byzantine', in *Polychronion, Festschrift Franz Dölger zum 75 Geburtstag*, ed. P. Wirth (Corpus der griechischen Urkunden des Mittelalters und der neueren Zeit, Reihe D. Bd. 1) (Heidelberg, 1966) pp. 253-65.

W. JAEGER, 'Greek uncial fragments in the Library of Congress in Washington', *Traditio*, 5 (1947), 79-102.

PG: Patrologia Graeca, ed. J.-P. Migne (Paris, 1857-66).

PL: Patrologia Latina, ed. J.-P. Migne (Paris, 1844-55).

M. RICHARD, *Répertoire des bibliothèques et des catalogues de manuscrits grecs*, ed. 2 and Supplément I (1958-63) (Paris, 1958, 1964).

G. TSERETELI, *De compendiis scripturae codicum Graecorum*, ed. 2 (St. Petersburg, 1904).

N. G. WILSON, 'Litera Neritina', *Scriptorium*, 21 (1967), 73-4.

One important publication since 1973 must be added here because many of its contributions deal in detail with the classification and localization of styles of writing: *La paléographie grecque et byzantine*. Paris, 21-25 octobre 1974. (Colloques internationaux du Centre National de la Recherche Scientifique No. 559, Paris, 1977).

NOTES ON PLATES, DESCRIPTIONS AND TRANSCRIPTIONS

PLATES

All reproductions are the size of the original manuscripts.

DESCRIPTIONS

Information is based on personal inspection of the manuscripts in the case of those in Florence, Grottaferrata, London, Milan, Oxford, Paris, the Vatican, Venice, and Vienna. A detailed description of each is not given here; this may (or may not) be found in the relevant library catalogue (where one exists) listed in Richard.

There is space usually only to give evidence without spelling out conclusions, and never room to state arguments on both sides in controversy. The following notes list ways in which descriptions have had to be abbreviated, and include some general statements which are not repeated under individual items.

Dates. 947/8 means between 1 September 947 and 31 August 948. 1491-2 means during the years 1491 and 1492.

Scribe and place. Here alone I abandon brevity in order to give precise data from the subscription, because a summary place-name heading almost always misleads. Anything not explicit in a subscription or other evidence is enclosed in ( ).

Measurements. Figures in ( ) give the size of the writing space.

Shelfmarks of manuscripts illustrated or referred to. The full names of libraries, alternative shelfmarks from different catalogues, etc. are given only in the index of manuscripts.

Subscription and transcription. Spelling, breathings, and accents are given exactly as in the manuscripts; only word division is imposed. ( ) enclose the expansion of an abbreviation mark which stands for specific letters. [ ] enclose letters supplied.

Dating. When the year and indiction numbers in a subscription do not agree by one year, the indiction is assumed to be correct (unless otherwise argued) because at least up to the twelfth century this is more often found to be the case when there is an independent check.

Style of writing. I have avoided giving mere descriptions of styles or comparisons with others illustrated here, in short anything that can be seen or deduced from the plates. General accounts of the characteristics, duration, or place of a particular style are not repeated from the introduction, where the numbers of the facsimiles which illustrate each statement are given in the margin to ease reference between plates and introduction.

Details of scribal practice are described by numbers which refer to the following standard uses:[1]

Abbrevations: (1) *nomina sacra* without accents, (2) *nomina sacra* with

[1]A number against any of these headings in the description of a manuscript does not mean that the usage in question is invariable in that manuscript.

accents, (3) ν omitted at line ends represented by ‾, (4) καὶ represented by ϗ or ς, (5) normal syllabic abbreviations used only at line ends or in marginalia, (6) normal syllabic abbreviations used in mid-text, (7) arbitrary abbreviation by omitting the ends of words, (8) abbreviation signs enlarged, rounded, and flourished.
Accents: (1) enlarged; joined to (2) abbreviation signs, (3) breathings, (4) letters.
Breathings: (1) all angular, (2) mixed, (3) all round.
Diaeresis over ι and/or υ used (1) to mark one of two consecutive vowels not forming a diphthong, (2) initially (including the beginning of the stem in compound words), (3) anywhere in mid-word.
Mute ι (1) adscript, (2) adscript below the level of the writing, (3) subscript.
Ruling: the writing (1) stands on (2) is guided by (3) hangs from the ruled lines.

Other manuscripts by the same scribe. I include only those I have seen personally or in facsimile. But this is not the place for exhaustive lists (which need to include manuscripts incorrectly ascribed); my intention is only to give examples for reference. Where there is a published study of a scribe I cite that instead of giving my own list; but I do not refer under separate manuscripts to the lists in Vogel and Gardthausen, revised by others, which are cited in the bibliography and should be consulted on any individual scribe.

Comparable script. Undated manuscripts listed are likewise only a selection, and include only classical texts. Comparison with documentary hands is not made for the later personal hands where the kinship is obvious.

Other facsimiles and publications. With rare exceptions, the reproductions listed are only those in the main collections of facsimiles. Besides these there is space to give references only to major discussions of particular manuscripts or palaeographical questions.

TRANSCRIPTIONS

Because the transcriptions were separated from the descriptions of the plates only at a late stage in the printing, the two parts must be read together: e.g. the names of authors, works referred to as "ibid." etc. will be found in the corresponding description. See also *Subscription and transcription* above.

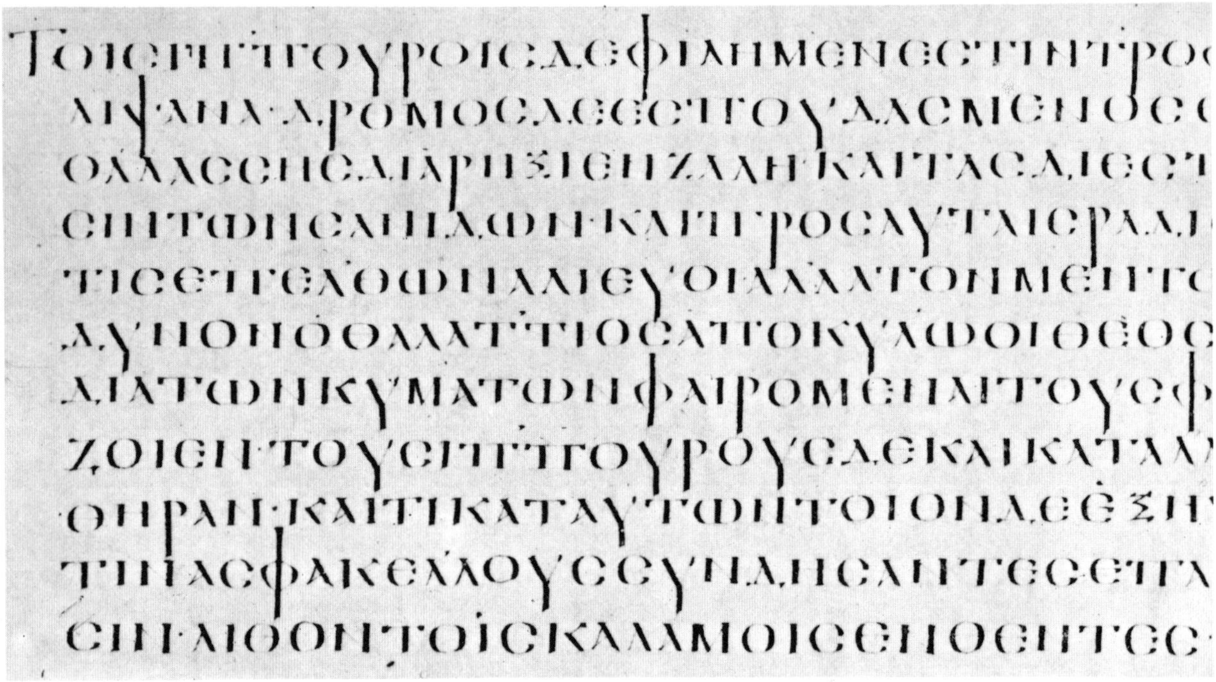

1

2

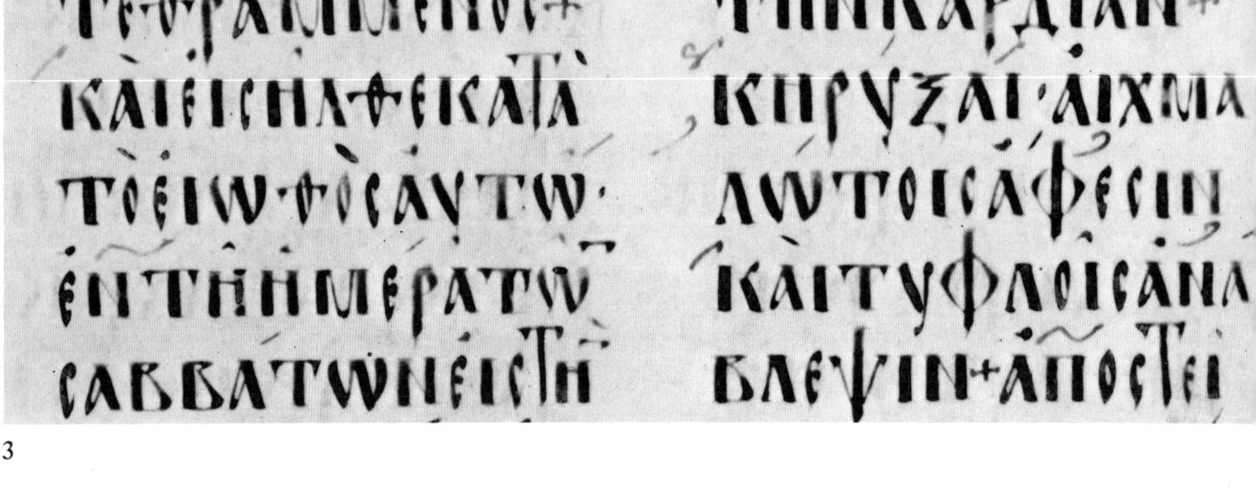

3

1 Probably before 527/8 or 513/14 — For Juliana Anicia in Constantinople

Dioscorides etc. — Parchment, 360/70 × 300 mm

Vienna, Nationalbibliothek MS.Med.gr.1

Fol. 6^{v} dedication to Juliana Anicia (d.527/8) in which she is praised by the people of Honoratai as the builder of a church (presumably that of the Theotokos ἐν τοῖς ὀνωρατοῖς on the Asiatic shore of the Bosphoros, of which she is described as foundress by Theophanes in his narrative of events of 513/14). Fol. 1-6 form a separate quire; there is therefore no proof, merely strong probability given no proof of the contrary, that this dating applies to the whole volume; the fact that the uncial hand of the main text supplied the names labelling figures in the illustrations on fol. 2^{v} and 3^{v} is not such proof.

'Biblical' uncial at the beginning of its decadence. Occasional breathings and accents; sometimes a horizontal stroke over a vowel, initially or in mid-word. Diaeresis (1), (2), and occasionally (3). Mute ι (1). Abbreviations (3), (4), and occasionally *ανος*. The reading of a difficult text full of plant and animal names is aided by the frequent use (common in book-hands from the second century) of an apostrophe at the ends of non-Greek words and words ending in some consonants, or to divide syllables especially between double consonants, or to mark elision. Ruling (1). Undated manuscripts with comparable script include B.M. Add. 17210 *(Iliad)*.

Other facsimiles : (complete) *Dioscurides. Codex Aniciae Iulianae* ..., ed. J. de Karabacek (Codices Graeci et Latini ... X, Leiden, 1906); and *Vollständige Facsimile-Ausgabe des Wiener Dioskurides*, ed. H. Gerstinger (Graz, 1966); Maunde Thompson, facs. 47; Pal. Soc. I. 177; Steffens, Taf.6. See also Cavallo, pp. 93-8, tav. 84.

2 Between 813 and 820

Astronomical tables — Parchment, 280 × 200 mm

Vatican MS. Vat. gr. 1291

Fol. 17^{r} the list of emperors with lengths of their reigns, in the first hand, includes Michael I (811-13); Leo V (813-20) was added later over an erasure.

The latest dated example of 'biblical' uncial. Breathings (1) and accents are used sporadically.

Other facsimiles : New Pal. Soc. II. 184-5

3 27 May 995 — Konstantinos πρεσβύτερος

Gospel lectionary — Parchment, 350 × 260 (245 × 160) mm

London, British Museum MS. Harl. 5598

Fol. 376^{v} *ἐγράφη δια χειρὸς κωνσταντίν(ου)· πρεσβυτέρ(ου) μη[νι] μαΐω κζ ινδ[ικτιωνος] η ἔτου ϡφγ.*

Uncial in its final ossified state. Breathings (2) and accents are used always. Abbreviations (1), (3), (4). Ruling (1) or sometimes the writing between two ruled lines. Ecphonetic notation in red.

Other facsimiles: Maunde Thompson, facs. 51; Pal. Soc. I. 26-7.

4 Last half of sixth century — Dioskoros of Aphrodito

Autograph poem — Papyrus, 295 × 390 mm

P. Lond. inv. 1552

Documents from the Dioskoros archive are dated between 506 and 585. All were found in the village of Kom Ishqaw in the Thebaid, Upper Egypt, 225 miles S. of Cairo.
The only datable example of the plain sloping uncial which was probably the working hand used before the spread of minuscule in the ninth century. No breathings, and only an occasional accent (a horizontal stroke over the vowel). Diaeresis (1) and (2).
The poem is edited with a facsimile in H.J.M. Milne, *Catalogue of the literary papyri in the British Museum* (London, 1927) no. 98, pl. VII. Another facsimile : R. Seider, *Paläographie der griechischen Papyri* (Stuttgart, 1967-) II, Abb. 64, Taf. XXXV.

5 Between 879 and 883 — For the imperial family (in Constantinople)

Gregory of Nazianzus — Parchment, 435 × 300 (305 × 185) mm

Paris, Bibliothèque nationale MS. grec 510

Fol. B^{r},C^{v} labelled portraits of Basil I, his wife Eudocia (d. 883), and sons Leo and Alexander, but not Constantine (d. 879).
The latest dated example of an elegant style of sloping uncial. Breathings (1) and accents are used always. Diaeresis (1) and (2).
Undated manuscripts with comparable script include Rome, Bibl. naz. gr. 6 + Madrid gr. N. 71 (*Iliad* scholia; only the hypotheses are in uncial); Paris gr.2389 (Ptolemy).
Another facsimile : Omont, *Plus anciens manuscrits*, pl. XI-XII. See also Jaeger.

6 Soon after September 888 — Arethas of Patrae

Euclid — Parchment, 225 × 190 (150 × 110) mm

Oxford, Bodleian MS.D'Orville 301 — additions and marginalia

Fol. 387^{v} *ἐγράφη χειρὶ στεφάνου κληρικοῦ μη[νι] σεπτεμβρίωι ινδ[ικτιωνι] ξ ἔτει κοσ[μου] ϛτϥζ : ἐκτησάμην ἀρέθας πατρεὺς τὴν παροῦσαν βίβλον νο[μισματων] [ι(?)]δ.* The hand of this subscription, presumably that of Arethas since the last sentence is in the first person, added many of the scholia etc. throughout the manuscript. Since he describes himself as a native of Patrae (Patras, on the NW. coast of the Peloponnese), Arethas presumably no longer lived there; it is assumed from his close association with the emperors Basil I and Leo VI and the patriarchs Photios and Nicolas I that he lived in Constantinople from before 886 until he became archbishop of Caesarea in about 902, if not also afterwards; it is therefore likely that this manuscript was copied, and annotated by him soon afterwards, in Constantinople.
The small plain uncial used for marginalia between the late ninth and mid-tenth centuries. Breathings (1) and accents are not always used. Mute *ι* (1). Abbreviations (6) (but Arethas' notes are mostly marginalia) : as usual at this time, abbreviated *ηυ* and *ιυ* are not differentiated; the abbreviation for *δια* is used to represent *διαι* also; Arethas rarely uses the normal form of *προs*, but instead the suspension *πρ̊*; likewise, for the plural forms of *θεός* he uses, not contractions formed in the same way as those used for the singular *nomina sacra*, but ordinary suspensions, e.g. *θε̃* for *θεοῖs*.
Other manuscripts containing annotations by Arethas include no. **37** of 895, no. **61** of 888-901, Paris gr. 2951 + Flor. Laur. 60. 3 of 906/7, no. **97** of 913/14, B.M. Harl. 5694 of *c.* 913/14, no. **26** of 932, and Rome, Vallicell. F. 10 (79).
Other facsimiles of this manuscript showing Arethas' notes: Lake, II, MS.51, pl. 94,104; Lefort and Cochez, pl. 6; Pal. Soc. I.65; Wilson, pl. 13. On Arethas' library see P. Lemerle, *Le premier humanisme byzantin* (Bibliothèque byzantine. Études 6, Paris, 1971) chap. 8.

7 Before 20 November 991 — Loukas abbot of S. Zacharias in the Mercourion (Calabria)

Maximus confessor — Parchment, 230 × 180 (165/70 × 118) mm

Grottaferrata MS.B.a.IV

p. 1 contemporary note : *ἔτ[ει] ϛφ ἰνδ[ικτιωνι] ε λουκ(ὰς) ἡγ(ού)με[νος] μον(ῆς) τ(ῆς) λεγομέ[νης] τοῦ ἁγί(ου) π(ατ)ρ(ος) ζαχ[αριου] εἰς τὸ μερκούρι(ον) μη[νι] νοεμβριω εἰκαδ[ι] νοσήσ(ας) χρ[όνον] δεκαμηνί(ον) κεκοίμητ[αι] ἡμέ[ρα] σ[α]β[βατω] ... ὁ λεχθεὶς κ(αὶ) τ(ὴν) βίβλ(ον) ἔγραψε ταύτ(ην).* From descriptions in the lives of contemporary local saints, and the survival of the name in a tributary of F.Lao and in S.Giovanni di Mercurio near Orsomarzo, it seems most probable that the district known as the Mercourion was west of Castrovillari in N. Calabria; other suggested identifications are all in Calabria.
Breathings (1). Abbreviations (1), (4), and (6) within scholia.
Other facsimiles showing the uncial scholia : Lake, X, MS. 383, pl. 724-5; Lefort and Cochez, pl. 61; Pal. Soc, II. 104.

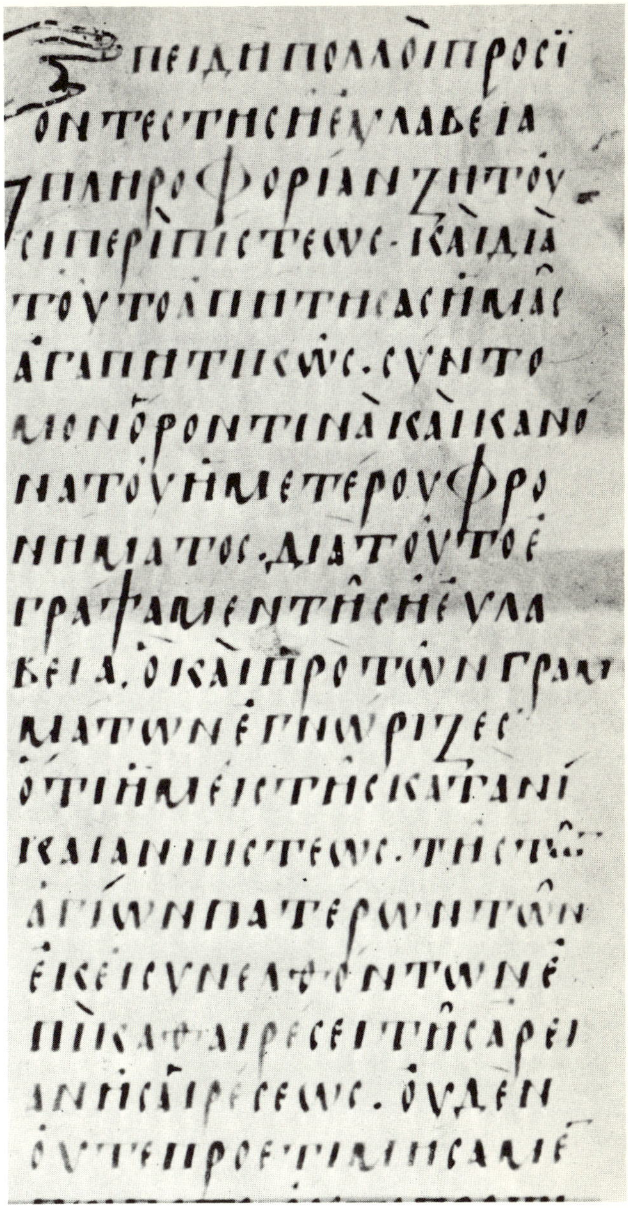

5

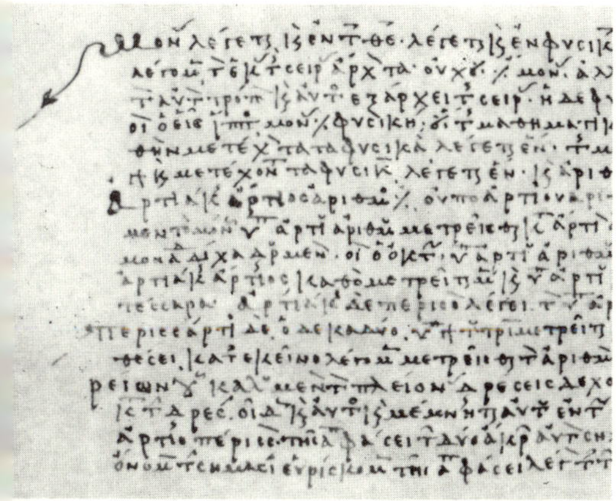

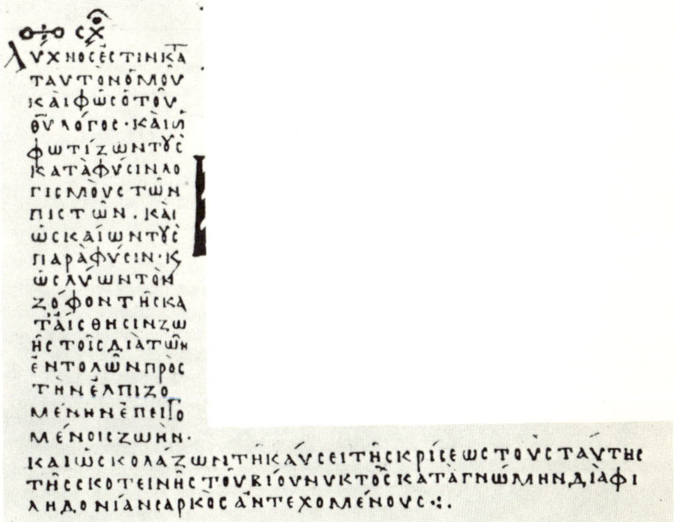

7

8

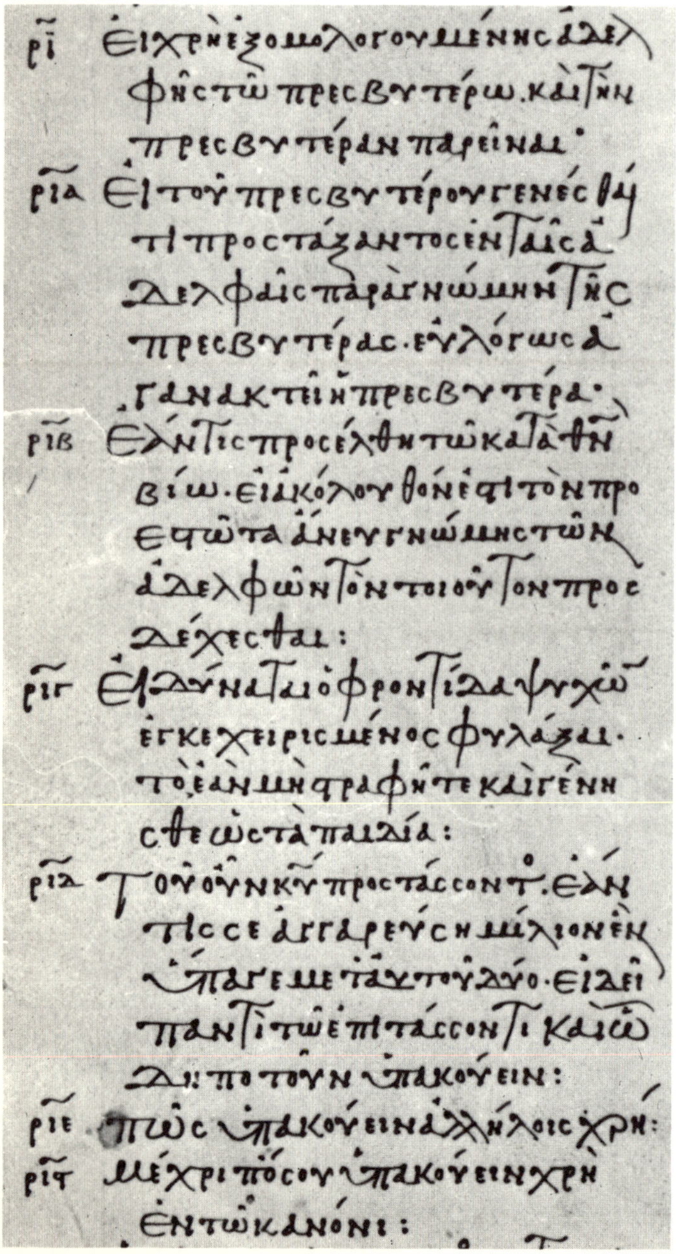

9

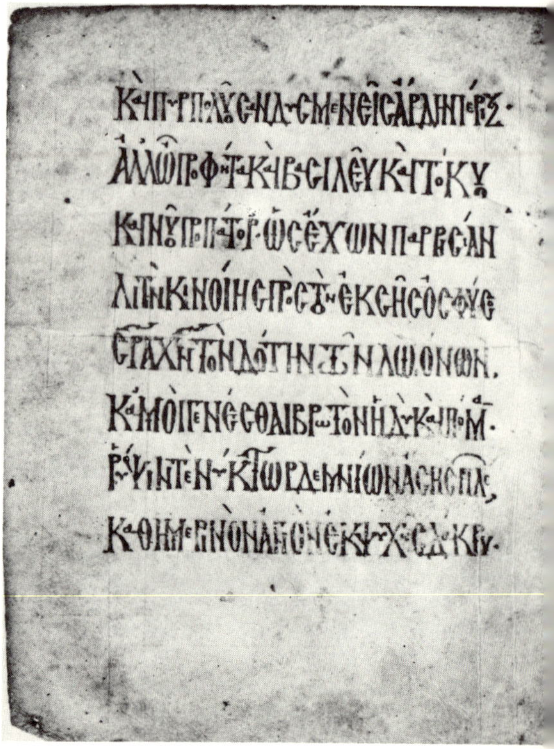

10

8 713, 719, or 724 — Alexandria

Paschal letter from patriarch of Alexandria — Papyrus, 450 mm × over 5 m (columns 380 × 380/400 mm)

P. Berol. 10677

The bilingual protocol restricts the date to between the Arab conquest of 641-6 and the substitution of all-Arabic protocols soon after 749 (date of the latest extant bilingual one). The letter fixes Easter on 16 Apr., on which day it fell in 640, 713, 719, 724, and 803.

The latest, and only, narrowly datable example of 'Coptic' uncial. Breathings (1) and accents are rarely used. Diaeresis (1) and (2). Abbreviations (1), (3), (4). An apostrophe is sometimes placed after words ending in a consonant. All the classical texts copied in 'Coptic' uncial of which facsimiles exist are in relatively less set and mannered hands, which suggest dates earlier than this letter; the nearest in style is perhaps PSI 1302 (Aristotle). That the greater artificiality and exaggerated forms of **8** might be not so much an effect of later date as a characteristic of ecclesiastical chancery scribes is ruled out by the plain style used in the Paschal letter of 577 or 672 (P. Lond. inv. 729).

The letter is edited with 2 plates in *Altchristliche Texte*, ed. C. Schmidt and W. Schubart (Berliner Klassikertexte VI, Berlin, 1910), pp. 55-109. Other facsimiles : *Papyri Graeci Berolinenses*, ed. W. Schubart (Bonn, 1911), Tab. 50; R. Seider, *Paläographie der griechischen Papyri* (Stuttgart, 1967-), II, Abb. 66, Taf. XXXVI. See also Irigoin, 'L' onciale grecque'.

9 21 April 1086 — Ioannes *μοναχὸς καὶ πρεσβύτερος* of monastery of the Theotokos or S. Aberkios in the patriarchate (Constantinople)

Basil — Parchment, 365 × 235 (280 × 170) mm

Moscow, Historical Museum MS. 121

Fol. 272^{r} *ἐτελειώθ[η] σὺν θ(ε)ῷ ἡ βί[βλος] αὕτ[η]. μηνὶ ἀπριλλ[ιω] κα̅· ἰνδ[ικτιωνος] θ̅ : ἔτους ϛ φ ϟδ δ(ιὰ) χειρ(ὸς) ἰω[άννου] τοῦ εὐτ[ε]λ[οῦς] [μον]αχ[οῦ] κ(αὶ) πρε[σβυ]τέ[ρου] τοῦ ναοῦ τ(ῆς) υπ[εραγιας] θ(εοτό)κου, ἤτοι τ(οῦ) ἁγίου ἀβερκιου τ(οῦ) ἐν τῷ π(ατ)ριαρχ[ειω].*

A late offshoot of 'Coptic' uncial, now used only for headings etc. Breathings (2). Abbreviations (2), (4), (5), (8). Ruling (3).

Another facsimile of an uncial page : Lake, VI, MS. 230, pl. 414.

10 *c.* 1077/8

Psalter — Parchment, 103 × 87 (65 × 45) mm

Oxford, Bodleian MS. E.D. Clarke 15 fols. 3^{r} - 9^{v}

Fol. 254^{v}-256^{v} Easter tables for 1077/8 to 1106/7.

Ornamental capitals, widely used for headings etc., are used here for preliminary matter to the Psalter. Ligatures, and small letters squeezed between others, are used to keep each metrical line within the writing space. Breathings (1) of the primitive ⊢ ⊣ shape (which are used also throughout the minuscule text, unusually at this late date). Diaeresis (1). Mute ι (1). Abbreviations (1), (2) on compound *nomina sacra*, (5), occasionally (6). The writing is between two ruled lines.

Other facsimiles of text in capitals: Lake, II MS. 60, pl. 110.

11 17 October 697 or 712 — Thebes (Egypt)

Firman from dux Thebaidos — Papyrus, more than 655 mm × 363 mm

New York, Metropolitan Museum Access. no. 24.2.4

Protocol dated not later than 695/6. Letter dated 20 Phaophi, 11th indiction. The sender of the letter, Flavius ʿAṭiyyah b. Juʿaid, is thought to have been dux Thebaidos only until 699; but the firman demands the payment of poll-tax by a monastery, for which there is no evidence before 704/5. Indiction 11 occurred in 697 and 712. Thebes was near the modern Luxor, 420 miles S. of Cairo.
A documentary hand foreshadowing minuscule: apart from the long ascenders and descenders, most letters and ligatures have the forms they have in the earliest minuscule; only ν, σ, and ω still have a partly uncial shape. No breathings or accents.
A reduced facsimile of the whole document is in H.I. Bell, 'Two official letters of the Arab period', *Journal of Egyptian Archaeology*, 12 (1926), 265-81, pl. XLVI.

12 and 13 7 May 835 — Nikolaos *μοναχός*

(in the Stoudion monastery, Constantinople)

Gospels — Parchment, 162 × 102 (110×60) mm

Leningrad, Public Library MS. gr. 219

Fol. 344[v] *ετελειωθη ... ἡ ϊερα αυτη ... βιβλος μηνι μαϊω ξ̅ ϊνδικτιῶν(ος) ιγ̅ ετους κόσμου ϡ̅ τμγ̅. δυσωπω δὲ πάντας τοὺς εντυγχάνοντας μνίαν μου ποιεισθαι του γραψαντος νικολαου αμαρτ[ωλου] μοναχ[ου]* ... Fol. 344[r] obits of Theodoros abbot of Stoudion, his uncle Plato who lived there, and his brother Ioseph.
The earliest dated manuscript written in minuscule.
Other facsimiles : Lake, VI, MS. 234, pl. 420, 432; Lefort and Cochez, pl.4; Tsereteli and Sobolevski, II, pl. I, I[a]; Wattenbach and von Velsen, tab. I.

12 Notes in a more current style than the text, with more of the characteristics of documentary hands, e.g. long ascenders and descenders, hooks on *η* and *κ*, tall *ι*. Breathings (1) and accents are very rarely used. Diaeresis (2). Abbreviations (1), (4), (5), (7).

13 Pure minuscule. Breathings (1) and accents are used always. Diaeresis (1) and (2). Abbreviations (2), (4); the use of accents on *nomina sacra* is very rare before the end of the tenth century. Only bounding lines and one central horizontal line are ruled. Undated manuscripts with comparable script include Oxford, Corpus Christi MS.108 (Aristotle); and in some respects Paris gr. 2935, fol. 27[r]-end (Demosthenes), Vat. gr. 1 (Plato), and 204, fol. 185- end (Euclid).

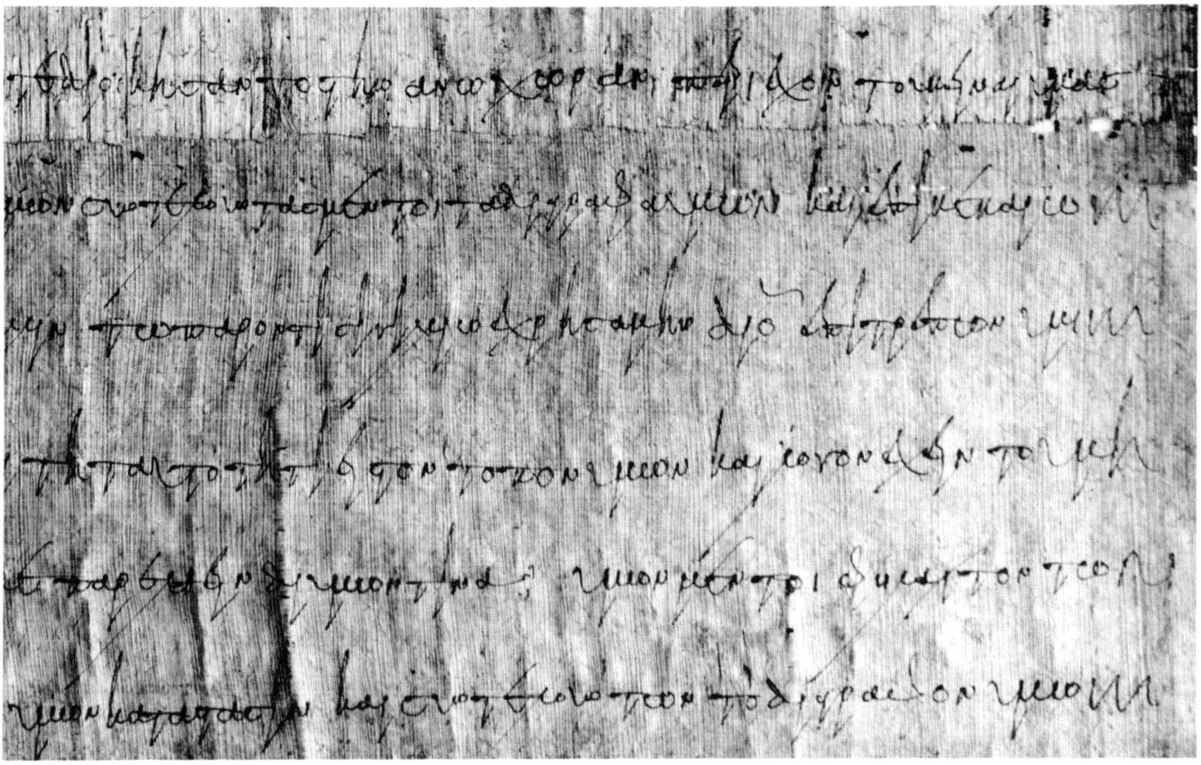

11

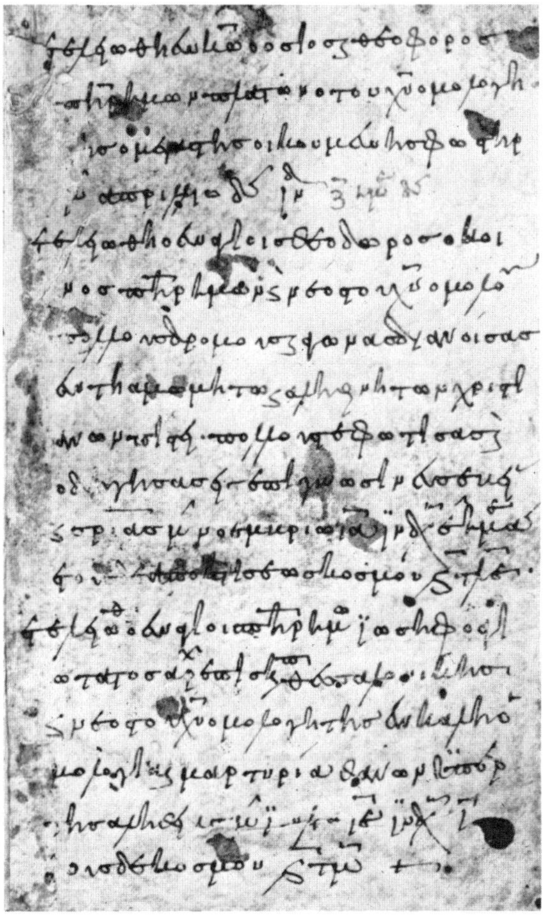

12

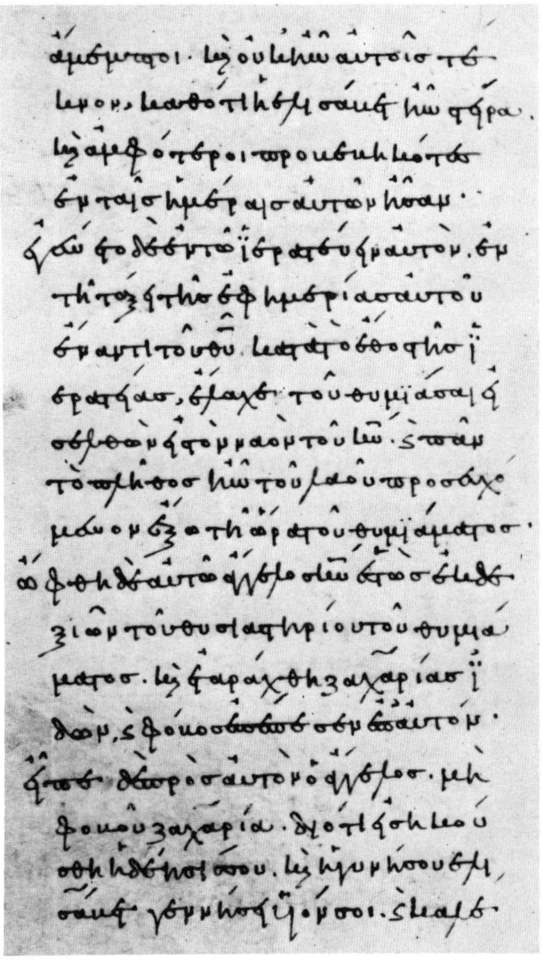

13

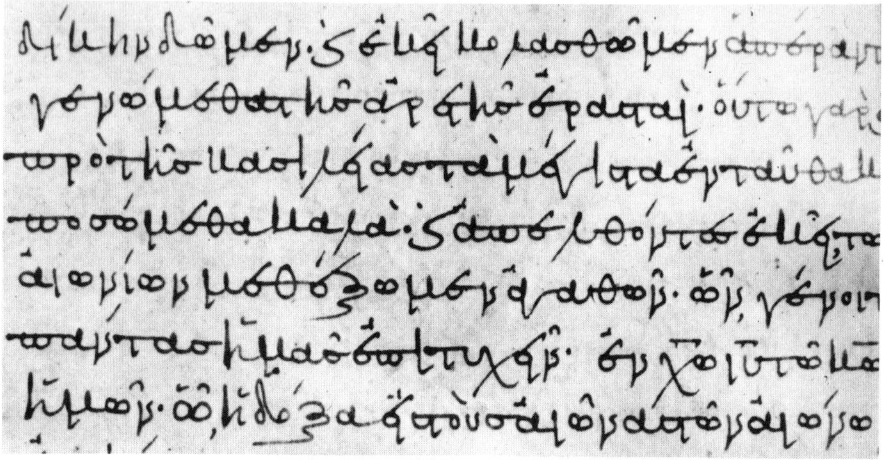

14

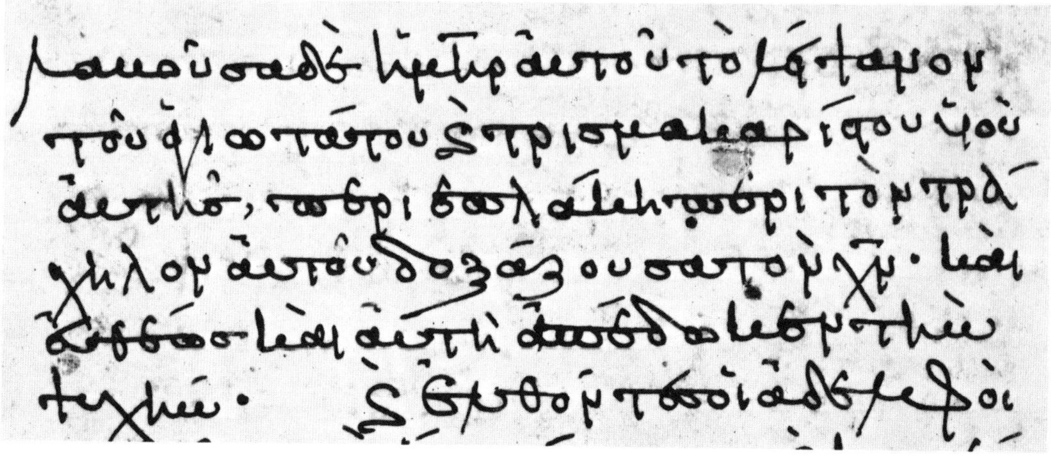

15

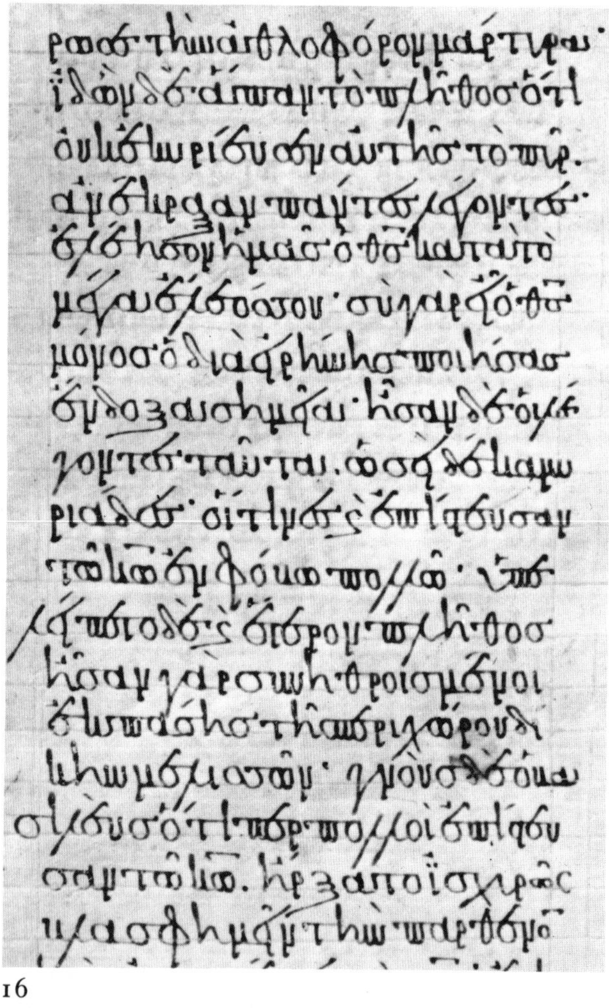

16

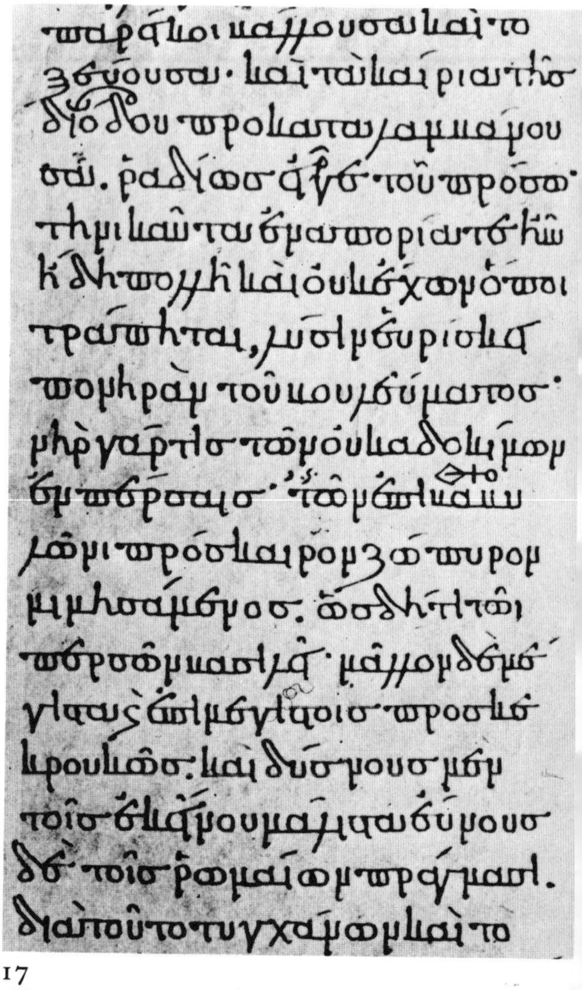

17

14 862/3 or 861/2 — Eustathios μοναχός, in the monastery of S. Anna, Kios, Bithynia

Chrysostom — Parchment, 288 × 175 (213 × 120) mm

Meteora, Metamorphosis MS. 591

Fol. 4r *Τριὰς μονὰς ἁγία ... τὸ πικρὸν ἕλκος τῶν ἁμαρτιῶν μου ἴάσαι. τοῦ τε κτησαμένου (καὶ) γράψαντος τὴν ἵερὰν ταύτην ... βίβλον εὐσταθίου ἐλαχίστου (καὶ) ταπεινοῦ μοναχοῦ: - εγραφη δε (καὶ) ετελειώθη ἡ ... αὕτη βίβλος ἐν τω ͵ϛ το ἔτη· ἐν τῇ ἑνδεκάτῃ ἰνδικτιόνη· ἐν τῇ μονὴ τῆς ἁγίας ἄννης τῆς διακειμένης ὑπὸ τῶν τῆς βυθινίας μερῶν ἐν τῇ ενορία τῆς κίου· ἐπὶ τῆς ἐξοριας τοῦ ἁγιωτάτου πατριάρχου ἰγνατίου:* - The year 6370 of the Constantinopolitan era was A.D. 861/2 but indiction 10, whereas 6370 in the Alexandrian era was 877/8 and indiction 11; but Ignatius was in exile from October 858 to November 867, therefore the Constantinopolitan year must have been intended; as usual at this period, the indiction is more likely to be correct than the year. Kios is the modern Gemlik, 17 miles N. of Bursa, on the E. shore of the Marmara. Pure minuscule. Breathings (2), the use of occasional round ones being very rare before the mid- tenth century. Diaeresis (1) and (2). Abbreviations (1), (4), and occasionally ϛ for αι at line ends. Only bounding lines are ruled; writing stands on the top and bottom lines.
Other facsimiles: Bees, I, pl. LXVIII-LXIX.

15 21 March 916 — Ioannes *μοναχός*, while Anatolios was abbot of the Stoudion monastery (Constantinople)

Menologion — Parchment, 320 × 200 (225 × 130) mm

Vatican MS. Vat. gr. 1660 fol. 1-24, 28-161, 162v-314, 323-end

Fol. 408r *τετέλεσται ἡ παροῦσα βίβλος· μηνὶ μαρτίω κα ινδ[ικτωνος] δ ἔτους κόσμου ͵ϛυκδ γραφεῖσα διὰ χειρὸς ἰωάννου ταπεινοῦ καὶ ἐλαχίστου μοναχοῦ, ἐπι ανατολίου τοῦ ὁσιωτάτου ἡγουμένου τῶν στουδίου:*
This and one of its companion volumes (see below) are the only examples of this early style explicitly connected with the Stoudion. Uncial λ, ν, ξ, and (at line ends) α are used. Breathings (1). Diaeresis (2). Abbreviations (1), (3), (4), and occasionally ϛ for αι at line endings. Rulings (1). Other volumes of the same menologion copied over a period of years are Vat. gr. 1669 and 1671 (when Timotheus was abbot of Stoudion). Undated manuscripts with comparable script include Heidelberg, Palat. gr. 252 (Thucydides); Flor. Laur. 81.11 (Aristotle); Milan, Ambros. L. 93 sup. (Aristotle).
Other facsimiles: Cavalieri and Lietzmann, tab. 12; Follieri, tab. 14; Lake, VII, MS. 260, pl. 461-3; Lefort and Cochez, pl. 20; Pal. Soc. II. 82.

16 April 890 — Anastasios

Menologion — Parchment, 325 × 230 (240 × 165) mm

Paris Bibliothèque nationale MS. grec 1470

Fol. 248v *μνήσθητι σ(ωτ)ερ ... τοῦ ἐμπόνως γράψαντος ἀναστασίου ... καμοῦ δὲ παύει τοὺς πόνους ἐν σαββάτω μηνὶ ἀπρηλλίω ἰνδικτιόνος η ἔτους ͵ϛτϙη.*
I know of no manuscript written in this compressed style at this early date where the place of copying is explicit. Occasional uncial λ and (at line ends) σ; it is probably the earliest dated minuscule hand to use any uncial form in mid-line. Breathings (1). Diaeresis (2). Abbreviations (1), (3), (4). Ruling usually (1), but sometimes (2) or (3). Anastasios also copied Paris gr. 1476 (Menologion). Undated manuscripts with comparable script, though less primitive and stiff, include Escorial Σ II.10, fol. 1-149 (Hippocrates), and Paris gr. 2934 (Demosthenes).
Other facsimiles: Lake, IV, MS. 134, pl. 226-8; Lefort and Cochez, pl. 7; Omont, *Manuscrits datés*, pl. I.

17 24 October 941 — Nikolaos *μοναχός* and Daniel, in Reggio Calabria

Gregory of Nazianzus — Parchment, 440 × 340 (340 × 255) mm

Patmos, S. John MS. 33

Fol. 190r *ἐγραφη κ(αι) πέρας εἴληφεν αὕτη ἡ ... βίβλος δια χειρὸς νικολάου μ(ονα)χου καὶ δανιὴλ υ(ιο)υ αὐτου ... εν τόπω ρηγίω τ(ης) καλαβρίας εν τῶ ὀκτωβρίω μηνὶ τῇ εἰκάδι δ ινδ[ικτιωνος] ιε εν ετει απο κτισεως κοσμ(ου) ͵ϛυν.*
One hand uses pure minuscule, the other uncial *λ* and (at line ends) *α* and *σ*. Breathings (1). Diaeresis (1) and (2). Mute ι (1). Abbreviations (2), (3), (4). Ruling (1). The similarity of style between this and a number of manuscripts of earlier date and unknown provenance is no argument for assigning them also to S. Italy; the unexpectedly late date for pure minuscule and for most of the scribal habits in this manuscript is consistent with its being a provincial product belatedly following models from one of the main centres of copying.
Other facsimiles: Komines, *Πιν.* 1; Lake, I, MS. 15, pl. 28-34.

18 September 888 Stephanos *κληρικός*, bought by Arethas of Patrae
Oxford, Bodleian MS. D'Orville 301
[for details see **6**]

Pure minuscule. Breathings (1) and accents are not always used. Diaeresis (2) used only on *ἴσος*. Mute ι (1). Abbreviations (4) and occasionally ς for αι at line ends. Ruling sometimes (1), sometimes (2).
Undated manuscripts with comparable script include Vat. gr. 1594, fol. 1-65, 68-277 (Ptolemy); and (though their style is more primitive and stiff) many of the group of manuscripts described by Allen, 'A group', especially Heidelberg Palat. gr. 398 (geographers), Paris gr. 1807 (Plato) and 1962 (Plato commentary), Vat. gr. 2197 (Proclus), Ven. Marc. gr. 246 (Damascius) and 258 (Alexander Aphrodisiensis).
Other facsimiles: Lake, II, MS. 51, pl. 94, 104; Lefort and Cochez, pl. 6: Maunde Thompson, facs. 53; Pal. Soc. I. 65-6; Wattenbach and von Velsen, tab. II; Wilson, pl. 13.

19 947/8 Kyrillos *μοναχός;* given to monastery of SS. Akepsima, Ioseph, and Aeithala on the island of Chalce
Climacus Parchment, 277 × 185 (205 × 125) mm
Oxford, Bodleian MS. Barocci 134

Fol. 219^r *ἐτελειώθη αὕτη ἡ πανήερος βίβλος τῶν ἁγίων ἱερομαρτύρων ἀκεψιμὰ ἰωσὴφ' καὶ ἀειθαλὰ· τῆς νήσου χάλκης· γραφὲν δια χειρὸς εὐτελοῦς κυρίλλου μοναχοῦ· ἔτους ϛυνq.* [mutil.] ... *δοθη μοι λυσις ἀμπλακ[η]μάτων κυρίλλω μο[να]χω κ(αὶ) ξενω τῶν ἐνθάδε: ταυτην τὴν δελτο[ν] προσφέρω τοῖς ἁγιο[ις] ἀκεψιμὰ ἰωσὴφ' ἀειθαλά τε: τῆς νήσου χάλκ[ης]* ... The manuscript was not necessarily copied on Chalce. No monastery dedicated to these saints is known on the island of this name either in the Sea of Marmara or near Rhodes.
Uncial *ζ, ν, ξ* are used. Breathings (1), occasionally (3). Diaeresis (1), (2), and occasionally (3). Abbreviations (1), (3), (4). Ruling (3).
Other facsimiles: Lake, II, MS. 53, pl. 96-7; Lefort and Cochez, pl. 30; New Pal. Soc. II. 29.

20 12 August 953
Basil Parchment, 334 × 230 (248 × 155/60) mm
Oxford, Bodleian MS. Auct. E. 2.12

Fol. 221^r *ἐπληρωθ[η] τὰ εἰς τὸν προφήτην ἡσαΐαν τοῦ ἁγίου Βασιλείου· μη[νι] αὐγούστω ιβ τῶν αγίων μ[α]ρ[τυρων] φωτίου κ(αὶ) ἀνικήτου· ἡμέρα παρασκευῆ· ὥρ[α]ῆ· ινδ[ικτιωνος] ια ἔτους ϛυξα.*
One of the latest dated examples of an elegant, mannered style which may have originated in Constantinople; this is suggested by (a) the probable origin of Athens suppl. gr. 641 (see below), (b) the sophisticated style of writing, and (c) the fine, white parchment used in most of these manuscripts. Uncial *γ, δ, ε, ζ, κ, λ, ν, ξ, π, ψ*, and (at line ends) σ are used; it contains one of the earliest appearances of the late form of β which was adopted from documentary hands but came into common use in literary texts only in the twelfth century (line 4). Breathings (1) and occasionally (3). Diaeresis (1) and (2). Abbreviations (1), (3), (4), and occasionally (5). Ruling (3).
The earliest dated example of this style is Venice, Marc. gr. 538 of 904/5 (Job with catena); the only example giving any indication of its origin is Athens suppl. gr. 641 of 913/14 (Old Testament), copied for Samonas as *πατρίκιος* which suggests that he had by then returned to the capital from exile. Undated manuscripts with comparable script include Flor. Laur. 69.2 (Thucydides), and in some respects Flor. Laur. 74.7 (medical works) and conv. soppr. 206 (Plutarch).
Other facsimiles: Lake, II, MS. 54, pls. 98-9; Lefort and Cochez, pl. 32; Pal. Soc. I. 82.

21 7 September 1052 Konstantinos *πρωτοπαπᾶς*, in Taverna (Calabria)
Gospels Parchment, 245 × 195 (185 × 145) mm
Vatican MS. Vat. gr. 2002

Fol. 117^r *γραφὲ[ν] δια χ[ειρος] κωνστ[αν]τ[ινου] ἁμαρτωλοῦ καὶ ταπεινου (πρωτο)π[α]π[α] οἰκῶν ἐν πολ[ει] ταβερνῶν· μηνὶ σεπτεμβρίω τελειωθ[εν] εἰς τὰς ζ ἡμε[ρα] β ὥρα δ ἔτους ϛφξα ινδ[ικτιωνος] ϛ ἡλίου κύκλ[ω] η σ[εληνης] κύκλ[ω] ε: παρῶν τῆς ἡγεμονίας γεωργιλὰ στρατηγοῦ καλαβρίας.* Taverna is on the S. slopes of the Sila, 8 miles N. of Catanzaro.
Nearly all distinctive uncial forms are used. Breathings (1). Circumflex accent sometimes (1) when over a breathing. Diaeresis (1) and (2). Mute ι (1). Abbreviations (1) and (4). Ruling (3).
Other facsimiles: Lake, VII, MS. 287, pl. 521.

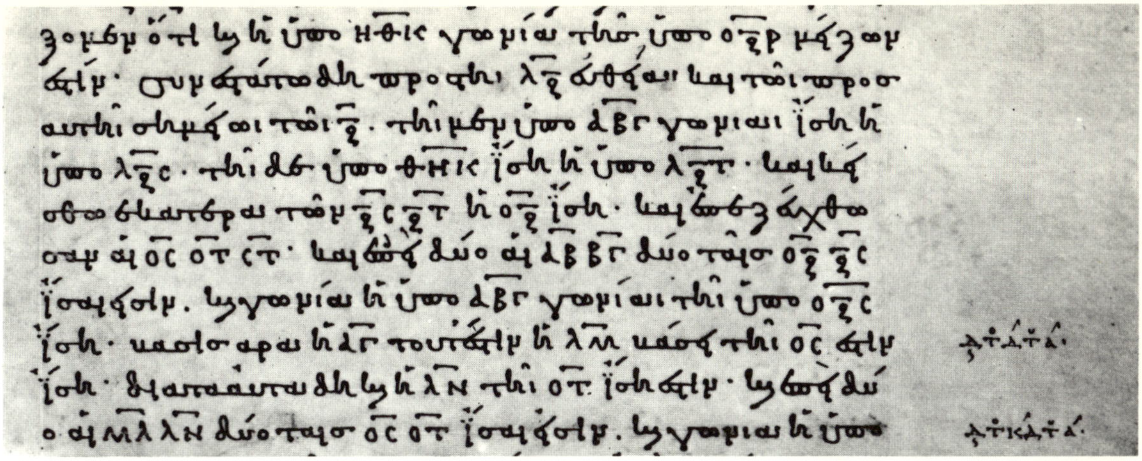

18

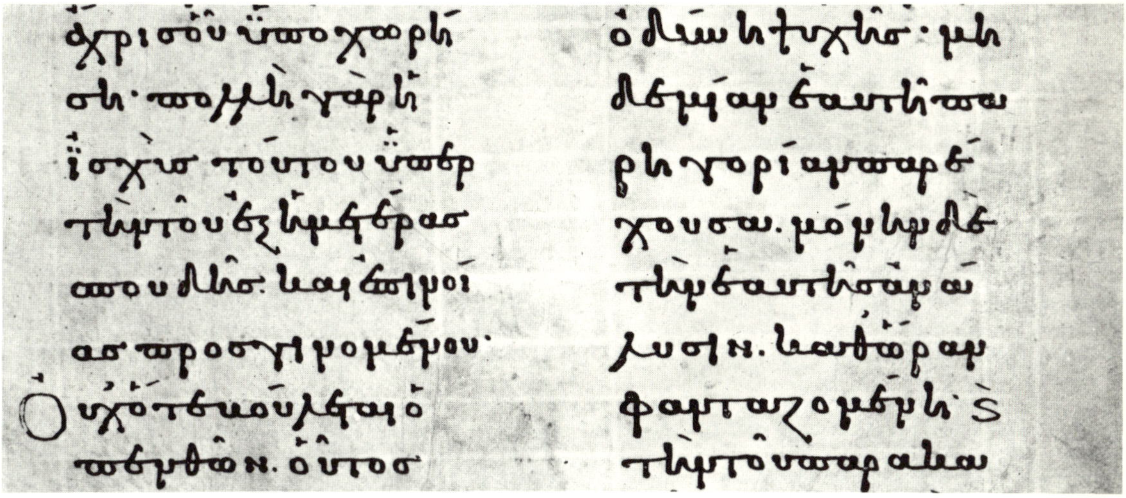

19

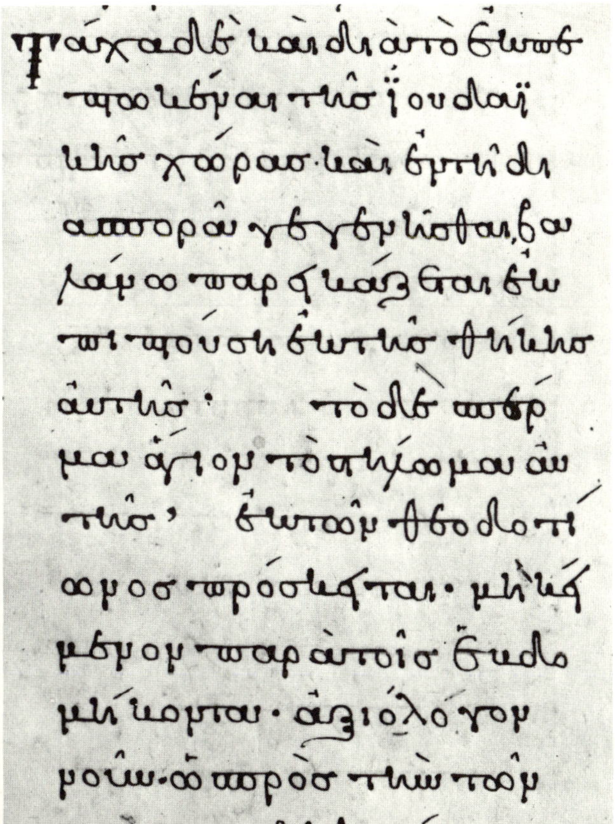

20

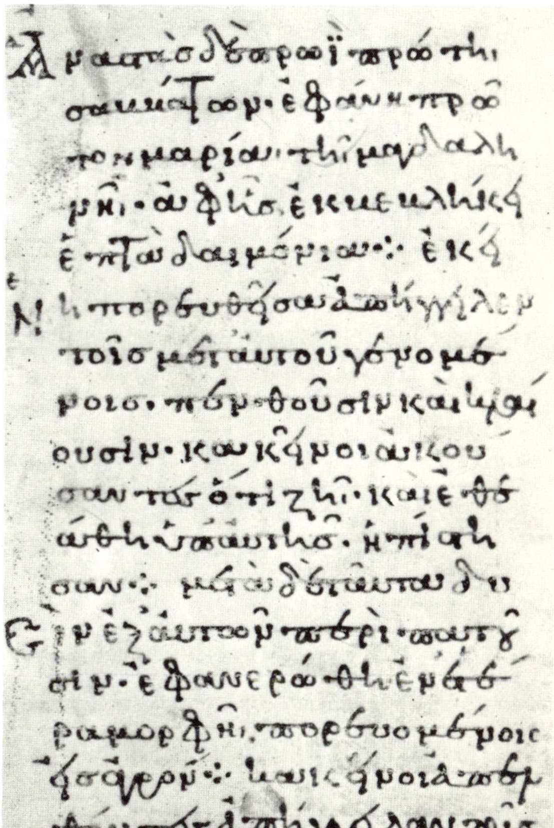

21

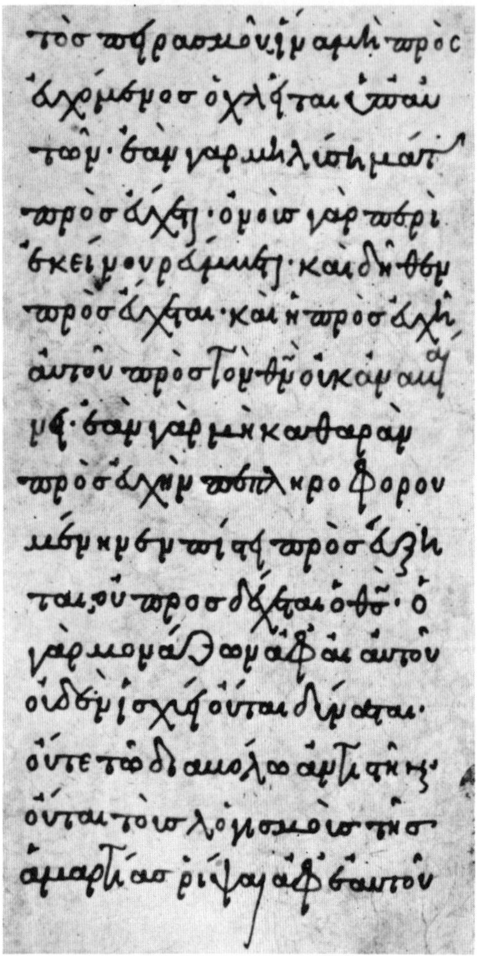

22

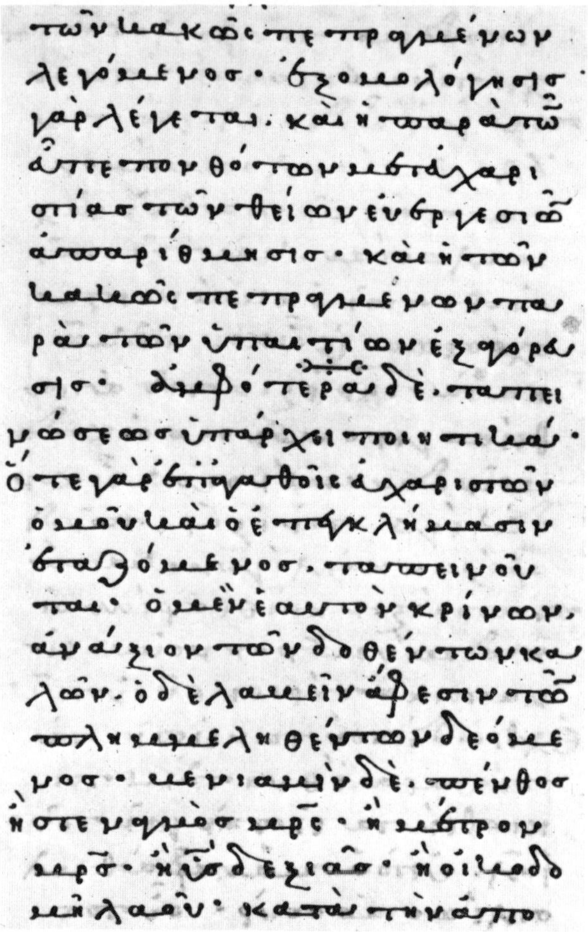

23

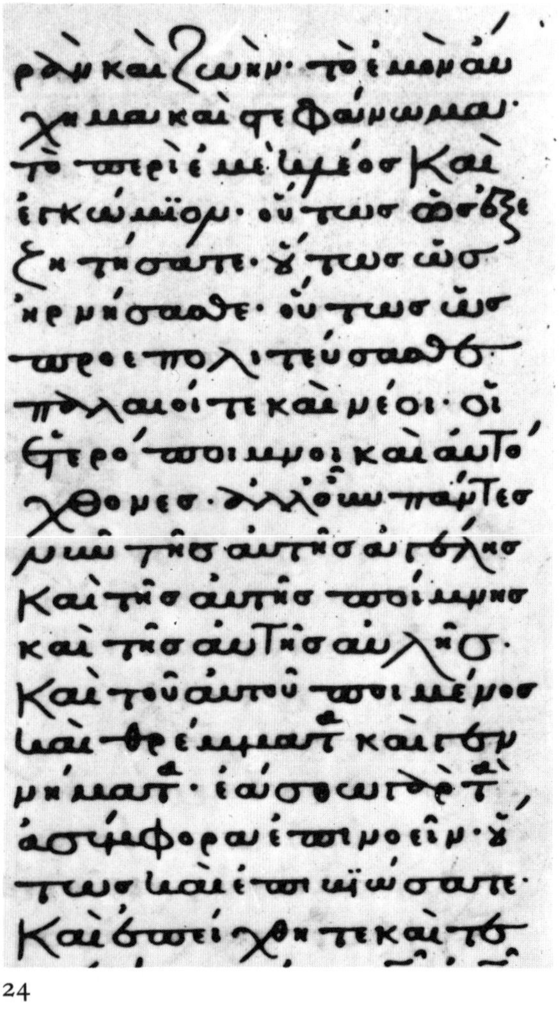

24

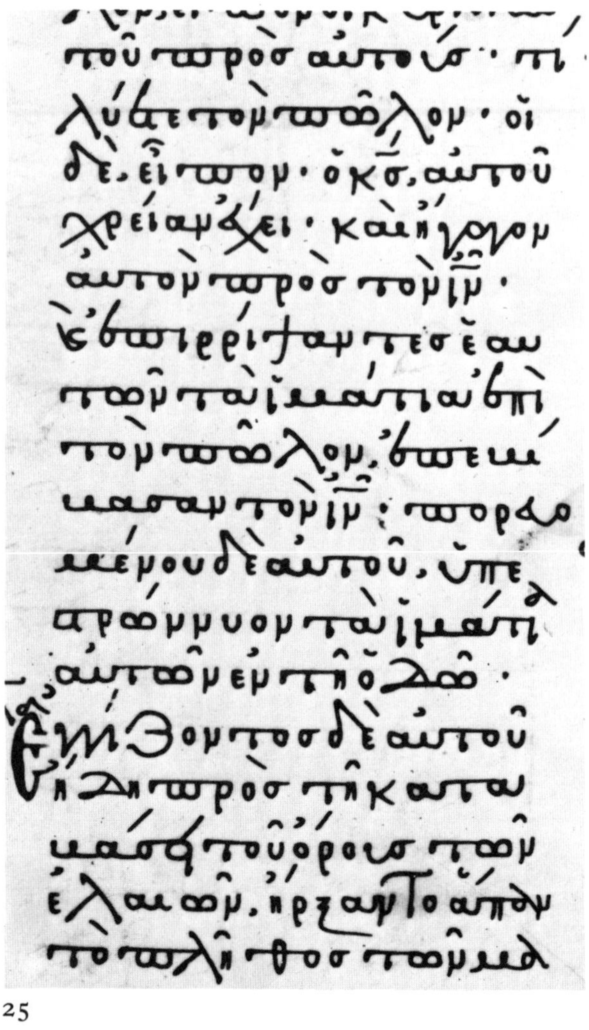

25

22 10 March 1104 — Gerasimos (?) *μοναχός* for Nikodemos abbot of monastery of S. Demetrios or *τοῦ Πoριανήτος*, Athos

Palladius etc. — Parchment, 245 × 190 (175 × 125) mm

Oxford, Christ Church MS. Gr. 70

Fol. 206[v] ... *τῶ εὐτὲλῆ [μον]αχ[ῶ]· νυκοδίμ[ω]· καὶ καθ[η]γουμέ[νω] τ(ῆς) μο[νῆς] τοῦ ἁγ[ίου] μ[ε]γ[αλο]μ[α]ρ[τυρος] δημητρ[ιου]· τ(ῆς) τοῦ πoριἀνή-τ[ος] λεγομέ[νης] κ(αὶ) ἐν τῶ ἁγ[ίω] ὄρη οὖσ(ης)· ... ἐγρά[φη] δὲ χειρὶ γηρα[σιμου(?)] [μονα]χ[οῦ] κ(αὶ) ἁμαρτ[ω]λ[οῦ] μη[νι] μαρτ[ιω] ῑ· ινδ[ικτιωνος] ῑβ̄ ἐν ἔτει ϡχιβ:* A monastery *τοῦ Πoριανήτος* is not known; the only one dedicated to S. Demetrios on Athos is a dependent house of Vatopedi.

Breathings (2). Circumflex accent sometimes (1) when over a breathing. Diaeresis (1), (2), and sometimes (3). Abbreviations (2), (4), (5), and sometimes (8) slightly. Ruling (3).

Other facsimiles: Lake, V, MS. 196, pl. 335-6.

23 24 October 1118 — Nikolaos of Reggio (Calabria)

Maximus confessor — Parchment, 308 × 254 (210 × 160) mm

Vatican MS. Vat. gr. 1646

Fol. 278[v] *ἐγράφη αὕτη ἡ βίβλος ... διὰ χειρὸς νικολάου χθαμαλοῦ ῥηγινοῦ· ἐν μη[νι] ὀκ[τωβριω] κδʹ· τοῦ ϡχκζʹ ἰνδ[ικτιωνος] ιβ:*

Breathings (2). Abbreviations sometimes (1), sometimes (2), (3), (4). Ruling (3).

Other facsimiles: Follieri, tab. 37; Devreesse, *Les manuscrits grecs* pl. IV.

24 12 June 1136 — Arsenios *μοναχός* for Maximos abbot of monastery of the Prodromos in Petra (Constantinople)

Theodore of Studium — Parchment, 313 × 243 (220 × 170) mm

Paris, Bibliothèque nationale MS. grec 891

Fol. 261[v] *ἡ βῖβλ(ος) αὕτη τῆς μονῆς τοῦ προδρόμου: τῆς κειμένης ἔγγιστα τῆς ἀετίου: ἀρχαϊκὴ δὲ τῆι μονῆι κλῆσις, πέτρα: ἐγράφη διὰ χειρ(ὸς) τοῦ μοναχοῦ ἀρσενίου ἐξ ἐπιταγῆς καὶ συλλογῆς τοῦ καθηγουμένου τῆς αὐτῆς μονῆς [μον]αχ[οῦ] κυροῦ μαξίμου· ... θ(εο)ῦ τὸ δῶρον ἡ γραφή δ' ἀρσενίου: Ἐτελειώθη μη[νὶ] ἰουνίωι δωδεκάτη· ἰνδ[ικτιῶνος] ιδ̄ ἔτους ϡχμδ βασιλεύοντ[ος] ἰω[άννου] τοῦ πορφυρογενν[ή]τ[ου].*

Breathings (3). Circumflex accent sometimes (1). Diaeresis occasionally (3). Mute ι (1) but shortened. Abbreviations (2), (4), (5). Ruling (3).

Other facsimiles: Lake, V, MS. 188, pls. 319, 321; Omont, *Manuscrits datés* pl. XLVII.

25 10 January 1197 — Athanasios *ἱερομόναχος*, for Ioannikios *λογοθέτης* abbot of monastery of S. Georgios *τῶν βεβαλίνων* (Calabria)

Gospels — Parchment, 265 × 210 (185 × 145 and 190 × 150) mm

Vatican MS. Vat. gr. 2290

Fol. 218[v] *ἐγρά[φη] (καὶ) ἐτελειώθη χειρὶ ἀθανασίου εὐτελοῦς (καὶ) ἁμαρτωλοῦ ἱερομονάζοντ(ος): μη[νὶ] ἰἀννου[αριω] ῑ, ἔτος ϡψ̄ε̄, τῆς ἰνδ[ικτίωνος] ιε̄, τῆ σπουδῆ τοῦ ... καθηγουμ[έν]ου κ[υροῦ] ἰω[αννι]κίου τοῦ λογοθέτου· τοῦτό τε προστατεύο(ν)τ(ος) τῆς μονῆς τοῦ ἁγ[ίου] μεγ[α]λ[ο]μάρτυρος γεωργ[ίου] τῶν βεβαλίνων.* This must have been the monastery S. Georgii de Bubalino recorded in 1324 in the diocese of Gerace, the most likely situation for it in this district being near the modern village of Bovalino in the E. foot-hills of Aspromonte 25 miles E. of Reggio Calabria.

One of the latest dated examples of a distinctive mannered elegant style associated with S. Italy and Sicily, but also found earlier in some manuscripts in which a Constantinopolitan origin is suggested by other features such as the ornament (e.g. Athos Esphig. 25 of 1129). Breathings (3). Accents occasionally (2). Diaeresis (1). Abbreviations (2), (4), (5). Ruling (3).

For a suggestion that this style was known as Litera Neritina from its association with Nardò and a list of some other manuscripts in which it is found, see Wilson, 'Litera Neritina'.

Other facsimiles: Lake, VIII, MS. 330, pl. 601-2; Devreesse, *Les manuscrits grecs*, pl. V.

26 April 932 — Stylianos *διάκονος*, for Arethas archbishop of Caesarea, Cappadocia

Polemical collection — Parchment, 275×200 (170×115) mm

Moscow, Historical Museum MS. 231

Fol. 169ʳ *στυλιανὸς διάκονος ἔγραψα ἀρέθαι αρχιεπισκοπωι καισαρείας καππαδοκίας. ἔτει κόσμ(ου) ςυμ ἰνδικτιων(ος) πέμπτης· μηνὶ ἀπριλίωι συμπληρωθέντος τοῦ τεύχους.* The manuscript was not necessarily written in Caesarea (Kayseri, in central Turkey, 165 miles SE. of Ankara) or by a local scribe.

Uncial forms are used in greater number than is common at this time: δ,ε,ζ,κ,λ,ν,ξ, occasionally α,β,η,π,ω, and (at line ends) σ. Breathings mainly (1) but sometimes with a tendency to roundness. Diaeresis (1). Mute ι (1). Abbreviations (1), (4), and occasionally ς for αι at line ends. Ruling (3).

Other facsimiles: Lake, VI, MS. 217, pl. 379-81, 384; Lefort and Cochez, pl. 25; Tsereteli and Sobolevski, I, pl. V-VI.

27 7 January 992

Ps. - Dionysius the Areopagite — Parchment, 320×255 (185×130) mm

Paris, Bibliothèque nationale MS. grec 438

Fol. 249ʳ *ἐτελειώθη ἡ παροῦσα βῖβλος μηνὶ ἰαννουαρίωι ζ̄ ινδ[ικτιωνος] ε̄ ἔτους ςφ.*

Breathings (2). Mute ι (1). Abbreviations (1) and (4). Ruling (3).

Other facsimiles: Lake, IV, MS. 144, pl. 245-7; Lefort and Cochez, pl. 62; Omont, *Manuscrits datés*, pl. IX.

28 1036/7 — Ioannes μοναχός

Climacus — Parchment, 285×215 (175/200×140) mm.

Paris, Bibliothèque nationale MS. Coislin 265

Fol. 259ᵛ *Ἐγράφη τὸ· θεόπνευστ[ον] τοῦτο βιβλίον· διὰ χειρὸς ἰωάννου μοναχοῦ ταπεινοῦ ξένου: ... ἔτ(ους) ςφμε (ινδικτιωνος) ε· Ἐπὶ ἀνακτ(ος) μιχ[αηλ] φιλοχρ[ιστου]:* The dating by the reign of Michael IV suggests, but does not prove, that the manuscript was copied in the Eastern part of the empire.

Though the style is formal, the hand is individual and unusual. Breathings (1). Mute ι (1). Abbreviations (1), (4), (5), occasionally (7) at line ends. Ruling (3).

Other facsimiles: Lake, IV, MS. 153, pl. 261, 264; Omont, *Manuscrits datés*, pl. XVI.

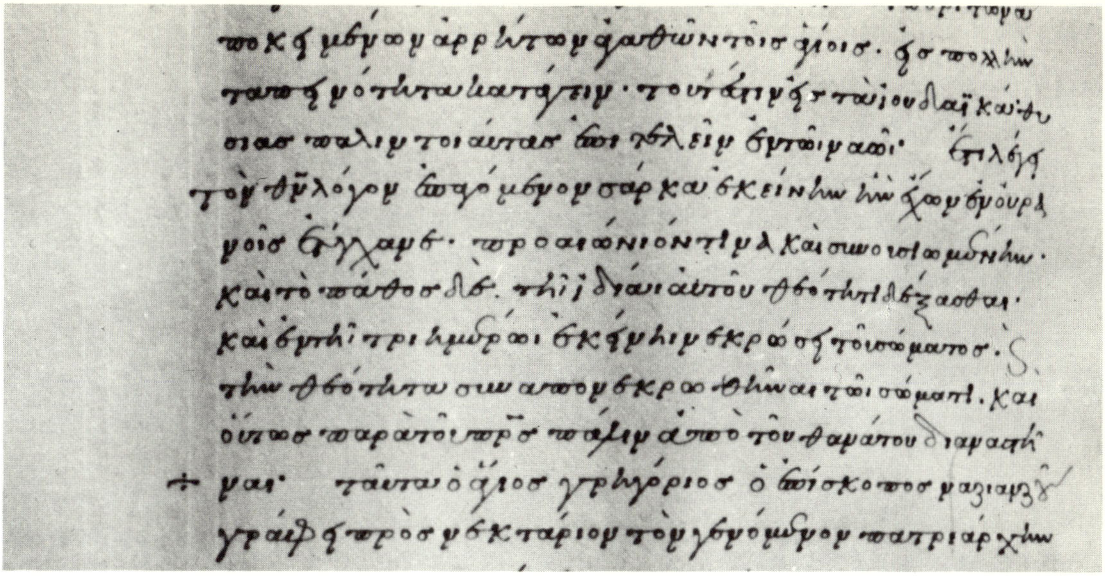

26

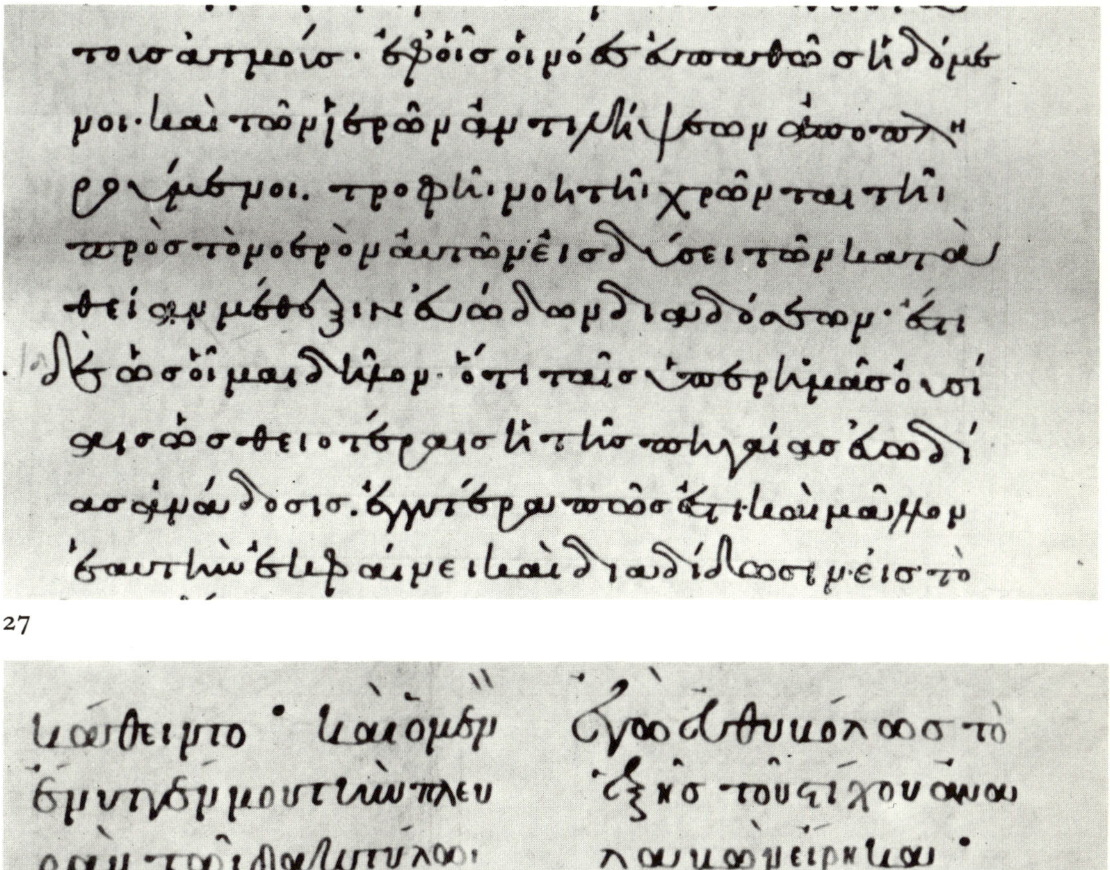

27

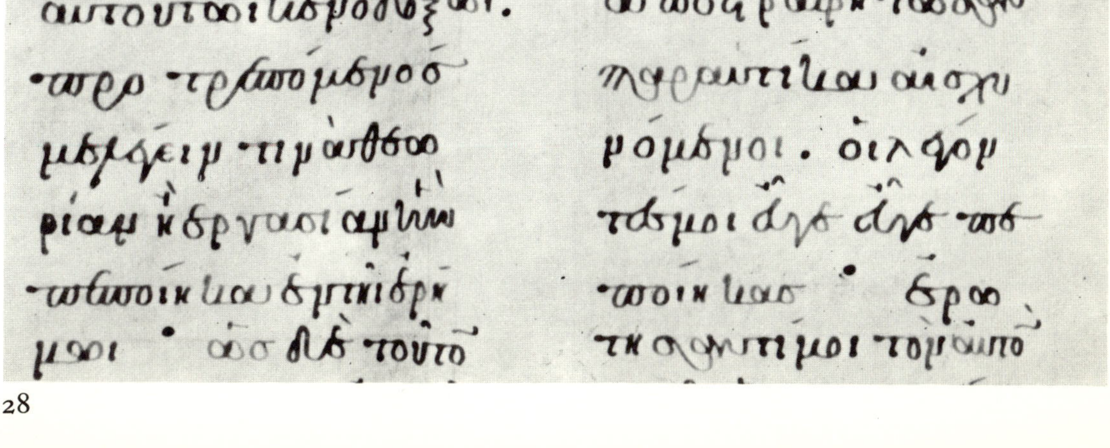

28

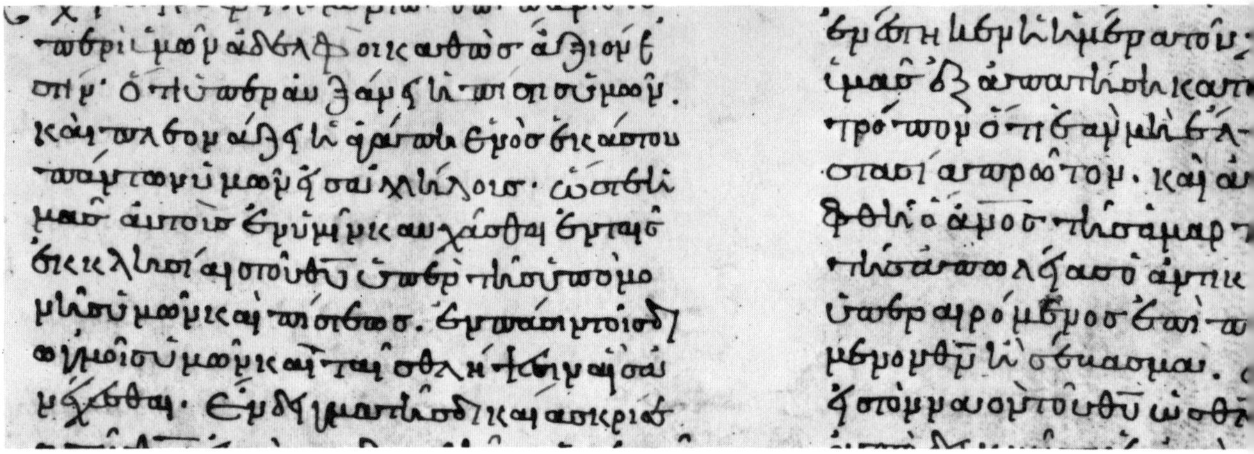

29

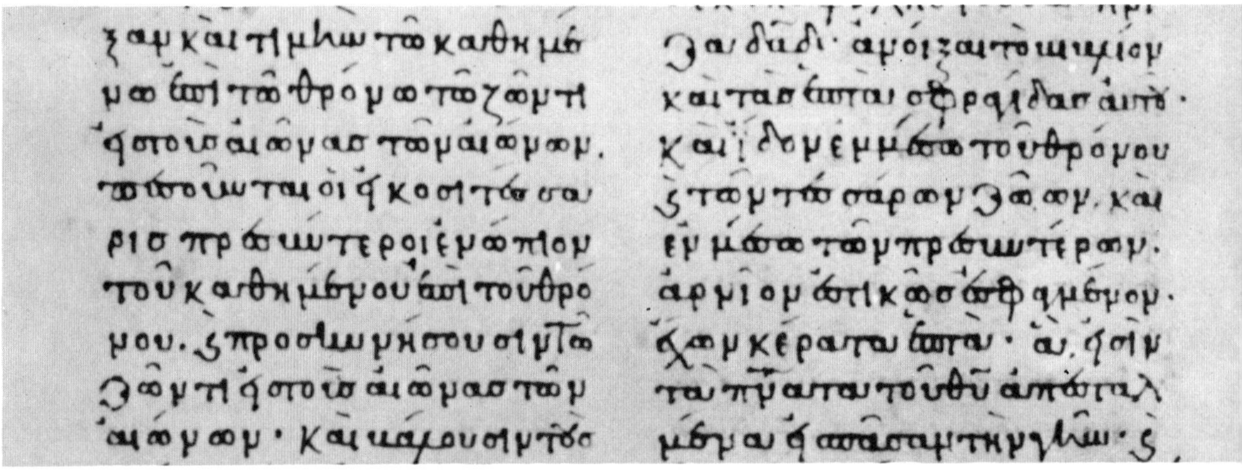

30

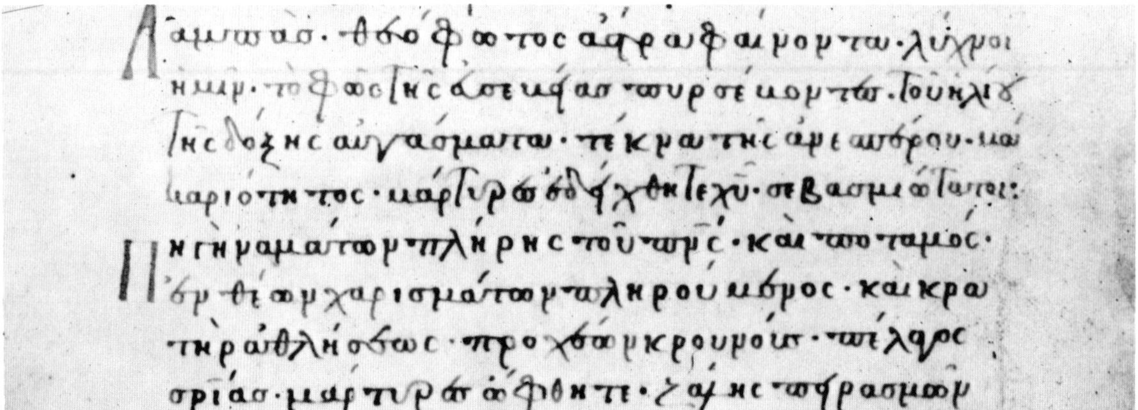

31

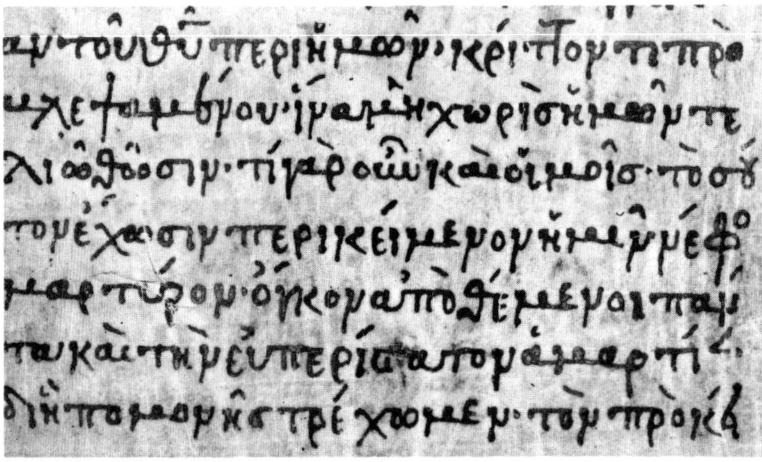

32

29 January 1037 — Theodoros *κληρικός* of Sicily, for Nikolaos archbishop of Reggio Calabria

Acts and Epistles — Parchment, 345 × 270 (260 × 180) mm

Vatican MS. Vat. gr. 1650 fol. 161-85

Fol. 185^{v} *ἔγραψε ταύτην νικόλαος ... ἐν ἐπισκόποις ἀρχιερεὺς ὑπάρχων· γαίας καλαβρίτιδος ριγίου πόλις· καὶ σικελίας θρηνακρίτιδος χώρας ... Fol. 186^{r} ... ἐγράφη αὕτη ἡ δέλτος διὰ χειρὸς θεοδώρου κληρικοῦ σικελιώτου κατ' ἐπιτροπὴν νικολάου επισκόπου κτήτορος ταύτης· ἐν ἔτει ἀπὸ κτίσεως κόσμου ἔτ[ει] ϛφμε̅ ινδ[ικτιωνος] ε̅ κυ[κλου] (σεληνης) θ̅ κυ[κλου] (ηλιου) κα̅ κ(αὶ) ἐπληρώθ[η] μη[νι] ἰαννουαρίω εἰς τὸν αὐτὸν χρ[ονον] ἡμέ[ρα] σα[ββατω] ὥρα γ̅.*

An ungainly hand, recognizably provincial. Breathings (2). Diaeresis (1) and (2). Mute ι (1). Abbreviations sometimes (1), sometimes (2), (4), and occasionally (5). Ruling (3).

Other facsimiles: Cavalieri and Lietzmann, tab. 22; Follieri, tab. 34; Lake, VII, MS. 283, pl. 510-16; of which only Lake, pl. 513-16, show Theodoros' hand.

30 26 July 1107 — Leontios *μοναχὸς πρεσβύτερος* in the monastery of S. Filippo di Fragalà (Sicily)

Climacus etc. — Parchment, 263 × 196 (225 × 142) mm

Escorial MS. X.III.6, fol. 35-end

Fol. 292^{r} *ἐτελιώθη ἡ βίβλος αὕτη μηνὶ ἰουλίω κϛ̅: ἔτους ϛχιε̅: γραφῆσα δια χειρὸς λεοντίου μοναχοῦ πρεσβυτέρου· ἀμαθοῦς (καὶ) ἰδιώτου· εἰς τὴν μονὴν τοῦ ἁγίου φιλίππ(ου) τοῦ μελιτυροῦ.* The existing monastery of S. Filippo di Fragalà is referred to in medieval documents by one or more of the epithets *τοῦ μελιτυροῦ*, de Mirtiro, de Demenna; it is near the village of Mirto in the N. foot - hills of Monti Nebrodi, 12 miles SW. of Patti. This extremely plain hand has no very marked provincial features. Breathings (2). Accents (not only the circumflex) are sometimes placed above or in front of breathings. Diaeresis (1) and (2). Abbreviations sometimes (1), sometimes (2), (4), and sometimes (5). Ruling (3).

Other facsimiles; Graux and Martin, pl. IX, facs. 32; and (with a detailed description of the manuscript) in G. Garitte, *Documents pour l'étude du livre d'Agathange* (Studi e Testi, 127, Vatican, 1946), pp. 150-61.

31 4 February 1316 — Markos *ἱερομόναχος*, for the Esphigmenou monastery (Athos)

Menaion — Parchment, 244 × 166 (175 × 120) mm

Athos, Esphigmenou MS. 58 + Leningrad, Public Library MS. gr. 355

Esphig. MS. fol. 162^{r} *ἐγράφη ἐν ἔτει ϛωκδ̅ ἰνδ[ικτιωνος] ιδ̅ μηνὶ φευρουαρίω δ̅ τελεσθὲν διὰ χειρὸς μάρκου ... ἁμαρτωλοῦ ιερομοναχου αφιεροθεν εις την αγ[ίαν] βασ[ιλικὴν] μονὴν τοῦ σ(ωτη)ρ(ο)ς μου χ(ριστο)υ τοῦ ἐσφιγμένου.*

An archaizing hand. Breathings (3). Abbreviations (2). Ruling (3).

Markos also copied Esphig. MSS. 55,56 and 57 (other volumes of the Menaia) in 1315 and 1316.

Another facsimile: Tsereteli and Sobolevski, II, pl. XLIII.

32 9 December 1373 or 1374 — Antonios *ἱερεύς* of S. Cristina (Calabria?)

Liturgy of S. Chrysostom etc. — Parchment (palimpsest), 172 × 128 (140 × 100) mm

Vatican MS. Vat. gr. 1973, fol. 1-69 (upper writing)

Fol. 57^{v} *Ἐγρά[φη] ἡ θεῖα, ἱερουργία αὕτη, διὰ χειρὸς, ἐμοῦ εὐτελ(οὺς) κ(αὶ) ταποινοῦ, ἱερέος ἀντωνίου, τῆς ἁγ[ίας] χριστίν(ας) ... ἐν ἔτει, ϛωπβ̅ ἰν[δικτιωνι] ιβ̅, μὴ[ν] δεκέβρι(ος) θ', ἡμέρ[α] σαβάτου:* The Byzantine year 6882 and indiction 12 ran from 1 Sept. 1373 to 31 Aug. 1374; but 9 Dec. was Friday in 1373, Saturday in 1374; if the scribe mistook the day of the week, he finished copying in December 1373; but if he had in mind the year beginning on 25 Dec. used in the papal and imperial chanceries, then he finished in Dec. 1374. Of several villages named S. Cristina in Italy and Sicily, the only one recorded before the sixteenth century is S. Cristina d'Aspromonte, on the N. slopes of Aspromonte, 20 miles NE. of Reggio Calabria.

Breathings (3). Circumflex accent occasionally (1) and (2). Diaeresis (1) and (2). Abbreviations (2), (4), (5), and (6). Ruling (2).

Other facsimiles: Follieri, tab. 58; Turyn, *Codices Vaticani*, tab. 146, 202b (with a full description of the manuscript).

33 1020/1 — Esaias, for Isidoros abbot of monastery of S. Ioannes *τοῦ ἀπείρου* (Campania)

Ascetic and hagiographical collection — Parchment, 395×335 (325×265 and 320×260) mm

Florence, Laurenziana MS. 11.9, fol. 1-215^{r}, 282^{v}-end

Fol. 282^{r} *Τὸ ... βιβλίον ... διὰ χειρὸς ἐγράφει λουκᾶ ἁμαρτωλοῦ μο[να]χ[ου]. κατ επιτροπὴν ἰσιδόρω θυεπίολω καὶ καθηγουμένω μονῆς τοῦ ἁγίου ιω[αννου] τοῦ ἀπείρου. τῶ ϛφκθ ἔτει του κόσμου· ινδ[ικτιωνος] δ'·* Fol. 282^{v} *δὸς χ(ριστ)ε χάριν τοῖς ἡσαΐου πόνοις ἀμήν·* (and similar notes on fol. 103^{v}, 129^{r}). The manuscript is a joint production of these two scribes. The monastery must have been near the modern village of S. Giovanni a Piro in Campania, 10 miles W. of Sapri.

Breathings (1). Diaeresis (1) and (2). Abbreviations (1), sometimes (2) on compound *nomina sacra*, (4), and sometimes (5). Ruling (3).

Other facsimiles: Lake, X. MS. 369, pl. 690-6; Lefort and Cochez, pl. 90-1; Vitelli and Paoli, tav. XXXVII.

34 April 1153 or 1152 — Georgios *ἱερεύς*, given to church of the Theotokos in Tiberias(?)

Gospel lectionary — Parchment, 302×205 (234×147) mm

Jerusalem, Mar Ibrahim MS. 18

Fol. 235^{v} *ἐτελειώθ[η], τὸ ... εὐαγγέ[λιον]· διὰ συνδρομ(ῆς) πόθου τὲ πολλ[οῦ] (καὶ) ἐξόδ[ου], τοῦ τιμϊωτ[ά]τ[ου] [μον]αχ[οῦ] καὶ ἱερέ(ως) γερασίμ[ου]: καὶ ἐτέθη εἰς τὸν πανύμνητον να(ὸν) τῆς ὑπὲρἀμώμου, ὑπερενδόξου δεσποίνης ἡμῶν θ(εοτό)κου, τῆς κατ[ὰ] τὴν τ(ῆς) βεριάδ(ος), ἀρχϊεπισκοπήν ... εὔχεσθ[ε] (δὲ) τῶ ... κτησαμ[έν]ω ... (καὶ) ἐμοὶ τῶ γραφ[εῖ] εὐτελ[εὶ] ἱερεῖ γεωργ[ιω]. ἔλαβε (δὲ) τέλ(ος) τὸ ... εὐαγγέλϊον, κατ[ὰ] τὸν ἀπρίλλ[ιον] μῆ[να] τῆς τρεχούσης α ἰνδικτιῶν(ος), ἔτους δὲ ϛχξ.* Fol. 150^{v} a painting of the Virgin and Child inscribed *μ(ητή)ρ θ(εο)ῦ ἡ τιβεριαδιότησσα.* This last makes it likely that the book was presented to a church (not now identifiable) in Tiberias; but uncertainty remains, for, although the omitted syllable in the subscription is understandable, Tiberias is not known to have been at any time an archbishopric. The year 6660 of the Constantinopolitan era (A.D.1151/2) was indiction 15, whereas in the Alexandrian era (A.D.1167/8) it was indiction 1; a mistake of one in either year or indiction number is rather more likely than the use of the Alexandrian era in Palestine at this time.

Breathings (3). Diaeresis (3). Abbreviations (2). Ruling (3). Ecphonetic notation in red.

Other facsimiles: Lake, I, MS. 11, pl. 19-22.

35 3 April 1154 — Symeon *νοτάριος*, for Paul abbot of monastery of the Theotokos *τῶν κεράτων* (Puglia)

Theophylact — Parchment, 385×270 (289/304×195/203) mm

Vatican MS. Vat. gr. 1221

Fol. 275^{v} *... διὰ χειρ(ὸς) συμ[ε](ῶν) τοῦ ταπεινοῦ καὶ εὐτελοὺς νοτ[αρίου] ... διὰ συνεργ[είας] του πανευλαβεστάτ[ου] ἡγουμένου τ(ῆς) υπ[ερ]αγ[ίας] θ(εοτο)κου τῶν κεράτ(ων) κυ[ροῦ] παύλ[ου]· ἀπριλλ[ίω] εἰς τ(ὰς) γ ἔτους ϛχξβ ἰνδ[ικτιωνος] β· ἐν τούτω (δε) τῶ ἔτ[ει]· καὶ ῥογέρι(ος) ο ... ἡμετέ[ρος] ρὶξ ἐξῆλθ[ε] του τῆδ[ε] βίου.* This is almost certainly the monastery of S. Maria delle Cerrate of which the church still stands about 10 miles NW. of Lecce.

This rather uncouth hand betrays its provincial (though not its known S. Italian) origin. Breathings (3). Circumflex accent sometimes (1) and (2). Abbreviations (2), (4), and sometimes (6). Ruling (2).

Other facsimiles: Lake, VIII, MS. 318, pl. 584, 586.

36 30 November 1405 — Iakobos, for Dorotheos patriarch in Jerusalem

Menaion — Paper, 278×178 (210×120) mm

Jerusalem, S. Saba MS. 229 + Leningrad MS. gr. 431

S. Saba 229 fol. 421^{r}-422^{r} *ἐτελειώθ[η] τὸ παρὸν δὴμηναίον ... τοῦ ἁγίου καὶ ζωοδόχου τάφου τοῦ κ(υριο)υ, δια συνεργείας τὲ καὶ ἐξόδου καὶ πολλῆς ἐπιμελείας τοῦ παναγιωτάτου ἡμῶν δεσπότου π(ατ)ρ(ὸ)ς καὶ π(ατ)ριἄρχου τῆς ἁγίας πόλεως ἱεροσολύμων κυροῦ δωροθέου τοῦ ἁγιονδρείτ(ου), εἶτα καὶ τῶ ἁγιωσαβίτου: καὶ εγράφη δια χειρὸς κἀμοῦ ἁμαρτωλου καὶ ταπεινοῦ ἰἀκώβου, ... Ἐγράφη εἰς τὰ ἱεροσόλυμα, ἐντὸς τοῦ σκολίου τὸν εὐλαβέστατον π(ατέ)ρα ἡμῶν κυροῦ παπᾶ σάδεκα, κληρικὸς τοῦ ἁγίου καὶ ζωοδόχου τάφου τοῦ κ(υρίο)υ: ἔτους ϛϡιδ ἐν μηνὶ νοεμβρίω: εἰς τὰς: λ': ἡμέρα δευτέρα, ὥρας θ': (ινδικτίων)ος* [blank].

Breathings (3). Accents (1), occasionally (2). Diaeresis (3). Abbreviations (2).

Other facsimiles: Tsereteli and Sobolevski, II, pl. LVI; A. Papadopoulos-Kerameus, *Ἱεροσολυμιτικὴ Βιβλιοθήκη* (St. Petersburg, 1891-1915), II, between pp. 356 and 357.

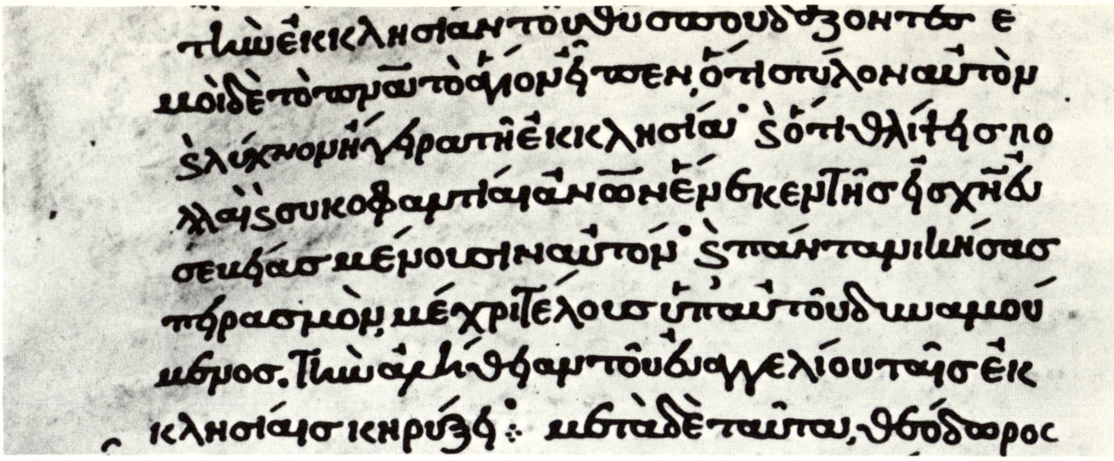

33

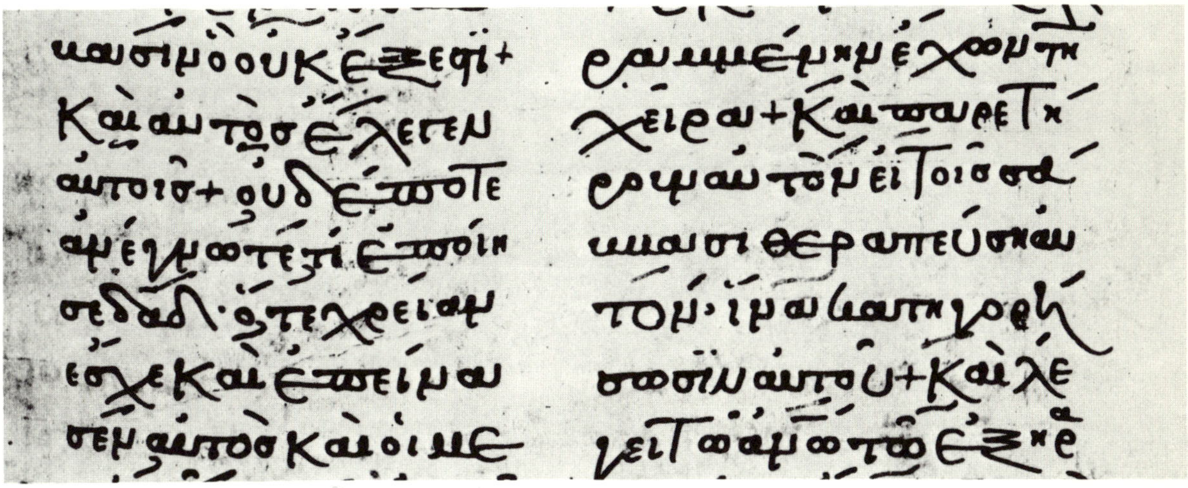

34

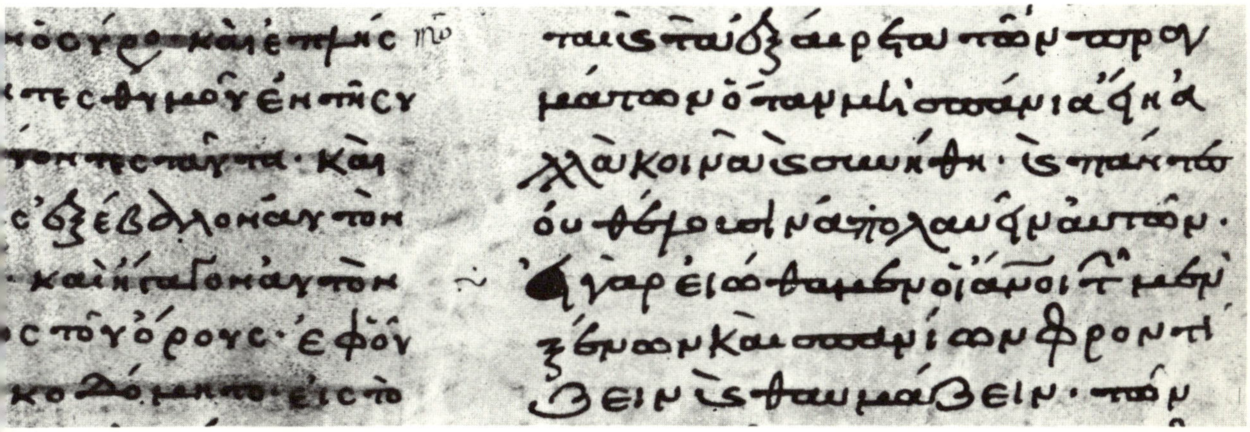

35

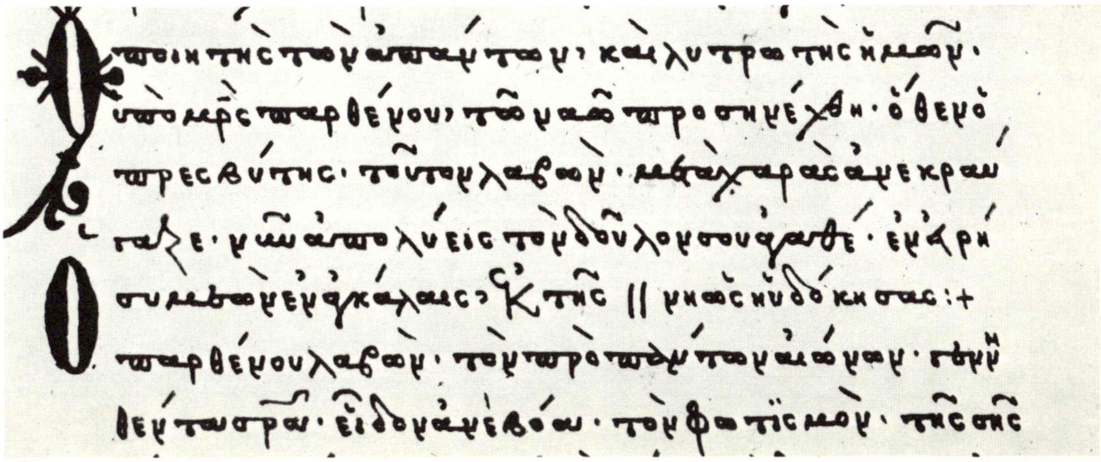

36

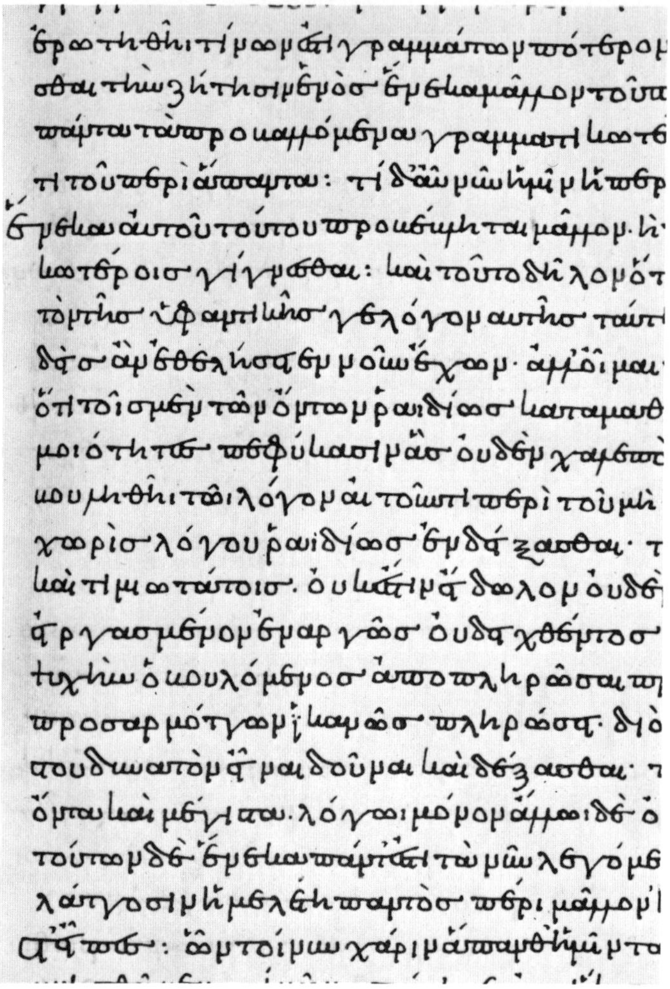

37

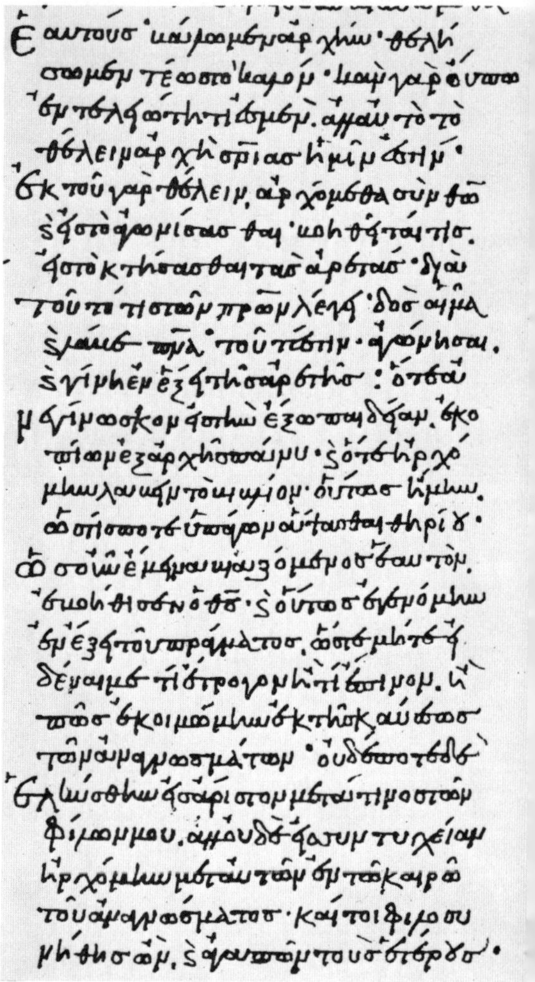

38

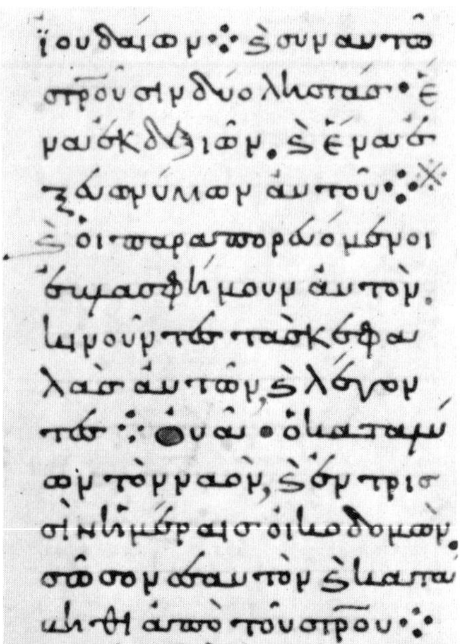

39

40

37 November 895 — Ioannes *καλλιγράφος*, for Arethas *διάκονος* of Patrae

Plato — Parchment, 320 × 220 (200 × 135) mm

Oxford, Bodleian MS. E.D. Clarke 39

Fol 418[v] *ἐγράφη χειρὶ ἰω[αννου] καλλιγράφου· εὐτυχῶς ἀρέθαι διακόνωι πατρεῖ· νομισμάτων βυζαντίνων δέκα κ(αὶ) τριῶν· μηνὶ νοεμβρίωι ἰνδικτιῶν(os) ιδ· ἔτει κόσμου ϛυδ βασιλείας λέοντος τοῦ φιλοχ(ριστο)υ υἱοῦ βασιλείου τοῦ ἀειμνήιστου.*

This manuscript is likely to have been copied in Constantinople, for the same reasons as **6**. Uncial forms of λ, ξ, and occasionally α,γ,ζ,κ, perhaps the first dated appearance of all except λ. Breathings (1). Diaeresis (2). Mute ι (1). Abbreviations (4) and occasionally (1). Ruling usually (3), sometimes (2).

Ioannes *καλλιγράφος* also copied Paris gr. 2951 + Flor. Laur. 60.3 (Aristides), and Venice Marc. gr. 447 (Athenaeus).

Other facsimiles: (complete) *Plato. Codex Oxoniensis Clarkianus 39* phot. ed. T.W. Allen (Codices Graeci et Latini photographice depicti III) (Leiden, 1898-9); Lake, II, MS. 52, pl. 95, 104; Lefort and Cochez, pl. 9; Maunde Thompson, facs. 54; Pal. Soc. I.81; Steffens, Taf. 8; Wattenbach and von Velsen, tab. III; Wilson, pl. 14.

38 964/5 — Neilos *μοναχός*, in Southern Italy

Dorotheus abbas — Parchment, 250 × 190 (180 × 120) mm

Grottaferrata MS. B.α. XX

Fol. 59[v] *τῶ ἑξακισχιλιοστῶ τετρακοσιοστῶ ἑβδομικοστῶ τρίτω του κόσμου ἔτει. ἔπαθεν τὸ φουσατον μανουὴλ τοῦ πατρικιου εις τ[α] ρηματ[α]· κ(αὶ) αὐτὰ τὰ ῥήματα ἐλείφθει· ... κ(αὶ) χειρὶ νεϥολχ [i.e. νειλου.* Code a = *ϑ* etc.] *μ[ονα]χ[ου]. ἐγράφει ἡ του αγιου δωροθεου πτυξ.*

This record (in the hand of the scribe of the whole manuscript) of the Arab capture of Sicily, makes it certain that it was copied in S. Italy.

Whether or not this is the hand of S. Neilos who founded Grottaferrata in 1004, the style is likely to be that practised by him, for it is found in a number of manuscripts from S. Italy in the last half of the tenth century when his influence as a calligrapher is known from contemporary sources to have been paramount there. Uncial *α,γ,ε,ζ,η,κ,λ,ν,ξ*, and π are used. Breathings (1). Diaeresis (2). Abbreviations (1) and (4). Ruling (3), but lines are not always ruled.

The same scribe copied Grottaferrata B.α. XIX (Marcus monachus etc.) and B.β.I. (Palladius). On manuscripts attributed to S. Neilos see S. Gassisi, 'I manoscritti autografi di S. Nilo juniore ...' *Oriens christianus*, 4 (1904), 308-70.

Other facsimiles: Lake, X, MS. 378, pl. 712, 730; Lefort and Cochez, pl. 38; S. Gassisi, op. cit., between pp. 310 and 311.

39 12 June 991 — Kyriakos *μοναχὸς πρεσβύτερος*, in Capua

Gospel lectionary — Parchment, 260 × 185 (175/80 × 115) mm

Vatican MS. Vat. gr. 2138

Fol. 52[r] *Κυριακὸς μ[ονα]χ[ος] πρεσβύτερος. ἐν ἄστεω καπούης ἔγραψεν.* Fol. 91[r] *Τετελείωται ... τὸ ἐκλογάδην τ(οῦ) εὐαγγελίου τοῦτου. διὰ χειρὸς κυριακοῦ πρεσβυτέρου· τλήμωνος τ(ου) καλογήρου: ἐν ἔτει ϛυϥϑ: ἰνδικτίωνος δ: μηνὶ ἰουνίω. εις τ[ας] ιβ: Ἀπὸ δὲ τῆς ἐνανθρωπήσεως τοῦ κ(υριο)υ ἡμῶν ἰ(ησο)υ χ(ριστο)υ. ἔτη ἐννακόσια, ενενήκοντα ἕν: λϥ α.*

A plain hand differing little from similar styles used in Eastern parts of the empire except in the use of a Western-type broad pen producing a marked contrast between thick and thin strokes. Uncial *α,ε,ζ,η,κ,λ,μ,ν,ξ* are used. Breathings (1). Diaeresis (2) and occasionally (1) and (3). Abbreviations (1), (2) on compound *nomina sacra*, (4). Ruling (3).

Kyriakos also copied Vat. gr. 2020 (Maximus confessor) in 993 in the monastery *φελλινος* in Capua.

Other facsimiles: Cavalieri and Lietzmann, tab. 17; Follieri, tab. 32; Lake, VII, MS. 266, pl. 472; Lefort and Cochez, pl. 60; Pal. Soc. II.87.

40 8 August 1105 — Bartholomaios *μοναχός*, in the monastery of the Theotokos, Rossano

Basil — Parchment, 287 × 230 (205/15 × 170) mm

Vatican MS. Vat. gr. 2050

Fol. 87[v] *ἐγρά[φη] χειρὶ βαρθολομαίου ἀνα[ξιου] [μον]αχ[ου].* Fol. 117[r] *ἐπληρώθ[η] ἡ παροῦσα βίβλος ... μη[νὶ] αὐγούστω. η· ἡμέ[ρα] γ ωρ[α] ια· τοῦ ϛχιγ ἔτ[ους]. ινδ[ικτιωνος] ιγ· τῶ ἐνιαυτῶ ὅτε καὶ ὁ ἁγιώτατος πάπα[ς] πασχάλιος σιγίλλιον ἐλευθερίας ἐποίησε τοῦ ἁγιοτατου π(ατ)ρ(ο)ς ἡμῶν Βαρθολομαίου εἰς τὴν ἁ[γιαν] αὐτοῦ μονὴν τὴν ὑπεραγίαν θ(εοτο)κον τὴν καλουμένην τοῦ ϡ λυλνϥθψβ* [i.e. *ροχονιάτη.* Code a = *ϑ* etc.] ... *τῶ αὐ[τω] δὲ ἐνιαυτ[ῶ] ἦν ὑποστρέψας ὁ βαϊμούνδις εἰς καλαβρίαν* [in the same code: *φεύγων ἐκ προσώπου ἀλεξίου: ἐκ τοτε δὲ εὗρεν ἀνάπαυσιν ἡ ἁγία μονὴ λυτρωθεῖσα ἐκ χειρῶν μαλαιίνων. πάνυ γὰρ ἐπολυόρκει αὐτὴν νικόλαος ὁ μαλαιίνος καὶ ἀρχ[ι]επίσκοπ[ος] μετὰ τῆς γενεᾶς αὐτοῦ].* These are known from other sources to be events in the history of the monastery later known as S. Maria del Patire near Rossano, which must therefore be the name decoded as *ροχονιάτη*.

Breathings (2). Diaeresis (2). Abbreviations (2) and occasionally (5). Ruling (3).

Bartholomaios also copied Vat. gr. 1992, fol. 118-274 (Gregory of Nazianzus, 1104), and Vat. gr. 2021 (Symeon of Chios, 1105).

Other facsimiles: Lake, VIII, MS. 306, pl. 561-3; Devreesse, *Les manuscrits grecs* pl. III.

41 April 981 — Dionysios *μοναχός*, while Epiphanios was abbot of the monastery *τῶν Ἀβραμιτῶν* (Constantinople)

Chrysostom — Parchment, 310 × 245 (225 × 155) mm

Vatican MS. Vat. gr. 2155

Fol. 357^{v} *ἐτελειώθη ἡ παροῦσα βίβλος. μηνὶ ἀπριλίω ινδ[ικτιωνος] θ̄· ἔτους ἀπο κτίσεως κόσμου ϛυπθ· Ἐπὶ ἐπιφανίου [μον]αχ[ου] τοῦ εὐλαβεστάτου ἡγουμένου μονῆς τῶν ἀβραμιτῶν· γραφεῖσα διὰ χειρὸς διονυσίου μοναχοῦ·*

An early dated example of a plain, light style. This is one of the earliest formal hands to use the open-ε ligatures which became common later (εν in lines 11, 17). Breathings (2). Diaeresis (2), sometimes (1). Abbreviations (1), (3), (4), and occasionally (5). Ruling (3).

Undated manuscripts with comparable script include Vat. gr. 284 (Galen and Dioscorides).

Other facsimiles: Cavalieri and Lietzmann, tab. 15; Follieri, tab. 21; Lake, VII, MS. 265 p. 470-1: Lefort and Cochez, pl. 54.

42 1062/3, — while Nicephoros *σεβαστοφόρος* was duke of Antioch

Chrysostom — Parchment, 380 × 280 (275 × 190) mm

Venice, Marciana MS. gr. 94

Fol. 216^{v} *ἐτελειώθ[η] ... ἡ ἱερὰ βίβλος αὕτη, ἐν τῶ ϛφοα ἔτει ἐπὶ τῆς βασιλείας κωνσταντίνου τοῦ δοῦκα· δουκὸς δὲ τῆς μεγάλης θ(εο)υπό[λεως] ἀντιοχ[είας] νικηφόρου σεβαστοφόρου: ἰνδικτιῶν(ος) ᾱ:*

Breathings (2). Circumflex accent often (1) when over a breathing. Diaresis occasionally (1). Mute ι (1) used only in the article. Abbreviations sometimes (1) sometimes (2), (4), (5). Ruling (3).

Other facsimiles: Lake, II, MS. 47, pl. 86, 90; Wattenbach and von Velsen, tab. XIII.

43 6 August 1072 — Michael *βασιλικὸς νοτάριος ὁ πανεργῆς*, for Michael VII Doukas

Acts and Epistles — Parchment, 112 × 78 (75 × 45) mm

Moscow, University Library MS. 2

Fol. 346^{v} *ἐτελειώθ[η] ἡ παροῦσα βίβλος μηνὶ αὐγούστω ϛ̄: ἡμέ[ρα] β̄ ἰνδ[ικτιωνος] ῑ: προστάξει τοῦ ... ἡμ(ῶν) βασιλέ[ως] κ[υρ]οῦ μιχ[αὴλ] τοῦ δοῦκ[α]: γραφεῖσα παρ' ἐμοῦ μιχ[αηλ] βασι[λικοῦ] νοτ[αρίου] τοῦ πανεργῆ: ἔτ[ους] ϛφπ:*

Breathings (2). Mute ι (1). Abbreviations (2) and occasionally (5). Ruling (3).

Other facsimiles: Tsereteli and Sobolevski, I, pl. XX.

44 24 July 1112 — Neilos *ἱερομόναχος*, at Grottaferrata

Menaion — Parchment, 240 × 180 (167 × 115) mm

Grottaferrata MS. Δ.α. II

Fol. 136^{r-v} *ἐγράφει δια χειρὸς του αμαρτωλοῦ ἱερομονάζοντος νεῖλου· [ἐν] τῆ μονῆ τῆς ὑπερενδόξου δεσποίνης ἡμ(ῶν) [θεο]τόκου τῆς ἐπονομαζομένης γρουτταφερράτα· κατ επιταγὴν τοῦ ταῦτης ... προεστῶτος ὁσιωτάτου νικολάου· ἐν ἔτει ϛχχ τοῦ κόσμου ἐν ἰνδ[ικτιωνι] ε̄ μηνὶ ἰουλίω· εἰκάδη δ̄:*

Breathings (2). Diaeresis (1) and (2). Abbreviations (1) and (4). Ruling (3). Early Byzantine notation in parts of the manuscript.

Other facsimiles: Lake, X, MS. 391, pl. 738-9; Tardo, tav. XIX.

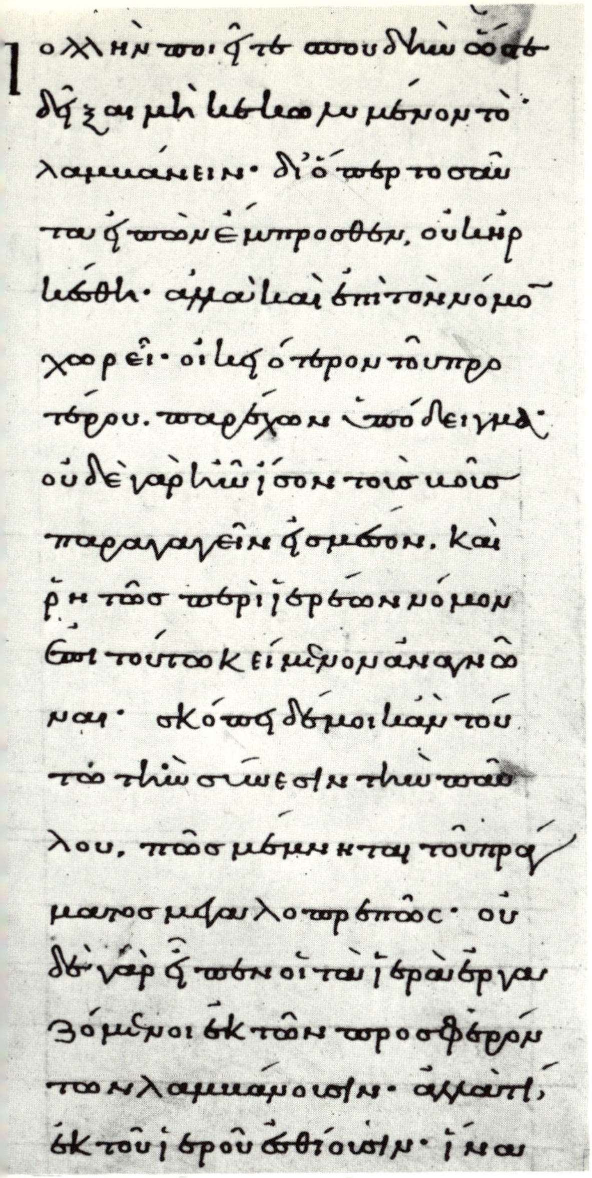

41

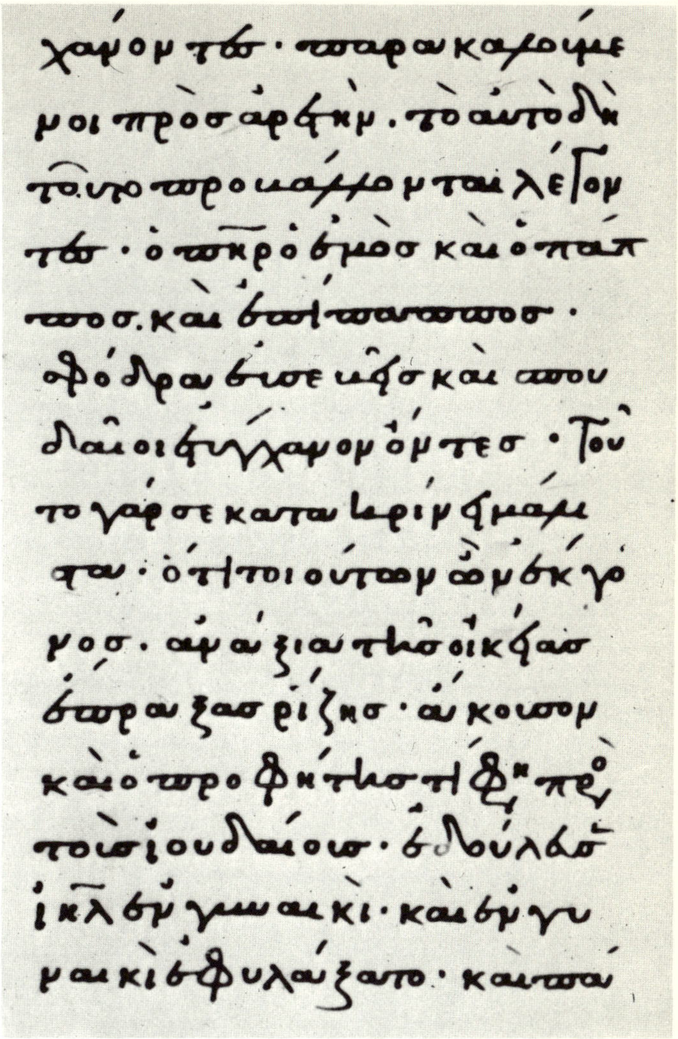

42

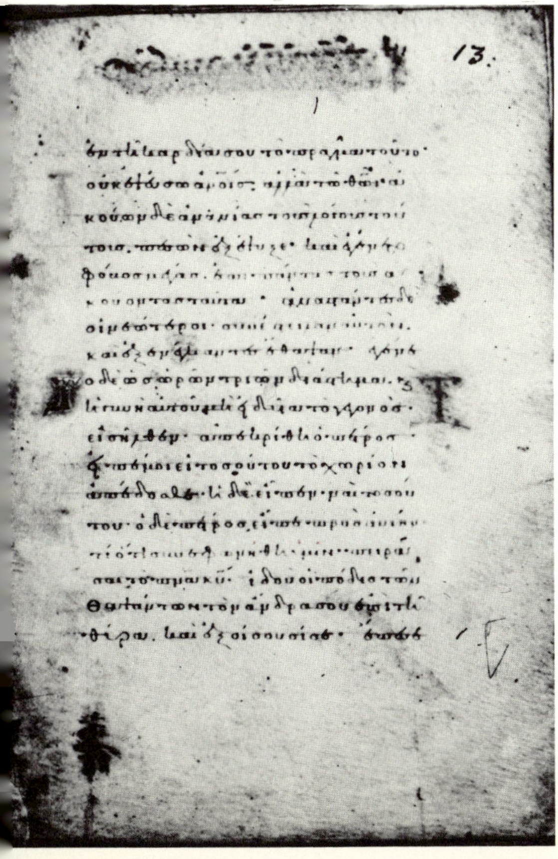

43

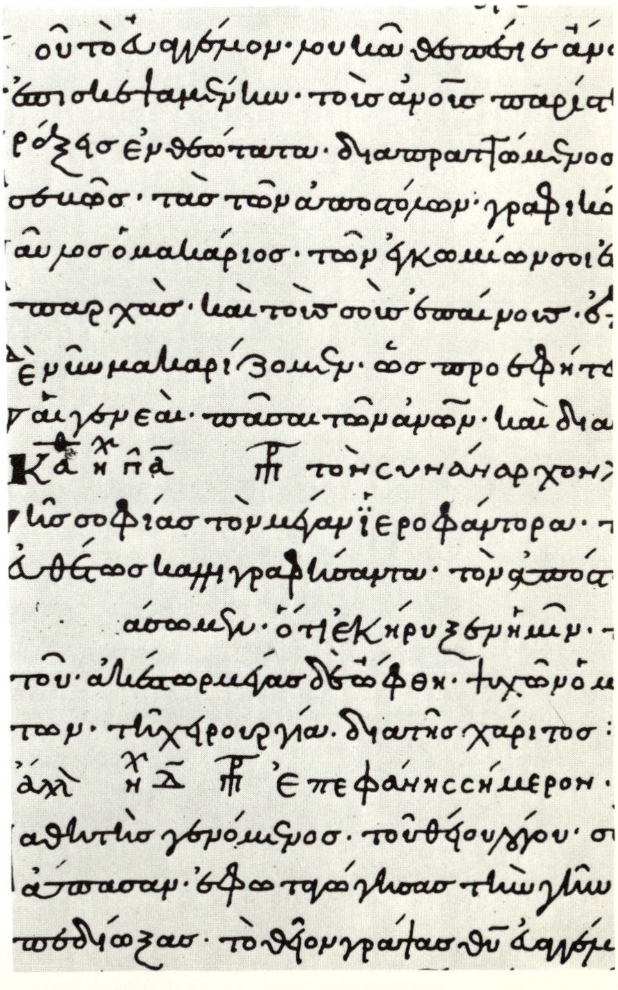

44

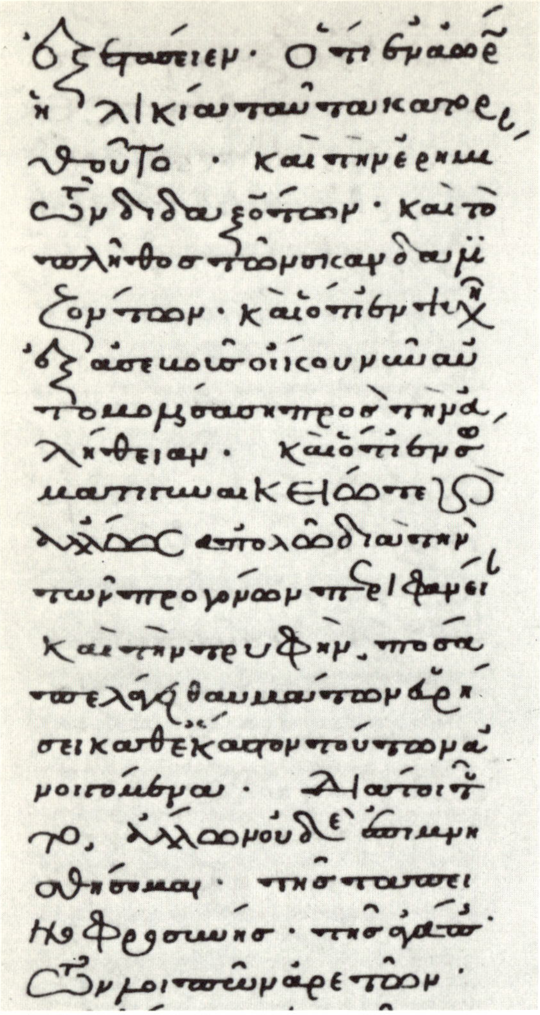
45

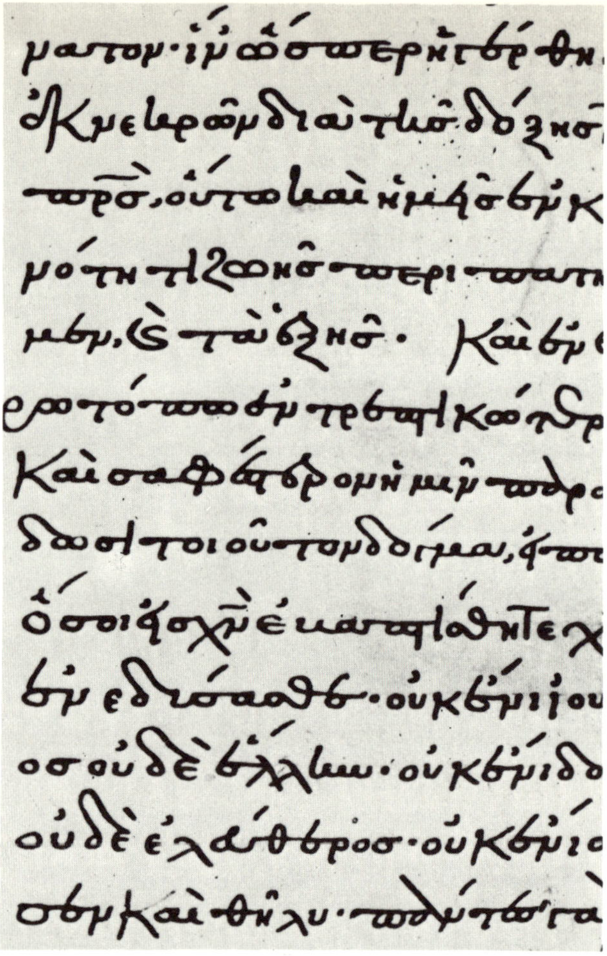
46

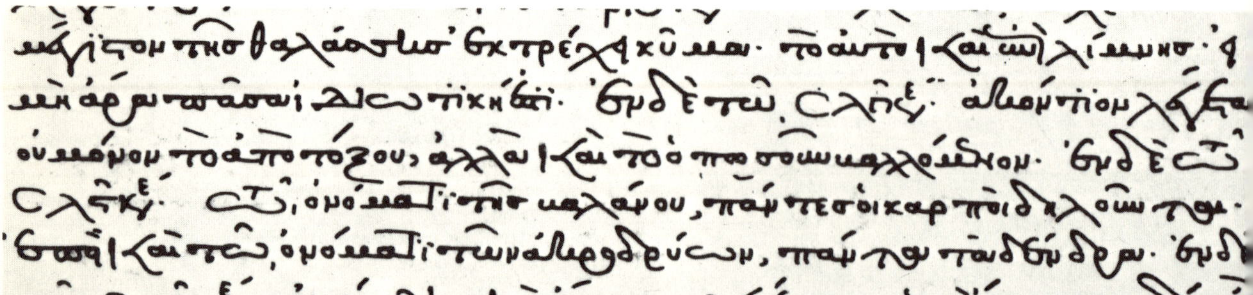
47

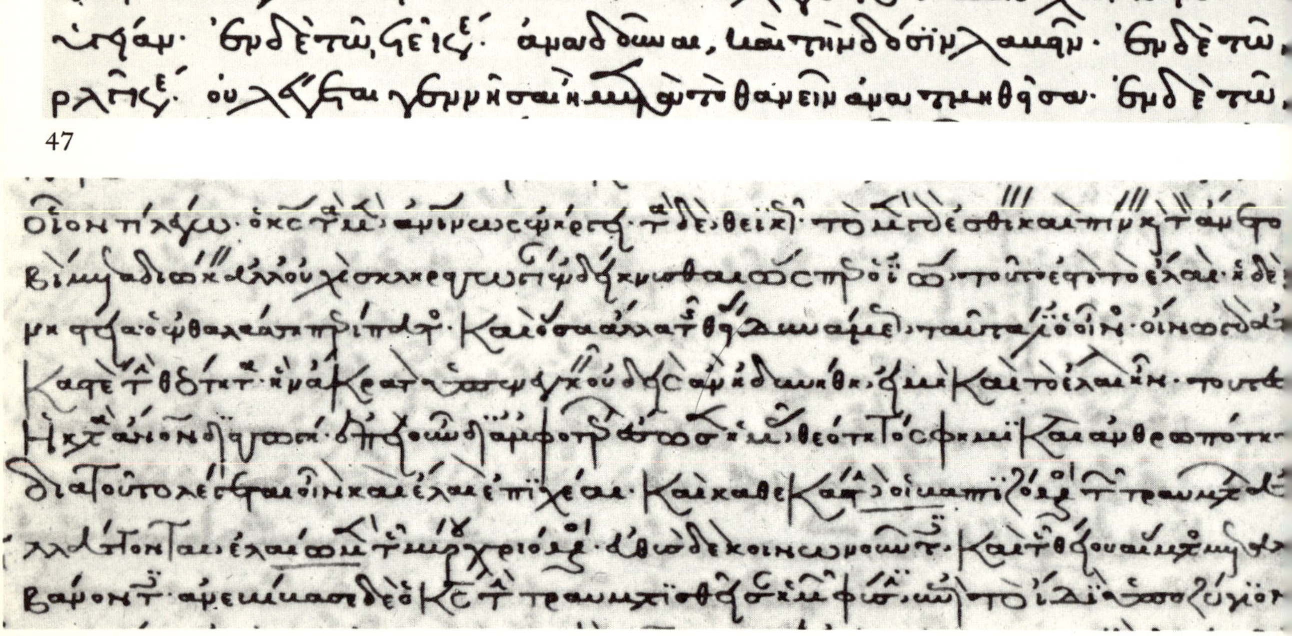
48

45 15 May 1129 — Konstantinos Tarsites of Athens, in Crete
Theological collection — Parchment, 295 × 205 (205 × 150) mm
Vienna, Nationalbibliothek MS. Theol. gr. 89

Fol. 245^{r-v} *Τέλος εἴληφα τῆς ... βίβλου ... χειρὶ εὐτελ(οῦς), κωνσταντίνου ταρσίτου· τοῦ ἐξ αθηνῶν, ἐν κρήτ[η] γεγονότ(ος)· ... μηνὶ μαϊῳ ιε* [added later] *(ἰνδικτιῶνος) ζ ἔτους ϛχλζ.*

Breathings (2). Diaeresis (3). Mute ι (2). Abbreviations (2), (4), (5), occasionally (6), (8). Ruling (2).
Other facsimiles: Bick, Taf. VII; Lake V, MS. 206, pl. 355-6; Lefort and Cochez, pl. 95.

46 October 1131 — Bartholomaios *μοναχός*, for Ioseph abbot of monastery *τοῦ παντεπόπτου σωτῆρος* (Constantinople?)
Basil — Parchment, 345 × 284 (250 × 210) mm
Messina, Biblioteca universitaria MS. gr. 24

Fol. 338^{v} *ἐγράφη ἡ παροῦσα βίβλος διὰ χειρὸς βαρθολομαίου [μον]αχ[οῦ]· προστάξει τοῦ καθηγιασμένου μου π(ατ)ρ(ὸ)ς τοῦ κυρ(οῦ) ἰωσηφοῦ καθηγουμ[έ]ν[ου] τ(ῆς) μο[νῆς] τ(οῦ) παντεπόπτ[ου] σ(ωτῆ)ρ(ο)ς· μη[νὶ] ὀ[κτωβρίῳ] (ινδικτιῶνος) ἰ τοῦ ϛχμ ἔ[τους].* No monastery with the precise dedication *τοῦ παντεπόπτου σωτῆρος* is known now; the epithet is used regularly only of the monastery *τοῦ Χριστοῦ τοῦ παντεπόπτου* in Constantinople. Of the numerous monasteries *τοῦ Σωτῆρος*, the great S. Salvatore in Messina seems unlikely to be the one in this subscription: it is usually called by various versions of 'de Acroterio' or 'de Lingua Phari'; the abbots from its (re?) foundation in 1131 had the title of archimandrite; the first of them, in power from possibly May 1131, was S. Luca. For the suggested identification with the nearby monastery of S. Salvatore di Bordonaro there is no evidence. The hand betrays nothing of its origin; the *ερ* ligature in line 7, though a favourite with some S. Italian scribes, was never peculiar to them; it is one of a class of ogee-arched *ε* ligatures (of which *εξ* is perhaps the most common), all of which are found (most often in early minuscule) in some manuscripts where there is no evidence of S. Italian origin and in some where all the probability is against it; from at least the twelfth century they occur in both literary and documentary hands from all parts (see **67**). Breathings (2). Accents slightly (1). Abbreviations (2) and (4). Ruling (3).
Other facsimiles: Lake, IX, MS. 350 pl. 645, 650. On these *ε* ligatures in the tenth century see P. Canart, 'Le problème'.

47 16 March 1167 — Georgios Kamarenos, in Crete
Synopsis Basilicorum — Parchment, 295 × 240 (225 × 170) mm
Vatican MS. Palat. gr. 13

Fol. 349^{v} *ἐτελειώθη το βϊβλΐον. κατὰ την ιϛ τοῦ μαρτ[ίου] μη[νὸς] τῆς ιε (ἰνδικτιῶνος) τοῦ ϛχοε ἔτους. βασϊλεύοντος τοῦ ... κυροῦ μανουὴλ τοῦ κομνηνοῦ. καὶ πορφυρογεννήτου. ἐν κρήτη, πρακτορεύοντος τοῦ ... κυροῦ ἀλεξίου τοῦ κοντοστεφάνου, ἐκ πόθου τοῦ καμαρηνοῦ γεωργΐου, καὶ κόπων ἰδίων.*

Breathings (3). Accents (1). Diaeresis (1) and (3). Mute ι (2) used only with the article. Abbreviations (2), (4), and occasionally (6). Ruling (3).
Other facsimiles: Cavalieri and Lietzmann, tab. 30; Follieri, tab. 28; Lake, VIII, MS. 319 pl. 585-6.

48 October 1196 — Paul, for Metrophanes abbot of monastery of the Theotokos *ἡ περίβλεπτος* (Constantinople)
Theophylact — Paper, 345 × 265 (250 × 180) mm
Vienna, Nationalbibliothek MS. Theol. gr. 19, fol. 62-314^{r}

Fol. 314^{r} *τὸ παρ(ὸν) βϊβλΐον προστάξει τοῦ ἁγίου μου π(ατ)ρ(ὸ)ς καὶ καθηγουμ[έν]ου τ(ῆς) σεβασμΐ(ας) μο(ν)[ῆς] τῆς περϊβλέπτ[ου] θ(εοτό)κου [μον]αχ[ου] κυ[ροῦ] μ(ητ)ροφά(νους) καὶ ϊερέ(ως), ἐγράφη κ(αὶ) ἐτελειώθ[η] κ[α]τὰ τ(ὸν) οκτ[ωβ]ρ[ί](ον) μῆ[να] τ(ῆς) ιέ (ἰνδικτιῶνος) τοῦ ϛψε ἔτ[ους] δϊὰ χειρ(ὸς) ἐμοῦ τοῦ ἁμαρτωλ[οῦ] παύλου·*

Breathings (3). Accents (1), the circumflex sometimes (2) and (3). Diaeresis (3). Mute ι occasionally (3) used only with the article. Abbreviations (2), (4), (6), (8). Ruling (3).
Other facsimiles: Bick Taf. XII; Lake, V. MS. 212 pl. 364-6.

49 November 954 — Ephraim *μοναχός*

Aristotle — Parchment, 308 × 228 (220 × 150) mm

Venice, Marciana MS. gr. 201

Fol. 183^{v} *εγϱ[αφη] χειϱὶ ἐφϱ[αιμ] μ[ονα]χ[ου] μη[νι] νο[εμβϱιω] ινδ[ικτιωνος] ιγ̄ ἔτ(ους) ϡυ̅ξ̅γ*
One of the earliest dated examples of the easy, plain, round style; an early example, too, of the stereotyped styles that began in the mid-tenth century to replace the earlier, more individual hands. Nearly all distinctive uncial forms are used. Breathings (2). Mute ι (1). Abbreviations (5) and occasionally (6). Ruling sometimes (2), sometimes (3).
Ephraim also copied Athos, Laura B.64 (Acts and Epistles); Vatopedi 949 (Gospels, 948); Vat. gr. 124 (Polybius, 947 ?); Venice Marc. gr. IV. 1, fol. 5-212 (Plato). Undated manuscripts with comparable script include Flor. Laur. 59. 32 (works on agriculture); Modena Archivio B^{a}1.I.1 (Thucydides); Paris gr. 1983 (Hermogenes); Ravenna 137.4A (Aristophanes); Vat. gr. 1164 (tactica).
Other facsimiles. Lake, II, MS. 44, pl. 80, 81, 85; Lefort and Cochez, pl. 34; Wattenbach and von Velsen, tab. V. On manuscripts copied by Ephraim see A. Diller, 'Notes on Greek codices of the tenth century II', *Transactions of the American Philological Association,* 78 (1947), 185-8.

50 11 February 1067 — Gregorios *μοναχὸς καὶ πρεσβύτερος,* while Timotheos was abbot of the monastery of the Theotokos *εὐεϱγέτης* (Constantinople)

Theodoret — Parchment, 235 × 180 (185 × 120) mm

Oxford, Bodleian MS. Auct. T.2.2

Fol. 173^{r} *Ἐπληϱώθη ἡ βίβλος αὕτη ... μηνὶ φευϱουαϱίω ια̅· ἰνδικτιῶνος πέμπτης· ἔτους ἀπὸ κτίσεως κόσμου ἑξακισχιλιοστοῦ φοε̅· ἐπι τιμοθέου τοῦ ὁσιωτάτου ἡγουμέ[νου] τοῦ καὶ μετὰ θ(εο)ν κτήτοϱος τῆς ὑπεϱάγίας* **ϑ(εοτο)κου τῆς εὐεϱγέτιδος. τοῦ καὶ ἐγκλήστου· δια** *χειϱὸς γϱηγοϱίου [μον]αχ[ου] καὶ πϱεσβυτέϱου·*
Breathings (2). Diaeresis (1) and (2). Abbreviations (1), (3), (4), (5) and occasionally (7). Ruling (3).
Gregorios also copied Venice Marc. gr. 101 (Chrysostom, 1065). Manuscripts with comparable script include B. M. Burney 86 (Homer) where the half-illegible subscription may give the date 1059 or (less likely in view of this resemblance) 1014; Paris gr. 1957 (Plutarch).
Other facsimiles: Lake, II, MS. 58, pl. 106-7; New Pal. Soc. II.30; Wilson, pl. 31-2.

51 27 February 1122 — Basileios *ἀναγνώστης,* for Georgios *χαϱτοφύλαξ,* both of the church of the Anastasis, Jerusalem

Typikon — Parchment 300 × 225 (235 × 165) mm

Jerusalem, Holy Cross MS. 43 + Leningrad MS. gr. 359

Holy Cross 43, fol. 152^{v}-153^{r} *ἐκτίσθ[η] ἡ δέλτος αὕτη κατὰ πϱόσταξιν τοῦ εὐλαβοὺς γεωϱγ[ίου] ἄϱχων κ(αὶ) κϱιτ[ὴς] τ(ῆς) ἁ[γίας] πόλε[ως] (καὶ) χαϱτοφύ[λακος]* **σακελλίου τὲ καὶ μεγάλου σκευοφύ[λακος] τῆς ἁγιας** *χ(ϱιστο)ῦ τοῦ θ(εο)ῦ ἡμ(ῶν) ἀναστά[σεως]: καὶ ἐδόθη παϱ' αὐτοῦ εἰς τ[ὴν] ἐκκλη[σιαν] τῆς ἁγίας ... αναστ[άσεως] ... ἐγϱάφη δὲ καὶ εἱϱμώσθη διὰ χειϱὸς βασιλείου τοῦ ἁγιοπολίτου· γϱαφεῦς τὲ καὶ ἐλαχίστου ἀναγνώστης τῆς ἁγίας ... ἀναστά[σεως] ἐν τῆι ἁγία πόλει ἱ(εϱουσα)λήμ. εἴληφεν δὲ τέλος ἡ αὕτη δέλτος ἡμέ[ϱα] β̅ ὥϱα γ̅ τῆς ἡμε[ϱᾶς] εἰς τ[ην] κζ̅ τοῦ φευϱουαϱίου μην(ός)· ἔτους* **κόσμ[ου] ἑξακισχιλιοστῶ· ἑξακοσίω τϱιάκοντα: ἰνδ[ικτιωνος] ιε:**
Breathings (2). Circumflex accent (1) when over a breathing. Diaeresis (3). Mute ι (1). Abbreviations (2) and (4). Ruling (3).
Other facsimiles: Lake, I, MS. 10, pls. 15-18; Tsereteli and Sobolevski, II, pl. XXV.

52 28 July 1141 — Bartholomaios *μοναχός* of Reggio Calabria, in the monastery of S. Salvatore (Messina)

Parchment, 253 × 210 (190 × 160) mm

Life of S. Symeon Styiites the younger

Oxford, Bodleian MS. Rawl. G. 199

Fol. 143^{v} *ἐγϱά[φη] ἐ[ν] [τ]ῆ σεβασμία (καὶ) πεϱιβλέπτ[ω] μο[νῆ] τ(οῦ) σ(ωτη)ϱ(ο)ς τ(ῆς) ἐν τῶ ἀκϱοτ[ηϱίω] ἀϱχιμανδϱεύοντ(ος) τότε λουκ(ᾶ) τοῦ πανοσι[ωτάτου] καὶ μεγάλ[ου] ἀϱχιμανδϱ[ί]τ[ου]· διὰ χειϱ(ὸς) βαϱθολ[ο]μ[αίου] εὐτελ[οῦς] [μον]αχ[οῦ] τοῦ ϱηγινοῦ· ἐν ἡμέϱ(αις) ῥογεϱ[ίου] τ(οῦ) πανευτυχε[σ]τ[άτου] ῥηγ(ός)· πληϱωθεῖσα μη[νὶ] ἰουλ[ιω] κη̅ (ἰνδικτιῶνος) δ̅· τοῦ ϛχμ̅θ ἔτους.* This is S. Salvatore at Messina, named sometimes de Acroterio from its original position at the end of the promontory forming the harbour, sometimes simply Archimandritatus from being the only monastery in Sicily with that status. Breathings (2). Accents sometimes (1). Diaeresis (1). Mute ι (1) or sometimes (2). Abbreviations (1) but more often (2), (4), (5), occasionally (6). Ruling (3).
Other facsimiles: Lake, II, MS. 63, pl. 114-15; Wilson, pl. 43.

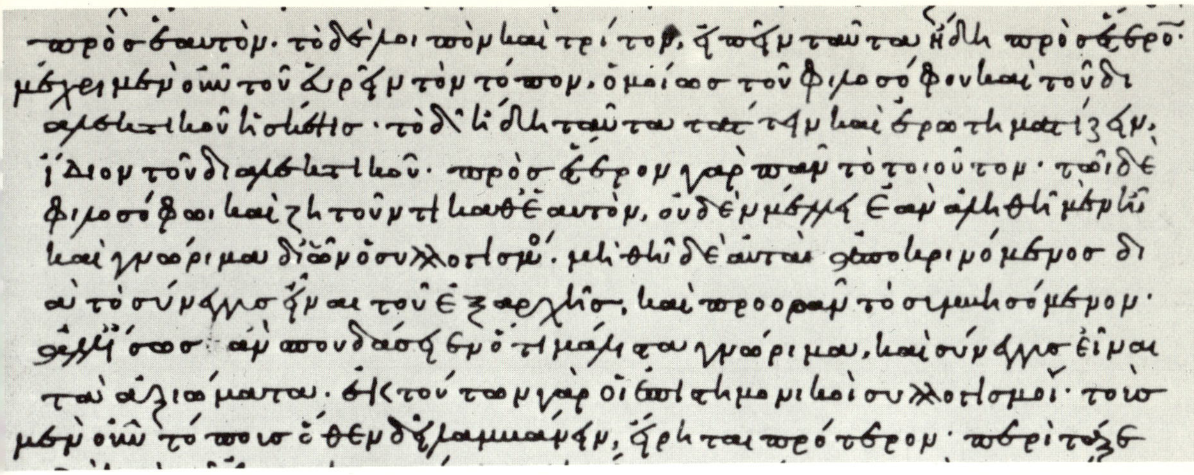

49

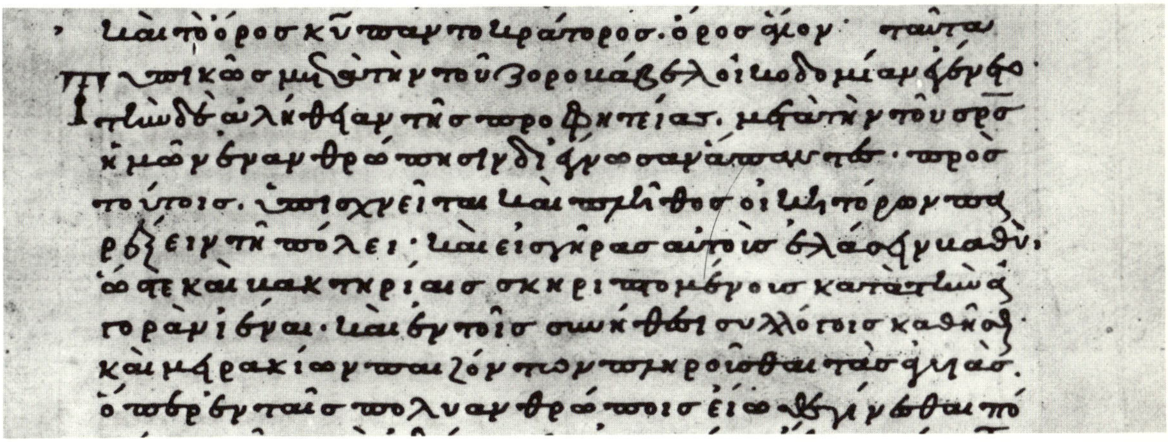

50

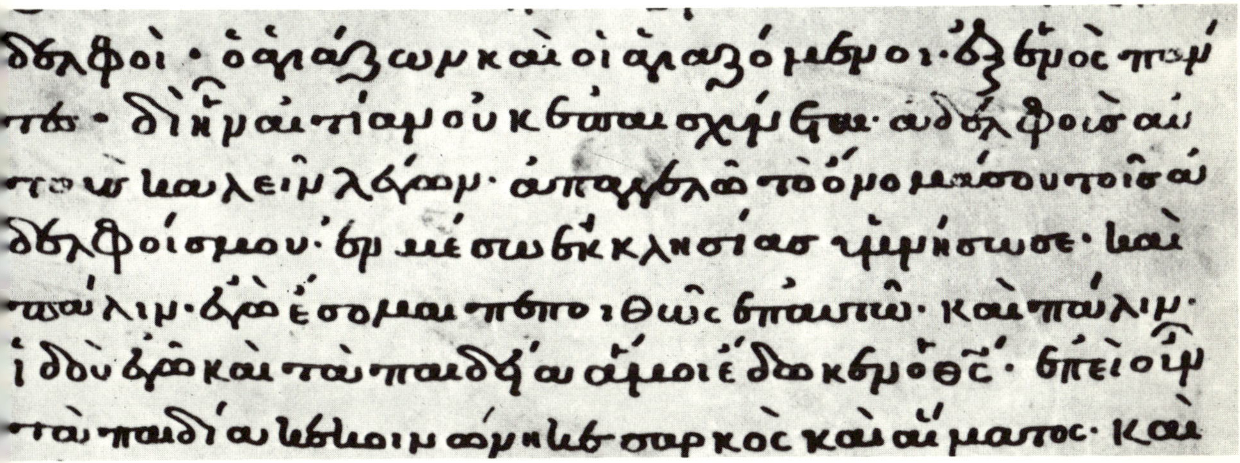

1

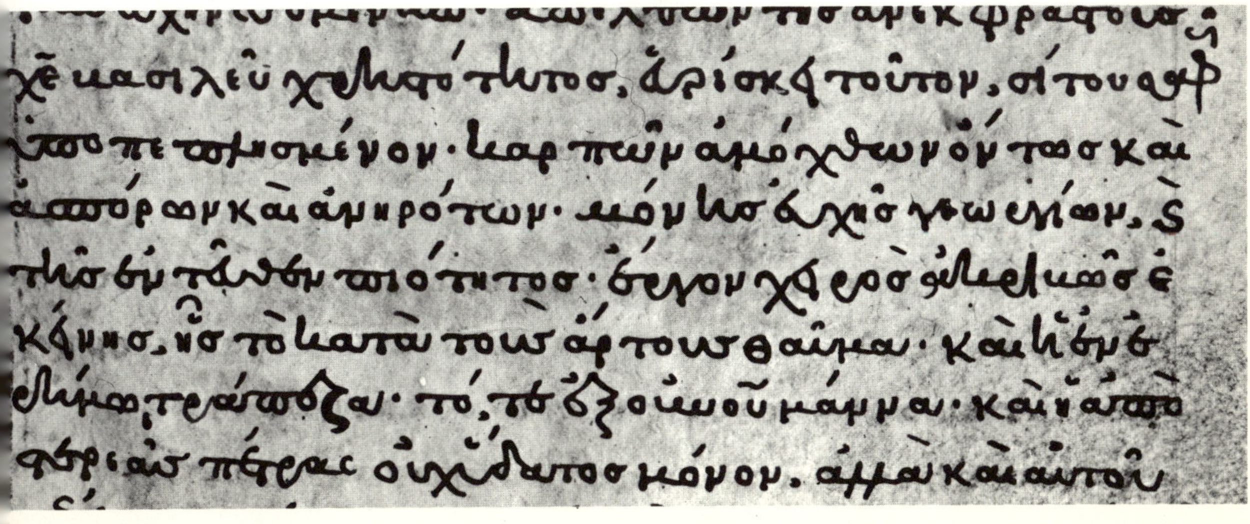

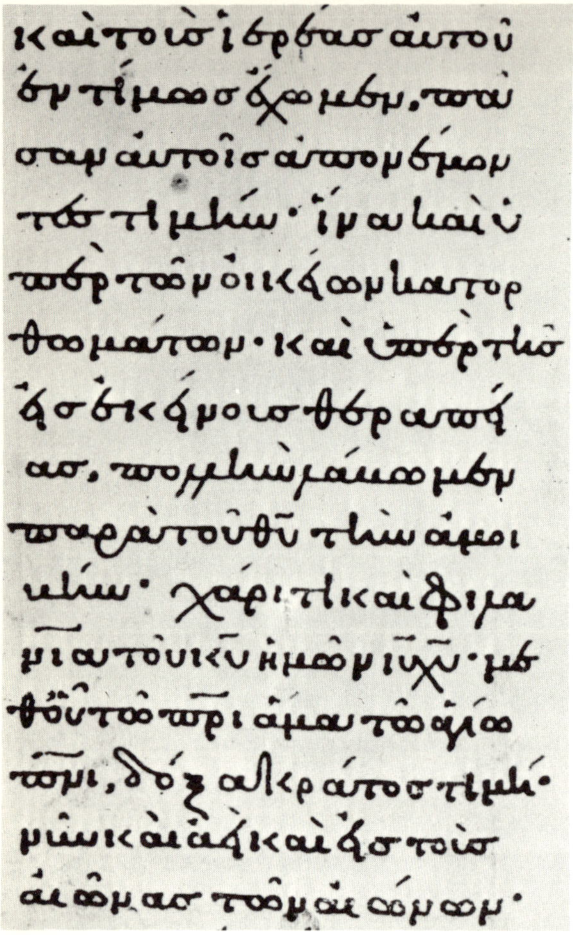

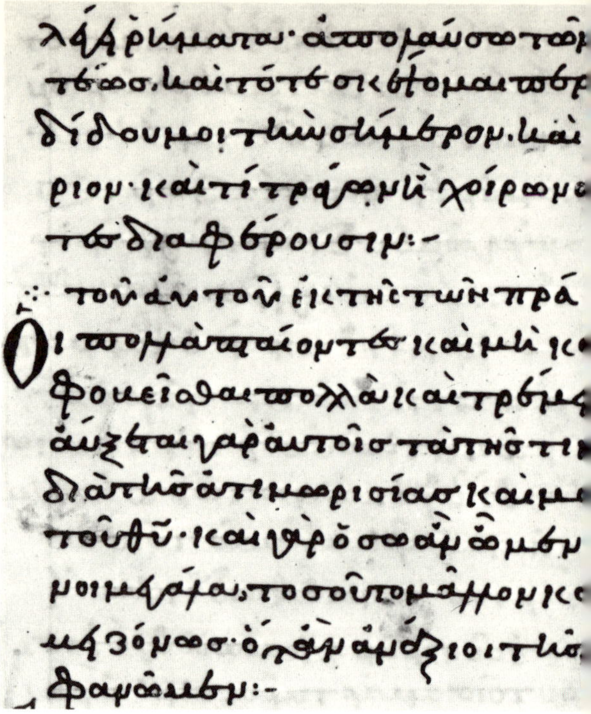

54

53

55

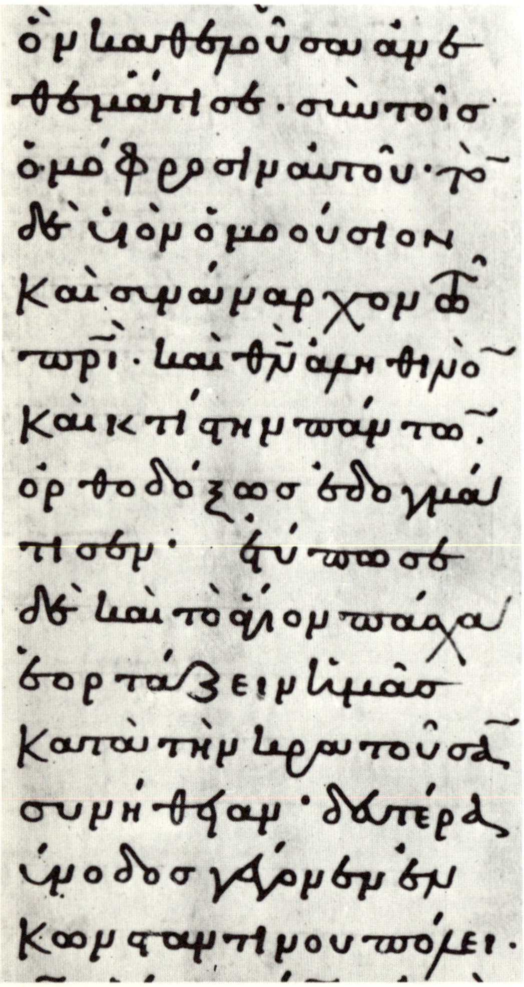

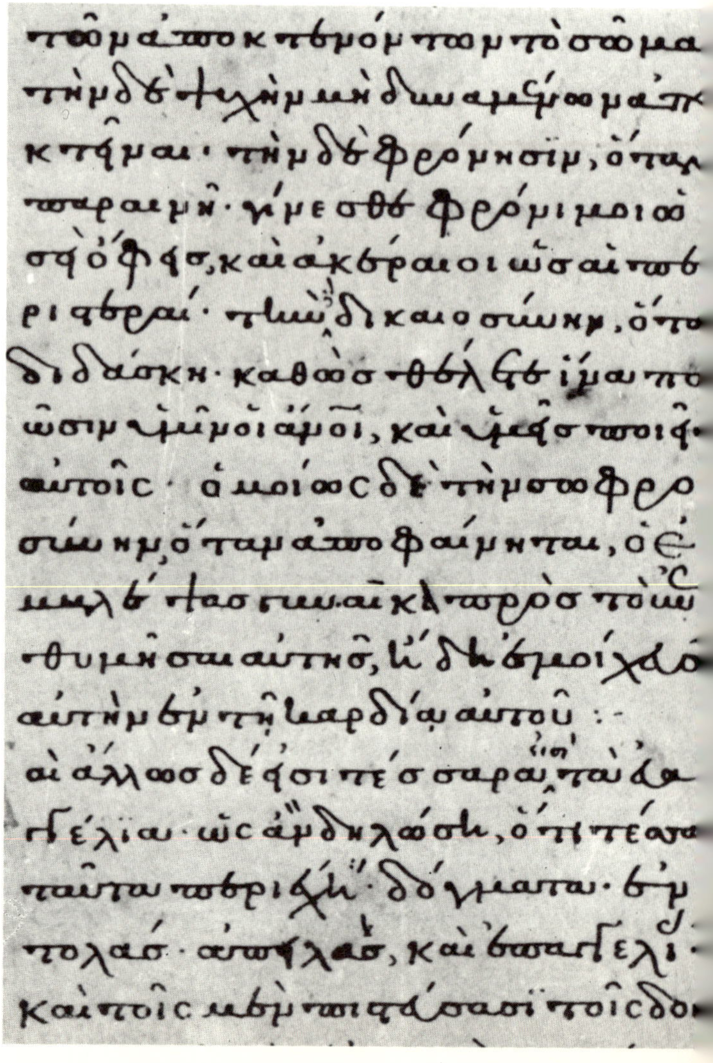

53 6 September 986 — Ioannes *μοναχός*

Chrysostom — Parchment, 320 × 260 (220 × 160) mm

Athos, Laura MS. Δ. 75

Fol. 292ᵛ *ἐγϱα[φη] ἡ παϱοῦσα ... βίβλος ... χειϱὶ ἰωάννου μοναχ[ου] ταπεινοῦ καὶ ἁμαϱτωλοῦ· καὶ ἐτελειώθη ... κατὰ τὴν ϛ̄τοῦ ἐνεστῶτος σεπτεμβϱίου μηνός· ινδ[ικτιωνος] ιε̄· ἔτ(ους) ἀπὸ κτίσεως κόσμου, ϛυϟε:* The year and possibly the indiction numbers look as if they might have been tampered with; but if so they cannot have been altered by much, given the apparently genuine dates 990, 992, and 993 in other manuscripts signed by this scribe. Since six out of seven identifiable as his work are now or are known to have once been in the Laura, it is possible (though not proved) that all were copied there.

A standard example of the widely used 'Perlschrift'. Breathings (1). Abbreviations (1). Ruling (3).

The same scribe also copied Athens 263 (Chrysostom, 991); Athos Laura A 19 (Gospel lectionary, 992), Γ 131 (Chrysostom, 995), Δ 70 (Psalter, 984); Moscow 101 and 108 (Chrysostom, 990 and 993).

Other facsimiles: Lake, III, MS. 91, pl. 160-1.

54 999/1000 or 1000/1 — Leon *κληϱικός*, in Egypt

Anastasius of Sinai — Parchment, 230 × 173 (180 × 120) mm

Paris, Bibliothèque nationale MS. grec 1085

Fol. 272ᵛ *ἐζϡθφβ ϙϥθ υεϥϡλω οέλνψλω ποβϡϥπλ̂χ· ἐν υόϡθ ἀιζχ́κψλχ·* [i.e. *ἐγϱαφη δια χειϱὸς λέοντος κληϱικôυ· ἐν χώϱα ἀϥγύπτου·* Code α = ϑ etc.] *ἐτους κοσμ[ου] ϛ̄φ̄θ̄ ινδ[ικτιωνος] ιγ̄.* **The Byzantine year 6509** was indiction 14; indiction 13 is more likely to be correct.

Breathings (2). Circumflex accent sometimes (1) when over a breathing. Diaeresis (1). Abbreviations (1), (2) sometimes on *ἄνθϱωπος*, (4), and occasionally (5). Ruling (2).

Other facsimiles: Lake, IV, MS. 145, pl. 248, 255; Lefort and Cochez, pl. 73; Omont, *Manuscrits datés*, pl. X.

55 Between 24 November 1059 and August / November 1060 — For the empress Eudocia (in Constantinople)

Theological collection — Parchment, 295 × 235 (200 × 155) mm

Paris, Bibliothèque nationale MS. grec 922

Fol. 4ʳ square of letters reading in every direction *ευδοκιας η δελτος αυγουστης πελει* · Fol. 5ᵛ verses with acrostic of the same words. Fol 6ʳ picture of the Virgin crowning an emperor and empress, flanked presumably by their sons. Of three Byzantine empresses Eudocia, the first (wife of Basil I, 867-86) is impossible palaeographically, and the last (wife of Alexios V, Feb.-Apr. 1204) had neither sons nor, presumably, time to acquire presentation volumes; therefore the figures here are plausibly assumed to be Eudocia Macrembolitissa, her first husband Constantine X Doukas (24 Nov. 1059 - 21 May 1067), and their sons Michael and Andronicus but not Constantine (born between Aug. and Nov. 1060).

Breathings (2). Diaeresis (1). Abbreviations (2), (5), and slightly (8). Ruling (3).

Another facsimile: Omont, *Plus anciens manuscrits*, pl. XLVI.

56 October 1292 — Symeon Kalliandres *ἱεϱεύς, νομικὸς καὶ πϱωτέκδικος* of Rhodes

Theophylact — Paper, 350 × 270 (270 × 200) mm

Escorial MS. Ω 1. 16

Fol. 408ᵛ *ἐγϱάφη ἡ παϱοῦσα ... βῖβλος χειϱῒ τοῦ ταπεινοῦ (καὶ) εὐτελοῦς καὶ ἀναξίου ἱεϱέως συμεὼν νομϊκοῦ (καὶ) πϱωτεκδῖκου τ(ῆς) ἁγϊωτάτης μ(ητ)ϱοπόλε[ως] ῥόδου τοῦ καλλϊάνδϱ[ου] ἐν μηνῒ ὀκτω[βϱίω] (ἰνδικτιῶνι) ϛ̧· τῶ ϛ̧ ω̅α̅ ἔτει· ἐγϱάφη δὲ τῶ τϊμϊωτάτω ἐν μοναχοῖς κυϱ[ῶ] χαϱί[τωνι(?)]*

An exceptionally conservative hand, preserving much of the even, close-knit appearance of late tenth-century Perlschrift. The impression of antiquity is belied by occasionally much-enlarged letters and by some minor details of scribal practice: breathings (3); circumflex accent sometimes (1) and (2); diaeresis (1) and (3); mute ι (3); abbreviations (2), (4) in the late inverted shape ϛ, (5), and slightly (8); ruling (3) with only alternate lines ruled.

Symeon Kalliandres also copied Leningrad, Bibl. Akad. Nauk 76 + Bibl. Publ. 311 (Gospels, 1281).

Other facsimiles: Graux and Martin, pl. XIII, facs. 48-50.

57 December 1062 — Symeon *μοναχός*, for Theodoros abbot of monastery *τῶν γαλακρινῶν* (Constantinople)

Gregory of Nazianzus — Parchment, 414 × 309 (250 × 180) mm

Vatican MS. Vat. gr. 463

Fol. 469v *αὔτη ἡ βίβλος πέφυκε θεοδώρου [μον]αχ[ου] πρεσβυτέρου. καὶ προεστῶτος τῆς τῶν γαλακρηνῶν μονῆς· ... γραφεῖσα δὲ τῇ αὐτοῦ προτροπῇ χειρὶ συμεὼν [μον]αχ[ου] τοῦ αὐτοῦ μαθητοῦ. καὶ τελειωθεῖσα μη[νι] δεκεμβρίω ἰνδ[ικτιωνος] πρώτης. ἐν ἔτει τῷ ϛφοᾶ· βασιλεύοντος τοῦ εὐσεβεστάτου κωνσταντίνου τοῦ δοῦκα. καὶ ἑβδοκίας τῆς αὐγούστης.* The district of Γαλακριναῖ was on the Asiatic shore opposite Constantinople.

An early, embryonic example of the evolution of Perlschrift towards the later more ornate styles by enlarging and flourishing some letters. Breathings (2). Circumflex accent (1) when over a breathing. Mute ι (1), but shorter than other letters. Abbreviations sometimes (1), sometimes (2), (4), (6), and sometimes (8). Ruling (3).

Undated manuscripts of comparable script include Venice Marc. gr. 453 (Homer).

Other facsimiles: Follieri, tab. 26; Lake, VIII, MS. 292, pl. 528-30.

58 12 June 1081 — Michael *μοναχός* of the monastery of Christ *πανοικτίρμων* (Constantinople)

Gregory of Nazianzus — Parchment, 255 × 190 (185 × 127) mm

Oxford, Christ Church MS. Gr. 6

Fol. 246r *Ἐγρά[φη] ἡ τοιαύτη βίβλ(ος) ... χειρὶ μιχ[αὴλ] εὐτελοῦ[ς] [μον]αχ[οῦ] καὶ ἀλιτροῦ· τῆς εὐαγοῦς μον[ῆς] τοῦ πανοικτίρμον[ος]· μηνὶ ἰουνίω ιβ ινδ[ικτιωνος] δ: ἔτους ἀπὸ κτίσεως κόσμου ϛφπθ.*

Breathings (2). Abbreviations (2), (5), (8). Ruling (3).

This is probably the scribe of **76**.

Other facsimiles: Lake, V, MS. 195, pl. 333-4.

59 12 June 1394 — Ioasaph, of monastery of the Theotokos *τῶν ὁδηγῶν* (Constantinople)

Acts and Epistles etc. — Parchment, 295 × 210 (185 × 128) mm

Vatican MS. Chigi R. V. 29, fol. 1r-230r, 238r-247v

Fol. 247v *ἔτους ϛϡβ (ινδικτιῶνος) β μηνὶ ἰουν[ίω] ιβ. θ(εο)ῦ τὸ δῶρον κ(αὶ) ἰωάσαφ πόνος. ἀπὸ τ(ῆς) σε[βασμί](ας) μο[ν](ῆς) τ(ῶν) ὁδηγῶν.* The date applies certainly only to fols. 238-47, but fol. 1-230 were also copied by Ioasaph.

Breathings (3). Diaeresis (1) and (3). Abbreviations (2). No ruling.

For a list of manuscripts ascribed to this Ioasaph, see L. Politis, 'Eine Schreiberschule im Kloster *τῶν Ὁδηγῶν*. I Der Schreiber Joasaph', *Byzantinische Zeitschrift*, 51 (1958), 26-34, Abb. 4-9.

Other facsimiles: Follieri, tab. 45; Turyn, *Codices Vaticani*, tab. 158, 205e (with a full description).

60 22 January 1471 — Ioannes Rhosos *ἱερεύς* of Crete, in Rome

Basil — Parchment, 222 × 138 (145 × 73) mm

Oxford, Bodleian MS. Canon. Gr. 108, fol. 26r-54r

Fol. 54r *μετεγράφη χειρὶ ἱερέως ἰωάννου ῥώσου κρητὸς τὸ γένος, ἐν ῥώμῃ· ἔτει αωυωοαω ἀπὸ τῆς χ(ριστο)ῦ γεννήσε(ως)· μηνὸς ἰαννουαρίου κβ.*

A descendant of the above styles brought to Italy in the fifteenth century. Breathings (3). Accents occasionally (1) and (3). Diaeresis (2) and (3). Mute ι (3). Abbreviations (2) and occasionally (4) and (5). Ruling (3).

Rhosos copied over 100 manuscripts, dated from at least 1455 to 1497, all in Italy, but many more have been incorrectly ascribed to him; among classical texts certainly copied by him are: Flor. Laur. 31.14 (Aristotle), 32.6 (Homer, 1465), 81.7 (Aristotle, 1475); Harvard MS. Typ. 18 (Homeric hymns etc.); B. M. Harl. 5600 and 5658 (Homer, 1466 and 1479), 5672 and 6325 (Homer), 6322, fol. 1-73 (Demosthenes); Naples III E 3 (Aristotle, 1493); Bodleian Canon. Gr. 7, fol. 1-40 (Aratus, 1488); Paris gr. 2352 (Euclid, 1487-8); Venice Marc. gr. 200 (Aristotle, 1457), 384 (Plutarch, 1456), 388 (Ptolemy), IV. 3 (Aristotle, 1494). Other scribes whose style was similar include Georgios Gregoropoulos, Ioannes of Patrae, Kaisar Strategos of Crete, Christophoros Trapezites.

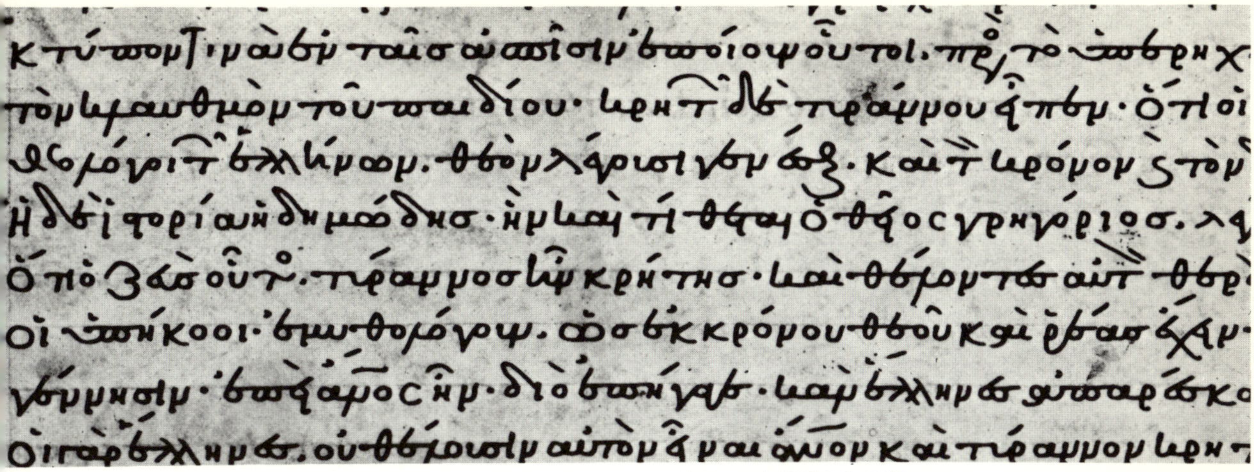

7

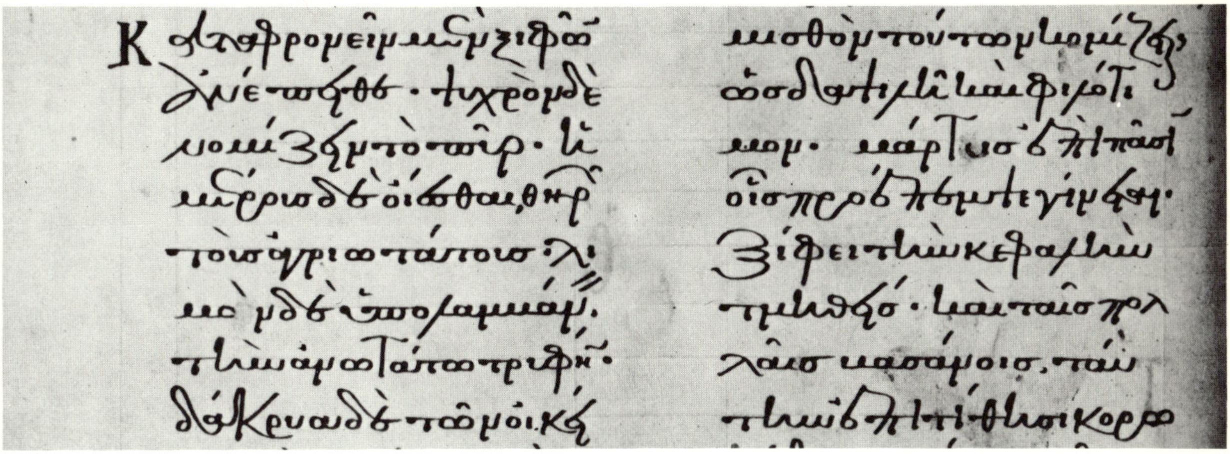

58

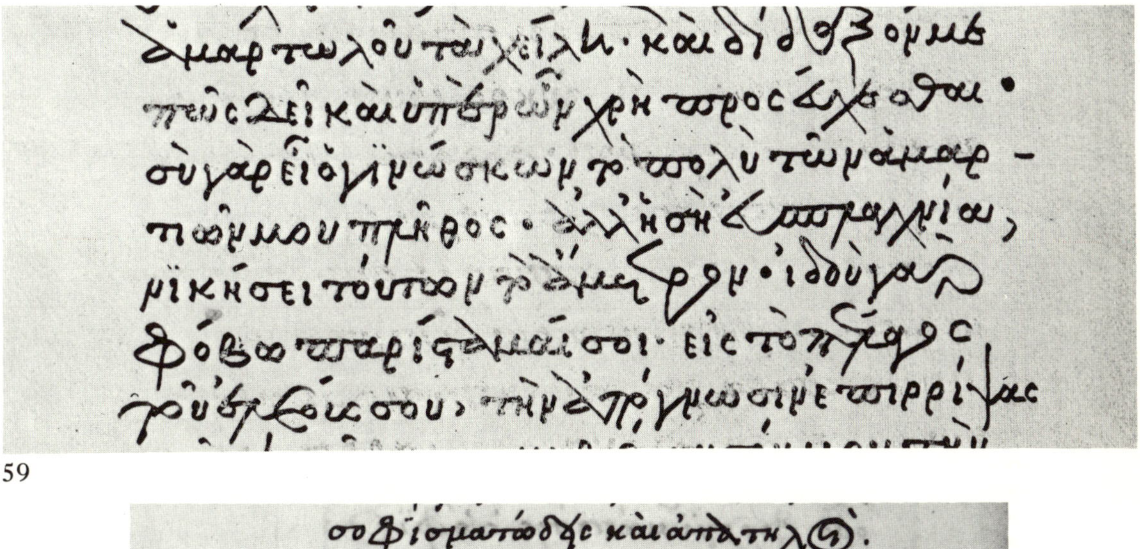

59

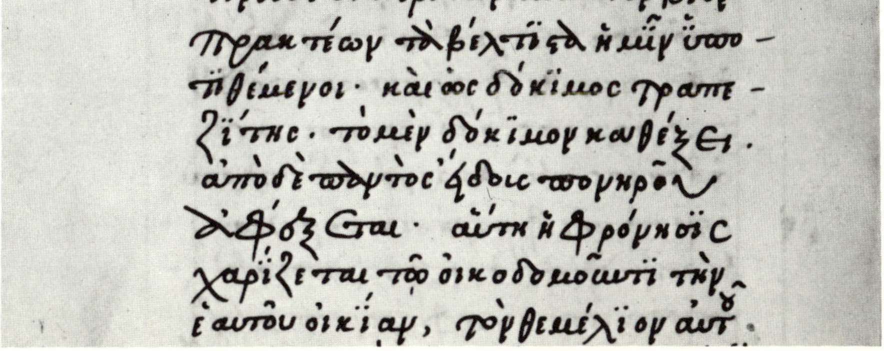

60

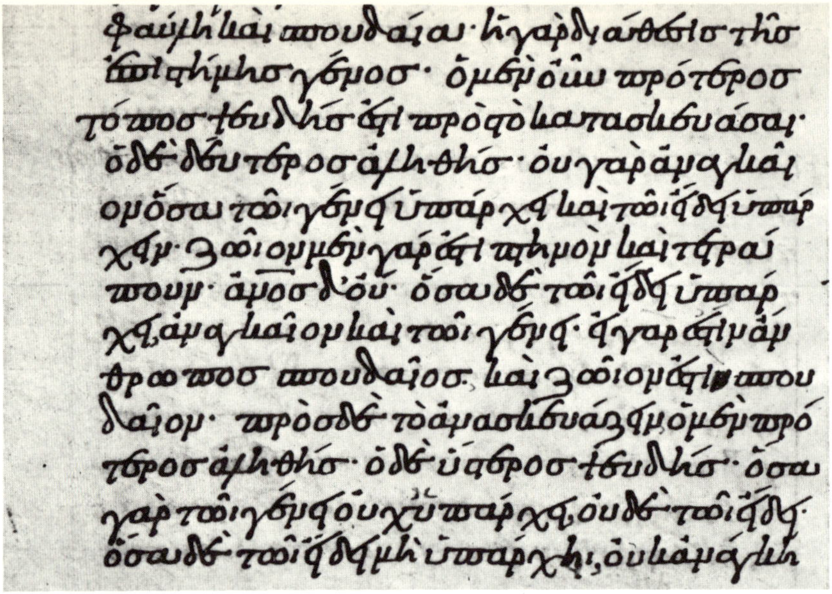

61

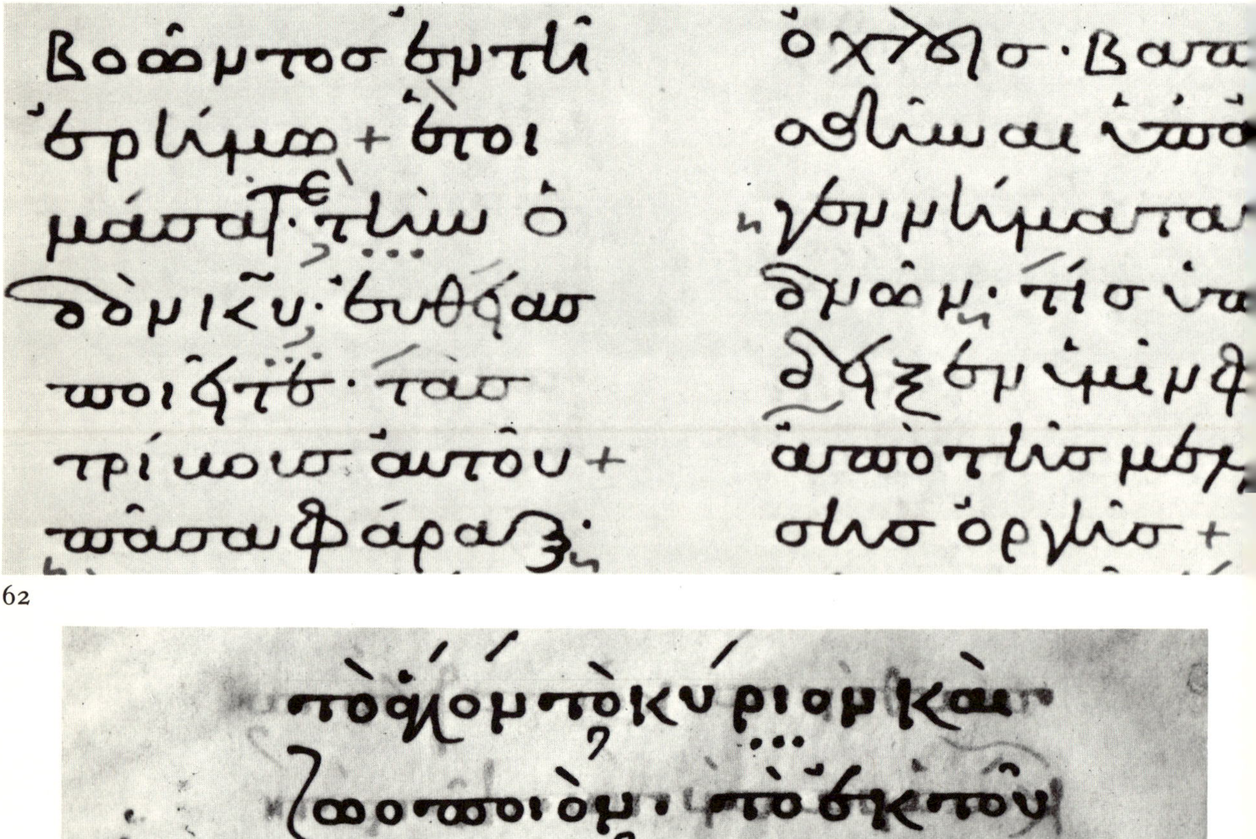

62

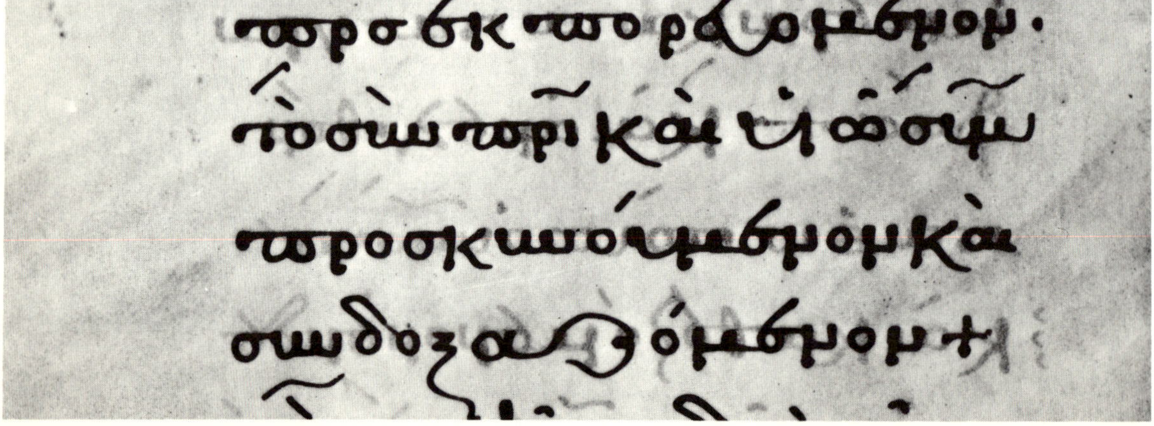

63

61 Between 888 and 901 — Gregorios *ὑποδιάκονος* for Arethas *διάκονος*

Aristotle — Parchment, 275 × 210 (136/40 × 94) mm

Vatican MS. Urbin. gr. 35

Fol. 441[v] *γρηγο[ριος] υπ[ο]διακο[νοσ] αρεθ[α] διακο[νω]*. Arethas was not yet a deacon in 888, and was archbishop of Caesarea in 901. The manuscript is likely to have been copied in Constantinople for the same reasons as **6**.

Uncial forms of λ and (at line ends) α are used. Breathings (1). Diaeresis (2). Mute ι (1). Abbreviations (1), (3), and occasionally (4). Ruling usually (3), sometimes (1).

Undated manuscripts with script comparable, though more developed, are Flor. Laur. 70.3, fol. 1-238[v] (Herodotus) and Venice Marc. gr. 395 (Dio Cassius).

Other facsimiles: Follieri, tab. 18; Lake, IX, MS. 333, pl. 606-8; Lefort and Cochez, pl. 13.

62 June 1008 — Theophanes *μοναχὸς καὶ ἱερεύς* of the Iveron monastery, Athos

Gospel lectionary — Parchment, 295 × 240 (210 × 168) mm

London, British Museum MS. Add. 36751

Fol. 141[v] *ἐτελειώθ[η] μ[ήνι] ιουνιω κβ̄*. Fol. 219[v] *Ετελειώθ[η] ἡ παρου[σα] ... βίβλ(ος) ... μ[ήνι] ἰουνιω ἰνδ[ικτιωνος] ϛ̄.ἔτ(ους) ϛ φιϛ:γραφεῖσα χειρὶ θεοφα[νους] μο[να]χ[ου] (καὶ) ἀναξίου ἱερ[εως] μο[νης] τ(ῶν) ι[βηρων εν] ἀ[θωνι]*. The last three words were read by the compiler of the 1907 catalogue but there now remains hardly any trace of them.

The fully developed heavy liturgical style. It is an early example among formal hands of the tendency to enlarge some letters disproportionately to the rest. Otherwise, details of scribal practice are predictably conservative: breathings (1), abbreviations (1), (3), (4). Ruling (3). Ecphonetic notation in red.

Theophanes probably also copied Athos Iveron 46 (Chrysostom, 1007); Moscow 62 (Chrysostom, 1006), 380 and 381 (lives of saints, 1022-3); Paris gr. 529 (Gregory of Nazianzus, 1020); Vat. Ottob. gr. 422 (Menaion, 1004).

Other facsimiles: Lake, II, MS. 67, pl. 121-3.

63 Between 1050 and 1052 — Theophylaktos patriarchal *κουβουκλείσιος καὶ δομέστικος* of Antioch

Synodikon — Parchment, 220 × 160 (155 × 105) mm

Oxford, Bodleian MS. Holkham Gr. 6

Fol. 170[v] [corner of page torn off, shown by ...] ... *ἠσθητι κ(υρι)ε τοῦ δούλου ... θεοφυλάκτου ἀνα ... ιου κουβου [κλεισιου] (καὶ) δομεστίκου ... ναγοῦς π(ατ)ριαρχικοῦ ... ρέτου ἀντιοχ[είας]*. Zoe (d. 1050) is the last of the dead emperors and empresses to be commemorated; the list of patriarchs of Anthioch ends before Peter III (appointed 1052).

Breathings predominantly (1). Circumflex accent (1) when over a breathing. Abbreviations (1) and occasionally (4) and (5). Ruling (3). Ecphonetic notation in red.

Other facsimiles: *Greek manuscripts in the Bodleian*, pl. VII; Wilson, pl. 30; and (with a detailed description of the manuscript) in R.J.H. Jenkins, C. Mango, 'A Synodicon of Antioch and Lacedaemonia', *Dumbarton Oaks Papers*, 15 (1961), 225-42; see also V. Laurent, 'La liste épiscopale du synodicon de la métropole de Lacédémone' *Revue des études byzantines*, 19 (1961), 208-26.

64 31 May 1106 — Anthes *ἱερεύς* (?), for Laurentios *μονότροπος καὶ δομέστικος* of the Vatopedi monastery, Athos

Sticherarion — Parchment, 265×205 (205×150) mm

Leningrad, Public Library MS. gr. 789

Fol. 258^v *Γράψαντ[α] προστάξαντ[α] χ(ρίστ)έ μου σῶσον· ἐκ προσταγῆς λαυρεντίω εὐτελῆ μονοτροπ[ω]· κ(αὶ) δομεστίκ[ω] τῆς σεβασμίας μο[νῆς]· τῆς ὑπεραγίας θ(εοτό)κου· τῆς τοῦ βατοπεδ[ίου]· τ(ῆς) ἐν τ[ῇ] ἁγίω ὄρει· ἐπιγράψαντι μὲν, κεφαλαίοις τὲ καὶ οὐδαμινοῖς χρυσοῖς γράμμασι καὶ ἐξομπλίοις· σὺν τοῦ ἀμφιάσματ[ος]· ὁ εὐτε[λῆς] ἱερε[ὺς] ἄνθης· ξένου πάσης ἀρετῆς, καὶ τ(ῶν) ἰδίω(ν). Ἐτελειώθ[η] δὲ τὸ παρὸν στιχηράριον· ἐπὶ βασιλείας ἀλεξίου μ[ε]γ[άλου] βασιλέ[ως] ῥωμαίω(ν)· τοῦ κομνηνοῦ· μη[νὶ] μαΐω λα· ἰνδ[ικτιῶνος] ιδ· ἔτους ϛχιδ.*

There are no breathings or accents in the body of the text, as is usual where there is musical notation. Abbreviations (4). Ruling (3). An early dated example of early Byzantine notation.

Other facsimiles: Lake, VI, MS. 243, pl. 437-9; Tsereteli and Sobolevski, II, pl. XXII, XXIIa.

65 9 June 1185 — Kosmas *μοναχός, ἐν κάστρῳ Ζαγορίων*

Gospel lectionary — Parchment, 280×210 (215×143) mm

London, British Museum MS. Add. 28817

Fol. 305^v *Συνεγράφη ἡ ... βίβλ(ὸς) ταύτ[η] διὰ χειρ(ὸς) κοσμ[ὰ] [μον]αχ[ου] ... μη[νὶ] ἰουνίω θ ἔτ(ους)ϛχϥγ διὰ συνδρομ(ῆς) κυροῦ βα[σι]λ[είου] τοῦ παπληνοῦ ... ἐτελιώθ[η] δὲ ... παρὰ βοηθεί(ας) κυροῦ θεοδ[ώρου] τοῦ καράβδ[ου] κ(αὶ) τ(ῆς) συμβιου αὐτ[οῦ] κυρ(ὰς) ζω(ῆς) ἐν τῶ οἴκω αὐτ(ων) ἐν τω κάστ[ρω] ζαγορί(ων).* Of the eight or more places now or formerly called Zagorion or Zagora, ranging from Yugoslavia to the Black Sea, perhaps the most likely one meant here is that near Volos in Thessaly; but wherever he was copying this manuscript, the scribe was not necessarily a native of the place, still less representative of any local tradition of writing.

The unusually flat appearance of this version of the heavy formal style, which makes it akin to the 'musical' hands, is due partly to the virtual absence of enlarged letters, exceptional at this date. Breathings (3). Diaeresis (1). Abbreviations (1). Ruling (3).

Other facsimiles: Lake, II, MS. 84, pl. 149-50.

66 1288/9 — Symeon *ἱερομόναχος*, for Pankratios *ἐκκλησιάρχης* of Grottaferrata

Kontakarion — Parchment, 324×240 (253×168) mm

Florence, Laurenziana MS. Ashburnham 64 fol. 1^r-116^v, 124^r-179^v, 200^r-257^r

Fol. 179^v *ἐτελιώθ[η] τὸ παρ(ὸν) ψαλτικ(ὸν), διὰ χὺρ(ὸς) ἐμοῦ εὐτελοὺς ἱερο[μον]άχ[ου] ῥακενδίτου συμεῶν(ος): ἐξ οἰκείου τε κόπ[ου] καὶ ἐξόδου κυ[ροῦ] παγκρατίου ἱερο[μον]άχ[ου] καὶ ἐκκλησιάρχ[ου] μον(ῆς) κρυπτοφέρρης ... : ἔτ[ους] ϛψϥζ (ἰνδικτιῶνος) β.* Fol. 44^r and 257^r have shorter versions of this note without the date.

The extreme flatness of the text hand here is produced by using the same pen as for the neumes, an exceptionally broad one held parallel to the line of writing. No breathings or accents. Diaeresis (3). Abbreviations (4). Ruling (2).

Other facsimiles: (complete) *Contacarium Ashburnhamense*, ed. C. Høeg (Monumenta Musicae Byzantinae, IV) (Copenhagen 1956); Lefort and Cochez, pl. 98; Turyn, *Dated manuscripts in Italy*, pl. 44, 229a,b,c.

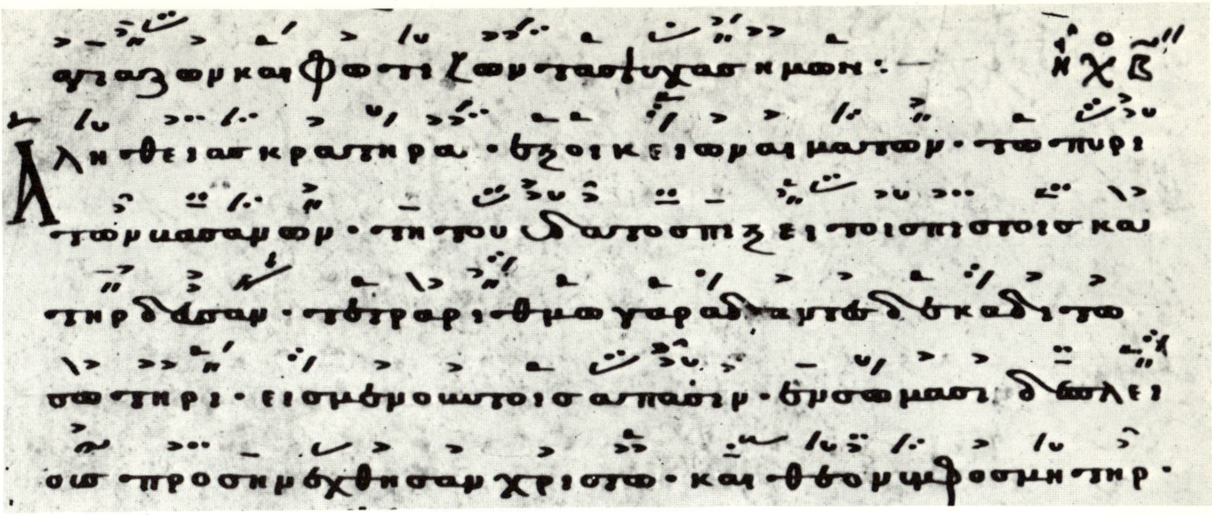

64

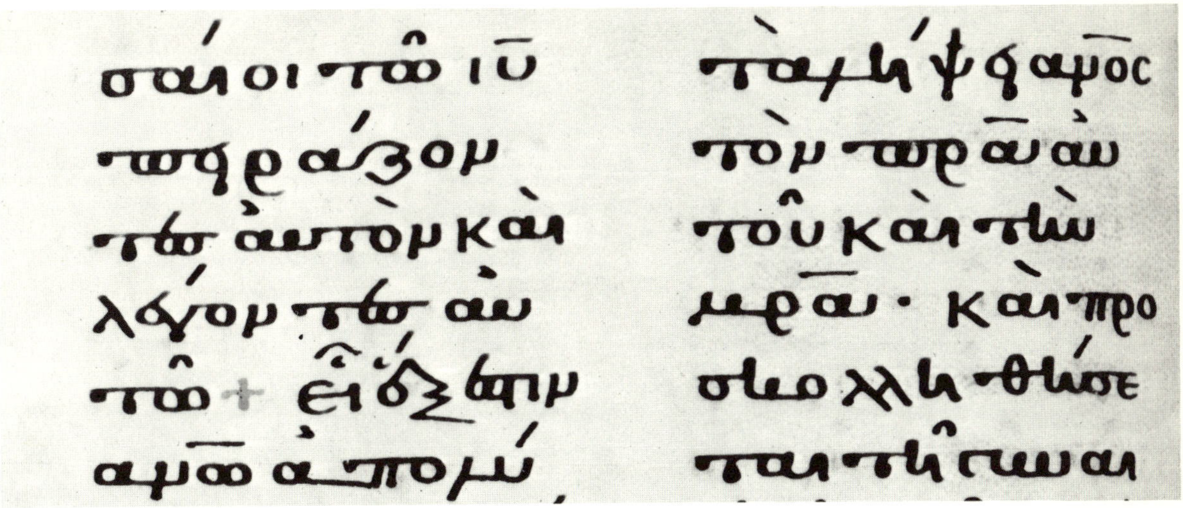

65

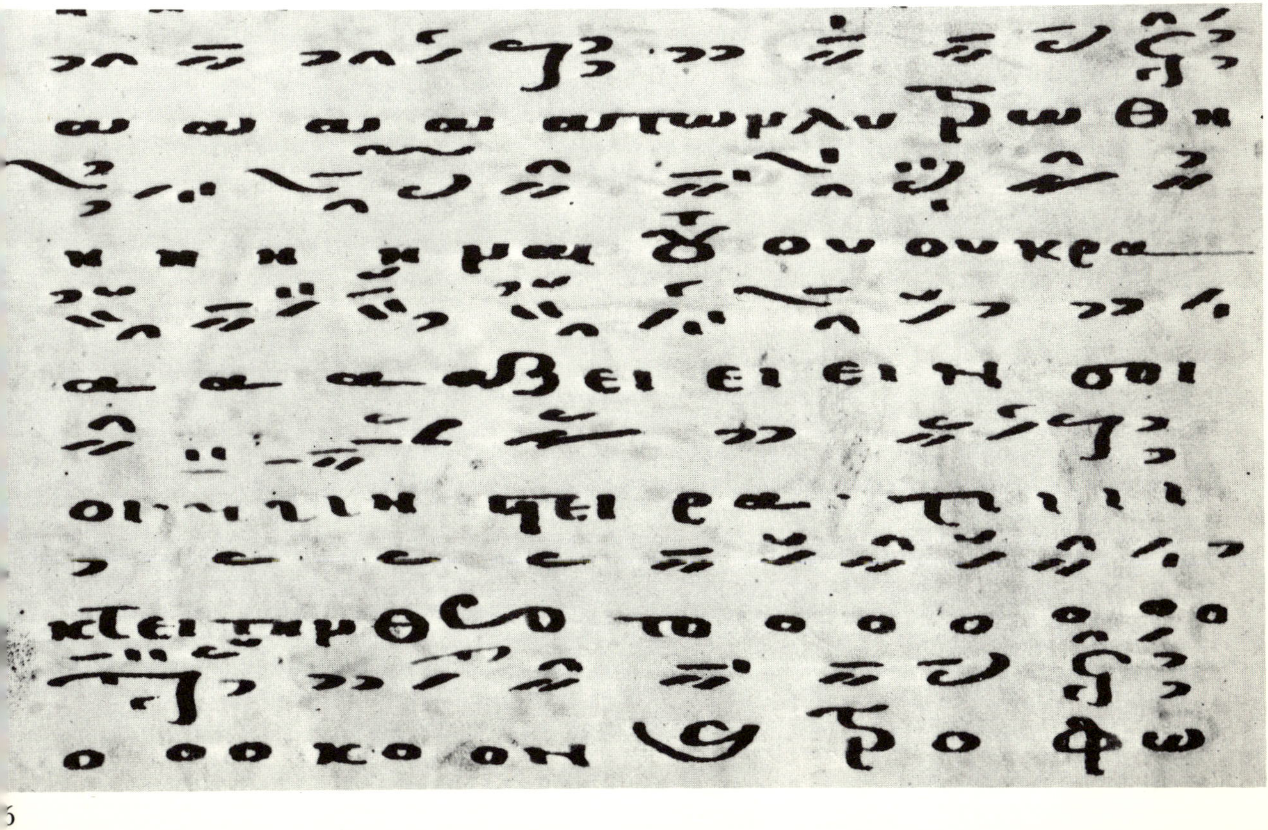

6

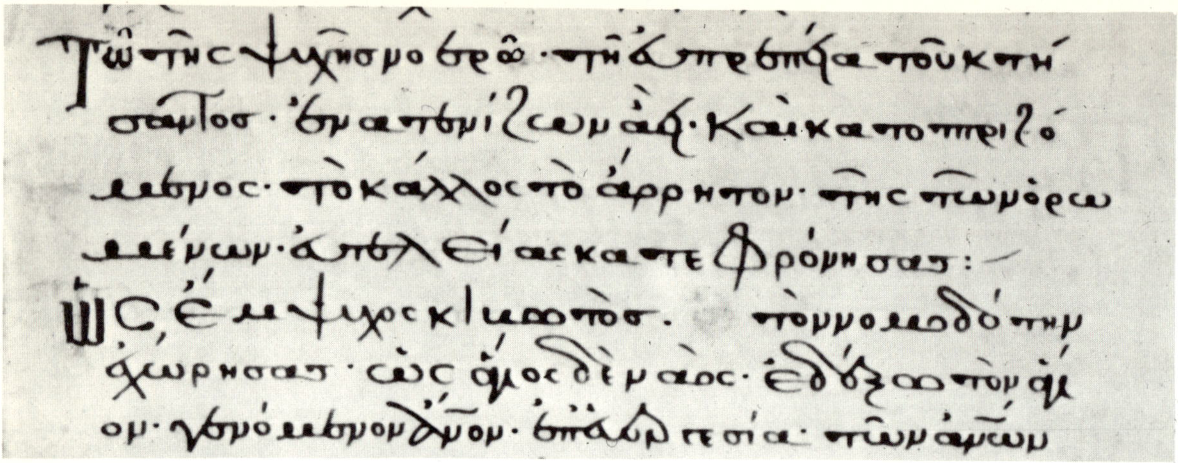

67

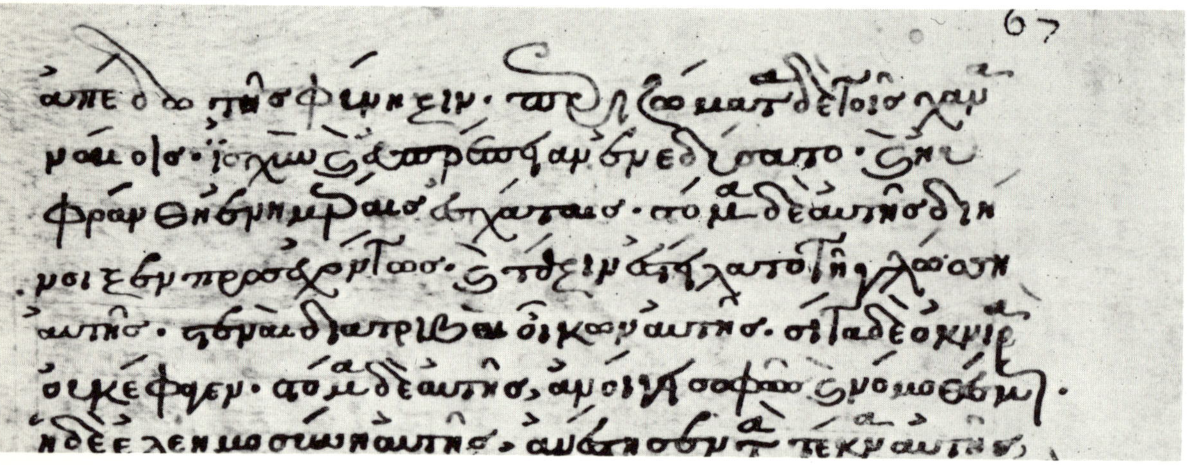

68

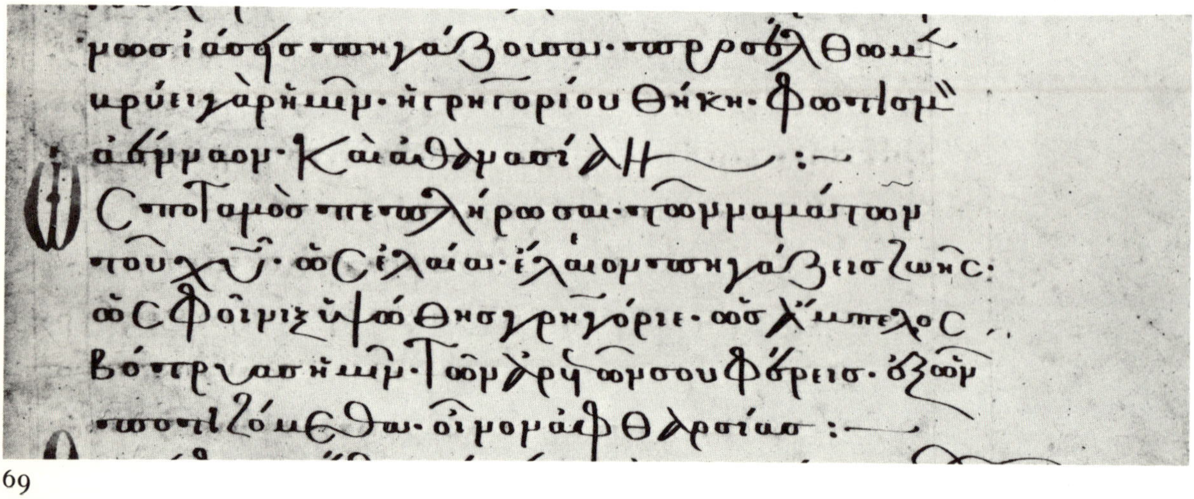

69

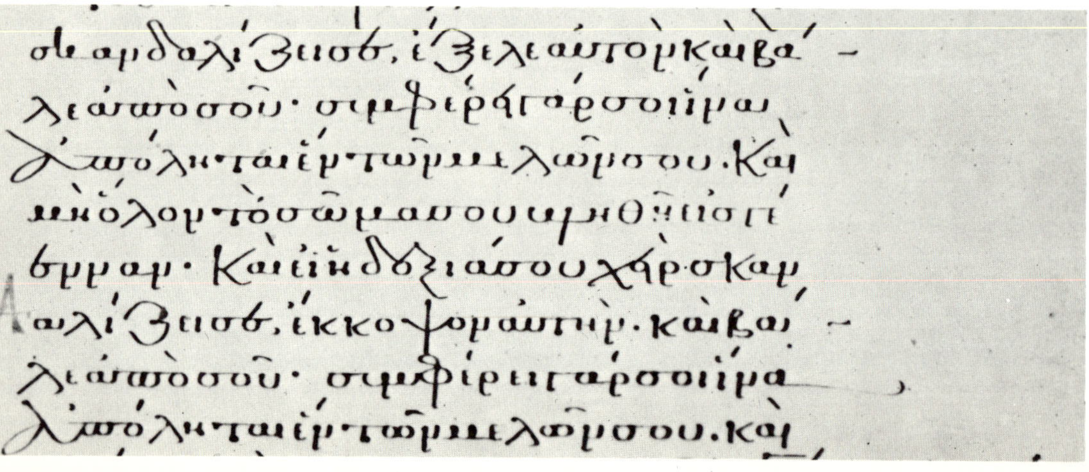

70

67 9 June 1127 — Theoktistos, for the monastery of the Prodromos in Petra (Constantinople)
Menaion — Parchment, 273 × 203 (193 × 130/7) mm
Paris, Bibliothèque nationale MS. grec 1570

Fol. 213[r] *ετελειώϑ[η] ὁ παρὸν νοέβρι(ος) μὴν, μη[νὶ] ἰουνίω ϑ̅· ὥρα ι̅ε̅ τ(ῆς) ἡμέρ[ας]· ἐπὶ τῆς βασιλείας ἰωάννου πορφυρογεννήτου τοῦ κομνηνοῦ· ἐν ἔτει, τῷ ϛχ̅λ̅ε̅· (ἰνδικτιῶνος) ε̅:* — Fol. 214[v] *ἡ βῖβλος αὕτη τῆς μονῆς τοῦ προδρόμου: τῆς κειμένης ἔγγιστα τῆς ἀετΐου: ἀρχαϊκὴ δε τῆ μονηῖ κλῆσις, πέτρα: ϑεῶ τὸ δῶρον· καὶ πόνος, ϑεοκτήστου.*

On the ερ ligature in line 7 see **46**. Breathings (2). Accents (1). Diaeresis (1) and (3). Mute ι (2). Abbreviations (2), occasionally (5). Ruling (3).

Theoktistos also copied Athos, Dionysiou 8 (Gospels, 1133).

Other facsimiles: Lake, V. MS. 186, pl. 316-17; Omont, *Manuscrits datés*, pl. XLV; Strunk, pl 101-8.

68 1279/80 — Makarios *μοναχός* from the monastery of S. Salvatore, Messina, for Blasios *ἐκκλησιάρχης* of Grottaferrata
Prophetologion — Parchment (palimpsest) 265 × 190 (190 × 130) mm
Vatican MS. Vat. gr. 770 upper writing

Fol. 106[r] *ἐγράφει αὕτη ἡ ... δέλτος χειρὶ ἀμελοὺς (καὶ) χϑαμαλ[οῦ] (καὶ) ἀναξίου μοναχ[οὺ] μακαρίω τοῦ ἀπ[ὸ] τ(ῆς) μεγ[ά]λ[ης] μον[ῆς] σ(ωτῆ)ρ(ο)ς ἀκροτ[η]ρ[ίου] μεσ[σ]αν[ης]· σπουδῆ ... βλασίω ἐκκλησιάρχ[ω] τ(ῆς) εὐαγοῦς μον[ῆς] ὑπ[εραγίας] ϑ(εοτό)κου κρυπτ[ο]φέρ-[ρης] ... Ἔτ(ος) ϛψπη′.*

Breathings (2). Accents (1), sometimes (3). Diaeresis (1) and (2). Abbreviations (2), (4), (8), and occasionally (5). Ruling (3).

Makarios of Reggio who copied Grottaferrata A.δ.VI, Δ. α. IV, and perhaps Δ. γ. XXXV, fol. 1-8, seems not to be the same scribe.

Other facsimiles: Turyn, *Codices Vaticani*, tab. 35,170a (with a full description of the manuscript).

69 1259/60 — Barlaam *μοναχός*, for the monastery of Galesion (near Ephesus)
Menaion — Parchment, 248 × 175 (170 × 117) mm
Vatican MS. Regin. gr. 63, fol. 1-31[r], 32[v]-end

Fol. 140[v] *ἡ βίβλος αὕτη, κτῆμα τοῦ γαλησίου χειρὶ γραφεῖσα, ἐσχάτου μονοτρόπ(ων), οἰκτροῦ βαρλαὰμ ... βασιλεύοντ(ος) ... ἀγγέλου κομνηνοῦ κυρ[οῦ] μιχα[ὴλ] τοῦ παλαιολόγου [καὶ ηγεμο]νεύοντος ἐν τῆ τοιαύτ[η] μονῆ κυρ[οῦ] ἰωσήφ. ἐν ἔτ[ει] ϛ̅ψξ̅η. (ἰνδικτιῶνος) ι̅γ̅.* The Byzantine year 6768 (1259/60) was indiction 3; the only indiction 13 in the reign of Michael VIII Palaiologos was 6778 (1269/70); but Ioseph abbot of Galesion was patriarch of Constantinople 1267-75 and 1282-3.

Breathings (3), occasionally (1). Accents sometimes (1). Diaeresis (1). Mute ι (3), usually only a dot. Abbreviations (2), (4), (5), (8). Ruling (3).

Other facsimiles: Cavalieri and Lietzmann, tab. 36; Follieri, tab. 50; Turyn, *Codices Vaticani*, tab. 19, 20, 165b (with a full description of the manuscript). On manuscripts from the Galesion monastery see F. Halkin.

70 1304/5 — Neophytos *ἱεροδιάκονος καὶ μοναχός* of Cyprus
Gospels — Parchment, 245 × 180 (160 × 105) mm
London, British Museum MS. Add. 22506

Fol. 219[r] *ἐγράφη ἐν ἔτη ϛ̅ω̅ι̅γ̅′: (ἰνδικτιωνος) γ̅: δϊ' ἐμοῦ τοῦ ἐν ἱεροδιακόνοις ἐλαχίστου οἰκτροῦ νεοφύτου· καὶ τάχα μοναχοῦ: τοῦ κϋπρίου:* The whole manuscript is in the same hand. The mention of the scribe's nationality suggests that the manuscript was not written in Cyprus.

Breathings (3). Diaeresis (1) and (3). Abbreviations (2), (4), (5), (8). Ruling (3).

Other facsimiles: Pal. Soc. I. 205.

71 Between sometime before 925 and 945 — Alexander bishop of Nicaea, or Jacob metropolitan of Larissa

Lucian — Parchment, 320×226 (240×165) mm

Vatican MS. Vat. gr. 90 marginalia

Fol. 305^{v} *Δ[ιωρθωσα] εγὼ αλέξανδ[ρος] ἐπίσκο[πος] ... νικαίας μ[ε]τ[α] ἰακώβου τοῦ ὁμαίμονος αδελφοῦ κ(αὶ) μητροπολίτου λαρίσσης*. Similar notes on fol. 34^{v}, 41^{v}, 45^{v}, 46^{v}, 92^{v}, 122^{r}, 124^{r}. Nicolaos Mysticus (d. 925) wrote to Alexander as bishop of Nicaea; in 945 he was deprived of the see.

Notes by Alexander and Jacob (there is nothing to show which one wrote which notes) are usually in uncial, but sometimes in this plain, current minuscule. Uncial β, γ, ε, η, κ, λ, μ, are used. Breathings (1). Abbreviations sometimes (5).

Undated manuscripts with comparable script include Vat. Palat. gr. 173 (Plato); and, though it looks somewhat earlier, Paris gr. 1741 fol. 1^{r}-37^{r}, 40^{r}-199^{r}, 246^{r}-293^{v} (Aristotle etc.). Compare also documentary hands, e.g. Athos, Iveron, archives (Dölger neg. N. 92, see *Schatzkammer* N. 56) of 995.

Facsimiles (showing only the uncial scholia): Cavalieri and Lietzmann, tab. 10; *Scholia in Lucianum*, ed. H. Rabe (Leipzig, 1906), pl. I.

72 Probably between 1013 and 1021

Gregory of Nazianzus — Parchment, 315×250 (195/205×155)mm

Paris, Bibliothèque nationale MS. grec 529, fol. 1^{r}, 3^{r}-16^{r}, 20^{r}-24^{r}, marginalia

Fol. 360^{v} *Ἐτελειώθ[η] ἡ παρου[σα] βίβλος μ[ηνι]* α[illegible]. *ἰνδ[ικτιωνος]* ‾ *ἔτ(ους) ϛφκ* [one illegible letter]: *γραφεῖσα χειρι θεοφα[νους] ταπ[εινου] μο[να]χ[ου] (καὶ) εὐτελ[οῦς] γερ(ον)τ(ος)*. The text must have been copied in one of the years 6521-9, and the scholia, though not in the same hand, are in one sufficiently alike to be contemporary.

Breathings (3). Diaeresis (1). Abbreviations (1) on names of the Trinity, (2) on lesser *nomina sacra*, (4), (6).

Undated manuscripts with comparable script include Jerusalem Patr. 36 (Euripides palimpsest).

Another facsimile showing scholia: Lake, IV, MS. 148, pl. 254.

73 23 October 986

Commentaries on Gregory of Nazianzus — Parchment, 160×125 (113×77/85) mm

Paris, Bibliothèque nationale MS. suppl. gr. 469^{A}

Fol. 7^{v} *Ἐπληρώθη τὰ σχόλια τῶν ἀναγϊνωσκομένων λόγων μ(ην)[ι] ὀκτωβρίωι κγ ἰνδ[ικτιωνος] ιε ἐν ἔτι τῶι ϛυϞε, ἡμε[ρα] σαββάτωι ὥρα γ*: — The whole manuscript is in the same hand.

The earliest dated example of the plain scholarly style used for the main text of a book, as in some classical texts. Breathings (2). Diaeresis (1). Mute ι (1). Abbreviations (1) for names of the Trinity, (2) for lesser *nomina sacra*, (4), (6), occasionally (7). Ruling (2).

A similar hand copied Patmos MS. 138 (Chrysostom, 988). Undated manuscripts with comparable script include Flor. Laur. 32. 9, fol. 127^{r}-189^{r} (Aeschylus), 32.15 (Homer); Leiden BPG 60^{A} (Sophocles palimpsest); Vat. gr. 1335 fol. 69^{r}-237^{v} (Xenophon); Venice Marc. gr. 454 (Homer; only the scholia are comparable with this manuscript, although text and scholia may be by the same hand). Compare also documentary hands, e.g. Athos, Iveron, archives (Dölger neg. N. 107, see *Schatzkammer* N. 108) written in the Laura in 984, and Protaton archives (Dölger neg. 7 ibid. N. 107) of 942.

Other facsimiles: Lake, IV, MS. 142, pl. 242; Lefort and Cochez, pl. 56; Omont, *Manuscrits datés*, pl. VIII^{I}.

74 Probably 1044/5 — *μοναχός* of monastery of *Ξηροχωράφιον* near Miletus

Ps. - Macarius the Egyptian — Parchment, 217×170 (167×120) mm

Paris, Bibliothèque nationale MS. grec 973

Fol. 309^{r} *ἐγρ(ά)φει ἡ βίβλος αὔτη* ... [illegible] *ἐλέ[ω] θ(εο)υ [μον]αχ[ου] γεν(ου)μέν(ου) ἀπὸ τ(ῆς) μον(ῆς) τ(οῦ) ξιροῦ χ(ω)ραφείου· θέματ(ος) θρακισίου· ἐγγὺς τῆς μιλίτ(ου)· ὁ δὲ τὸ ὄρ(ος) τ(ῆς) μον(ῆς) ἐπὶνοίμία καλῖται βραχιὰνὸς: Ἐν ἔτι ϛφνγ· ινδ[ικτιωνος] γ*: The Byzantine year 6553 (1044/5) was indiction 13; it is perhaps more likely that ι was accidentally omitted from the indiction number than that ϛφνγ is a mistake for ϛφμγ or ϛφνη (both indiction 13); all the figures are clearly written uncials. The monastery is the one later known as Hiera.

Breathings (2). Abbreviations (1), (4), and sometimes (6). Ruling (3).

Other facsimiles: Lake, IV, MS. 158, pl. 270; Omont, *Manuscrits datés*, pl. XVIII^{III}.

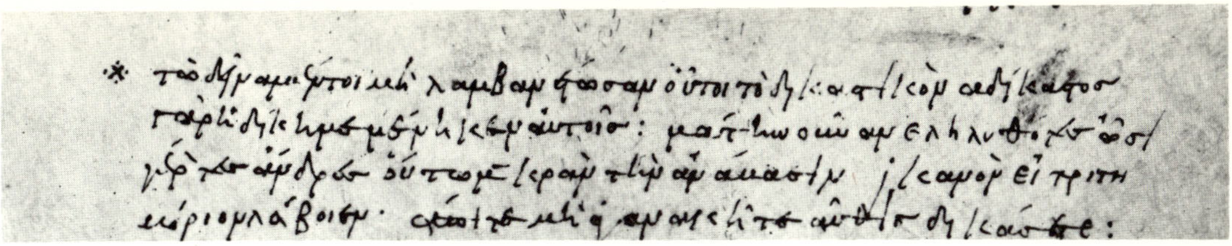

71

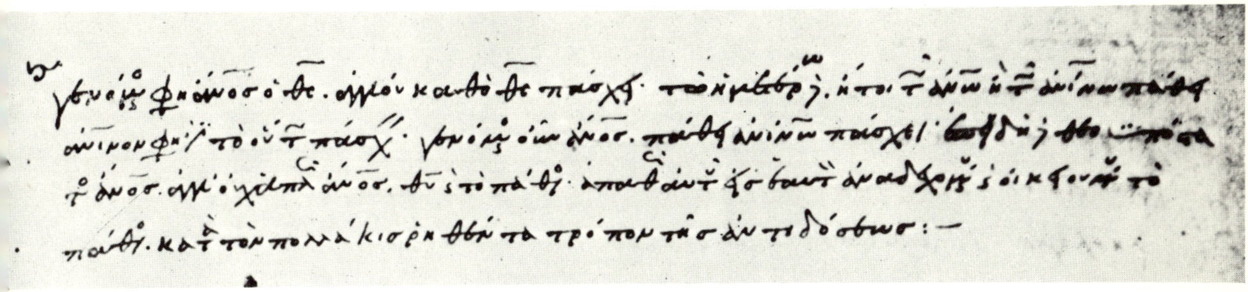

72

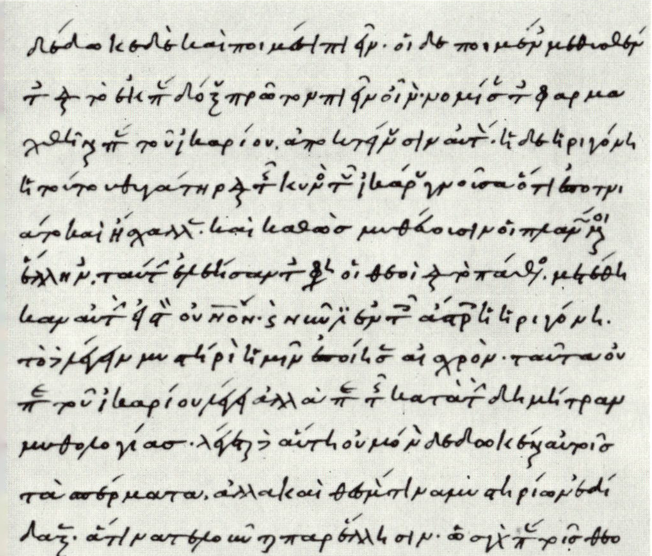

73

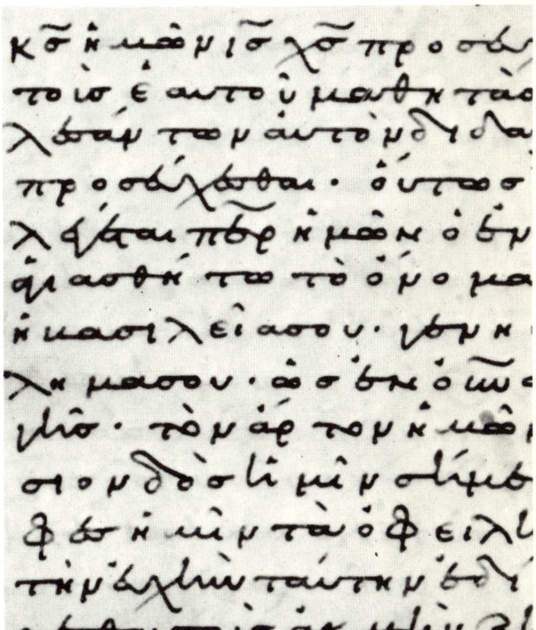

74

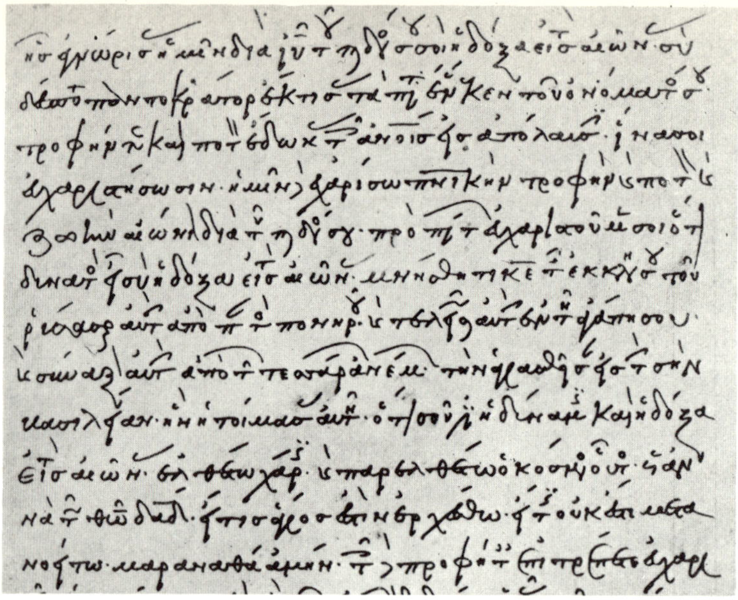

75

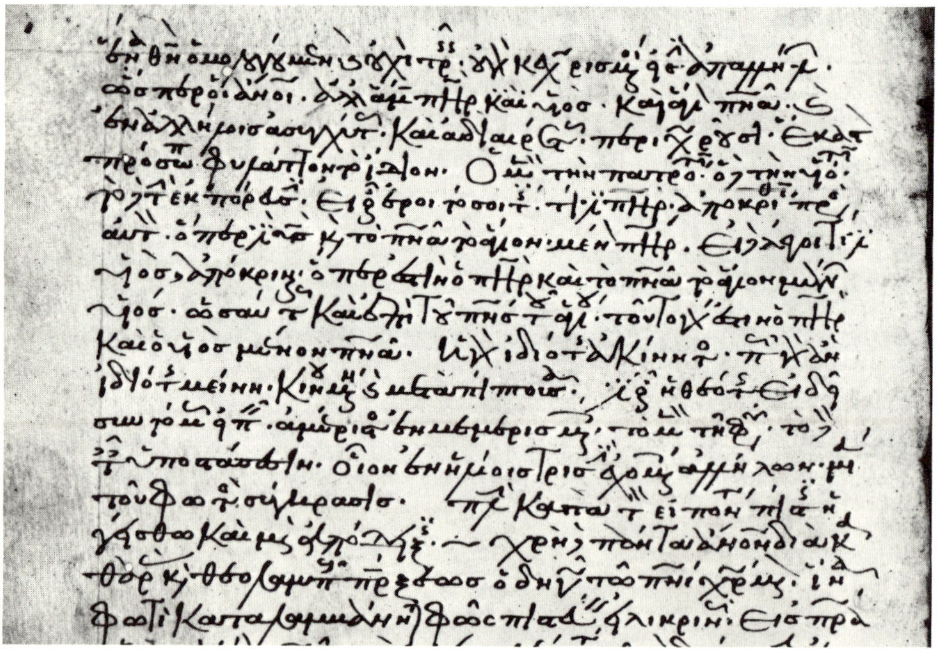

76

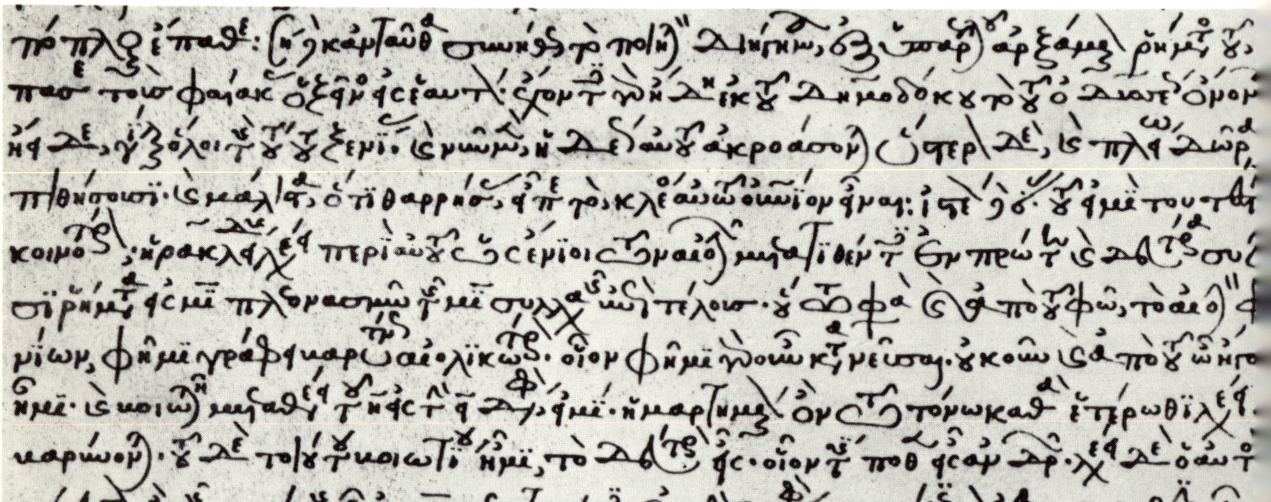

77

75 11 June 1056 — Leon (?) *νοτάριος*

Apostolic fathers — Parchment, 190 × 150 (145 × 95) mm

Jerusalem, Patriarchate MS.54

Fol. 120^r *ἐτελειώθ[η] μη[νὶ] ἰουνίω εἰς τ[ὰς] ια̅ ἡ[μέρα] γ̅ ἰνδ[ικτιῶνος] ϑ' ἔτ(ους) ϛφξδ χειρὶ λέ[ον]τ[ος] (?) νοτ[α]ρ[ίου] (καὶ) ἀλείτ[ου].*
One of the earliest dated appearances of minuscule η half-way towards losing its tall first stroke and acquiring a descending last stroke; also of the occasional use of ligatures reduced to their minimum possible shape (e.g.ꝗ) which became common only in the next century. Breathings (2). Circumflex accent sometimes (1). Diaeresis (1) but rarely used. Mute ι occasionally (1) used only with the article. Abbreviations (2), (4), (6), (7), (8). Ruling (3).
Other facsimiles: Lake, I, MS. 7, pl.11; Pal. Soc. II.48; *The teaching of the apostles*, ed. J. Rendel Harris (London and Baltimore, Md., 1887), pl. 1-X.

76 *c.* 1087/8 — Michael *μοναχός*, abbot of monastery of Christ *πανοικτίρμων* (Constantinople)

Psalms with commentary, etc. — Parchment, 175 × 130 (95×70) mm

Vatican MS. Vat. gr. 342, fol. 3^r-280^r

Fol. 20^v-23^v Easter tables for 1087/8 to 1158/9. Fol. 24^r verses on the Psalms ending *Μιχαὴλ μοναχῶ εὐτελεῖ καὶ ἀλύτρω*. Fol. 276^v *ὁμολόγ[ησις] Μιχ[αηλ] εὐτε[λοῦς] [μον]αχ[οῦ] κ(αὶ) καθηγουμ[έ]ν[ου] μον[ῆς] τ(οῦ) κ(υρίο)υ ἡμ(ῶν) ἰ(ησο)ῦ χ(ριστο)ῦ τοῦ πανοικτηρμ[ο]ν[ος] τοῦ ἀτταλ[ειατου]*. Commentary and additional matter are in a more current version of the hand copying the Psalms, presumably that of the abbot himself, to judge from the modest descriptive words used of him. The order of words in this heading suggests that the author was not the founder Michael Attaliates, but Michael abbot of 'the monastery of Christ *πανοικτίρμων* of [i.e. founded by] Attaliates', which is how the monastery is sometimes described; there is no evidence that Attaliates was ever abbot, nor any sign of his survival after 1080.
Breathings (2). Circumflex accent sometimes (1) and (2). Abbreviations (2), (4), (6), sometimes (7), and slightly (8). Ruling (3).
The same scribe probably copied no **58**.
Other facsimiles: Lake, VIII, MS. 298, pl. 544-5

77 Between *c.*1140 and 1195/6, probably before 1175 — Eustathios of Thessalonica (?) probably in Constantinople

Eustathius — Parchment, 405 × 275 (330 × 215) mm

Venice, Marciana MS.gr.460

Fol. 1^r note by Bessarion, who owned the manuscript before 1468: *εὐσταθΐου ἀρχϊεπϊσκόπου θεσσαλονίκ(ης) ἐξήγ[ησις] εἰς ὅλην τὴν ὀδύσσειαν· εἰσὶ δὲ γράμματα τῆς χειρ[ος] αὐτοῦ ἐκείνου.* No signed autograph of Eustathius is known, by which the truth of this statement can be tested; it could be the work of a secretary working closely with him, which the existence of another complete text of the same commentary in the same hand suggests, and which would be consistent both with some unintelligent copying mistakes and with some corrections such as an author would make to his own text. Whether Eustathius' hand or not, it is likely to have been a product of his tenure of various teaching posts in Constantinople between about 1140 and December 1174 when he went to the see of Thessalonica.
Breathings (3). Accents slightly (1) and occasionally (3) and (4). Diaeresis (3). Abbreviations (4), (6), sometimes (7), (8). Ruling (3).
The same scribe copied Flor. Laur. 59.2-3 (Eustathius on *Iliad*), Paris gr. 2702 (Eustathius on *Odyssey*).
Another facsimile: Wattenbach and von Velsen, tab. XLIX. On Eustathius' supposed autographs see E. Martini, 'Eustathianum', *Rheinisches Museum*, N.F. 62 (1907), 273-94; S. Peppink, 'De autographis Eustathianis cum codice Suidae comparatis', *Mnemosyne*, N.S. 60 (1933), 423-4; P. Maas, 'Verschiedenes zu Eustathios 4', *Byzantinische Zeitschrift*, 45 (1952), 2-3; B. Laourdas, *'Εἰς Εὐστάθιον Θεσσαλονίκης', Ἐπετηρὶς Ἑταιρείας Βυζαντινῶν Σπουδῶν*, 23 (1953), 544-7; *Eustazio di Tessalonica, Espugnazione di Tessalonica*, ed. S. Kyriakidis (Palermo, 1961), pp. XVI-XIX; V. Laurent, art. 'Eustathe, métropolite de Thessalonique § II' in *Dictionnaire d'histoire et de géographie ecclésiastiques*, 16 (1967), col. 35-6; *Eustathii ... Commentarii ad Homeri Iliadem pertinentes* ... ed. M. van der Valk (Leiden, 1971), praefatio; N.G. Wilson, 'The autographs of Eustathius', *Greek, Roman and Byzantine Studies*, 14 (1973), 226-8.

78 25 April 1063 — Theodoros *ὕπατος καὶ βασιλικὸς νοτάριος*

Isocrates — Parchment, 210 × 172 (160 × 110) mm

Vatican MS. Vat. gr. 65, fol. 5r -end (except 66r, 87v, 219r-20v, 238r, 251v)

Fol. 304v *ἐτελειώθη ἡ βίβλ(ος) αὕτη παρὰ θεοδώρου ὑπάτου (καὶ) βασ[ιλικου] νοταρίου· γραφεῖσα οἰκεία χειρὶ αὐτοῦ μηνὶ ἀπριλλίω κε̅ (ἰνδικτιωνος) α̅: τοῦ ἁγίου μάρκου: ἔτους ϛφοα.*
An early example of a personal hand of pronounced unevenness arising from variations in the size of different letters. Breathings (2). Accents sometimes (1), occasionally (2). Diaeresis (2) and (3). Abbreviations (1), (4), (6), (8). Ruling (3).
Other facsimiles: Lake, VII, MS. 293, pl. 531.

79 22 November 1079 — Nikolaos (?) *γραμματικός*, in Jerusalem

Climacus — Parchment, 310 × 240 (195 × 150) mm

Jerusalem, Patriarchate MS.21, fol. 1-175

Fol. 175v *ἐτελειώθ[η] ἡ δέλτ(ος) αὕτη, μη[νὶ] νοεμβρίω κβ̅: ἰνδ[ικτιῶνος] γ̅· τοῦ ϛφπη ἔτους.* Fol. 163v verses ... *γέγραφε δ' αὐτὴν γραμματικὸς τῇ τέχνῃ πρὸς ... ἱερουσαλὴμ ... ὁ συγγραφεὺς δὲ τῶν στίχων νικόλαος.* Nikolaos, author of the verses, was not necessarily the *γραμματικός* copyist.
Breathings (2). Accents slightly (1). Diaeresis (3). Abbreviations (2), (4), (5). Ruling (2).
Other facsimiles: Lake, I, MS. 8, pl. 12, 14.

80 14 October 1383 — Konstantinos Charases, *ῥεφερενδάριος, ἱερεὺς καὶ κληρικός* of S. Sophia (Constantinople)

Pentekostarion — Parchment (palimpsest) 320 × 240 (275 × 190) mm

Oxford, Bodleian MS. Canon. Gr. 102 upper writing

Fol. 70r *ἐτελειώθ[η] ἡ βίβλος αὕτη· διὰ χειρὸς ἐμοῦ ἁμαρτωλοῦ. (καὶ) ῥαιφερενδαρίου εὐτελ(οῦς) ἱερέ(ως). (καὶ) κληρϊκοῦ, τῆς τοῦ θ(εο)ῦ μεγ[α]λ[ης] ἐκκλησίας κωνσταντίνου τοῦ χαράση. ἐπὶ ἔτ(ους) ἐϛωϟβ̅. μη[νὶ] ὀκτωμβρίω εἰς τὰ ιδ̅. ἡμέρα δ̅.*
Breathings (3). Accents (1), (3), and occasionally (4). Diaeresis (3). Mute ι (3). Abbreviations (2), (4), (5), (8). Ruling (2) using the lines ruled for the underwriting.

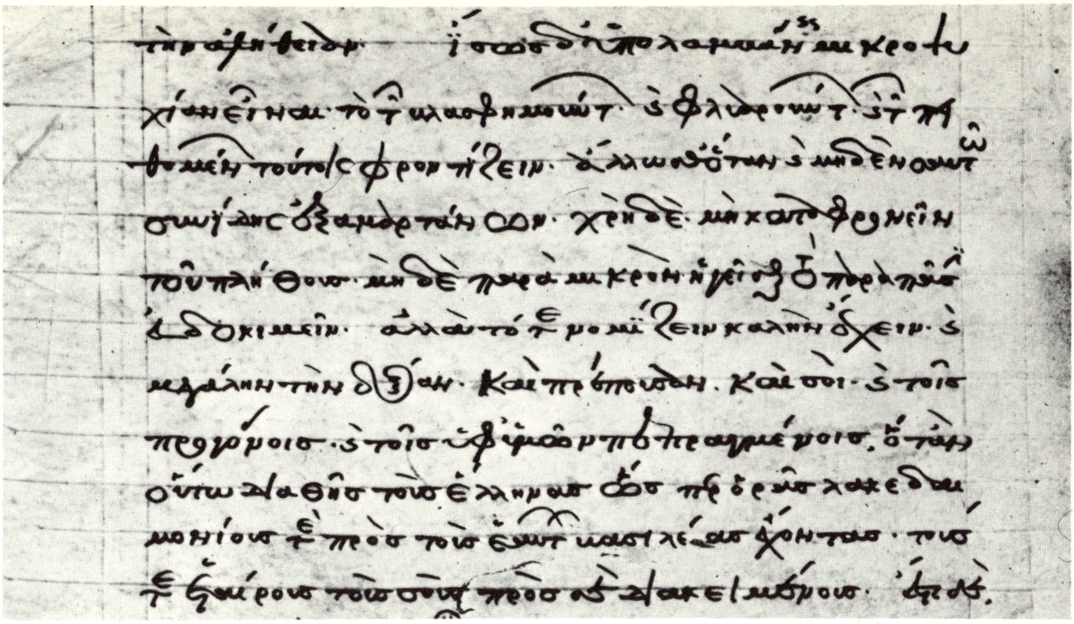

78

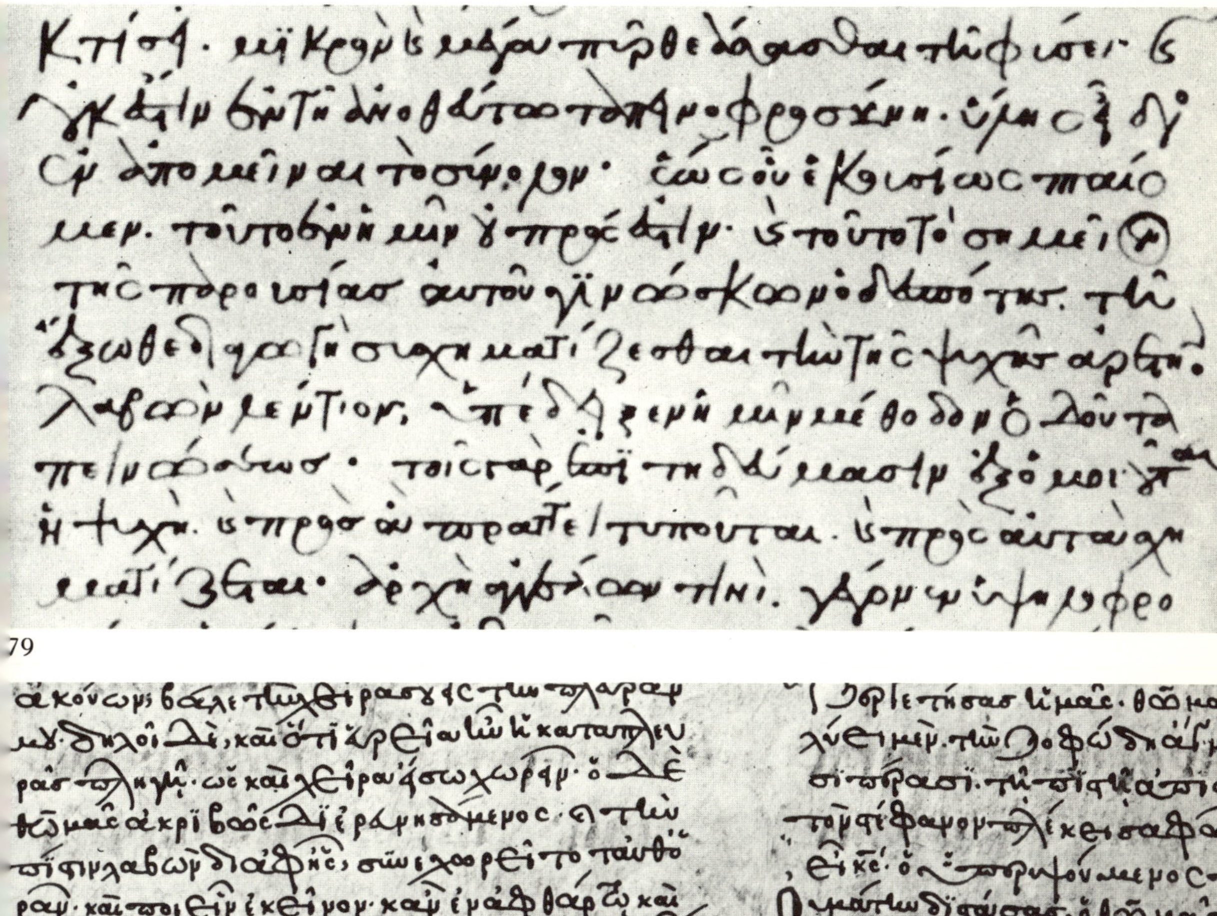

79

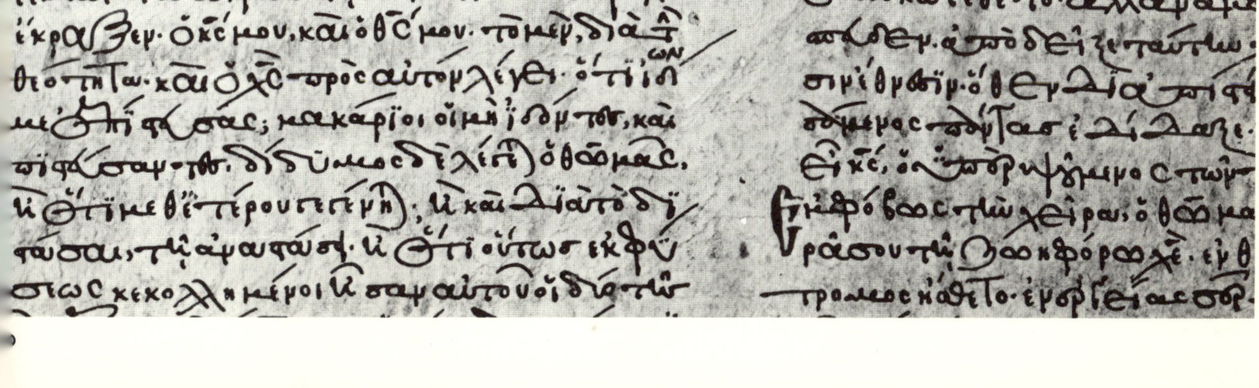

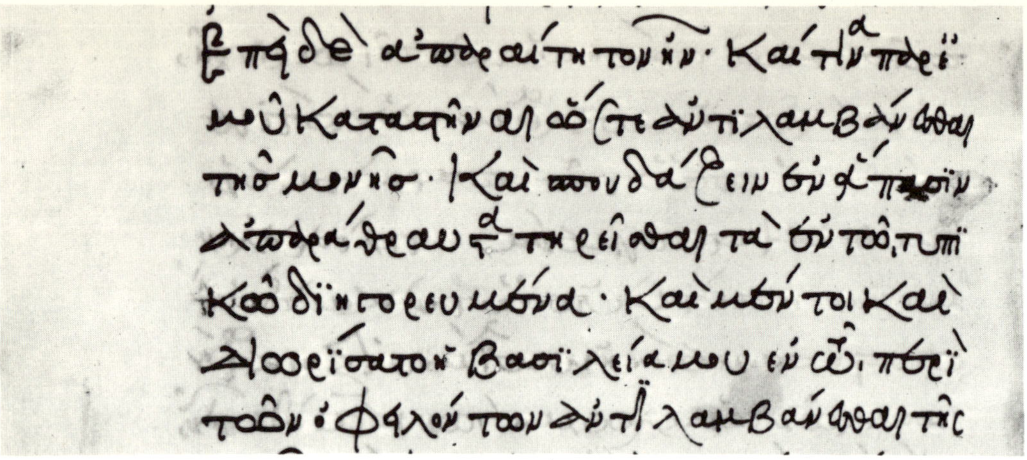

81

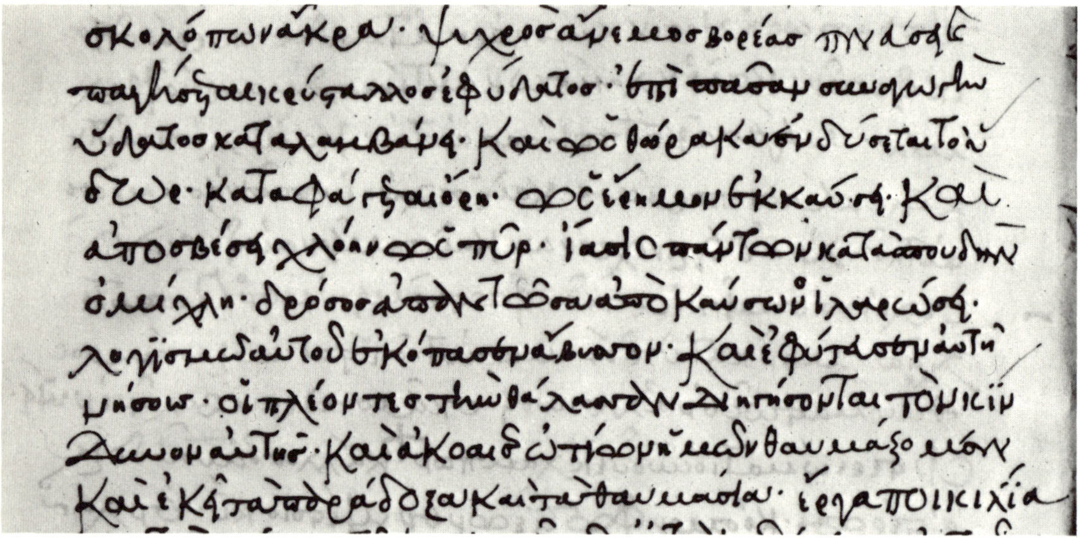

82

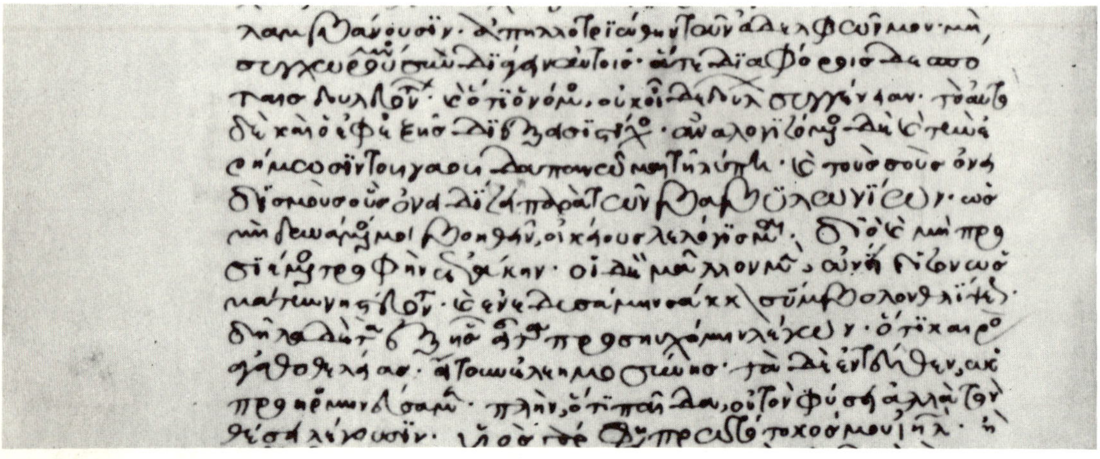

83

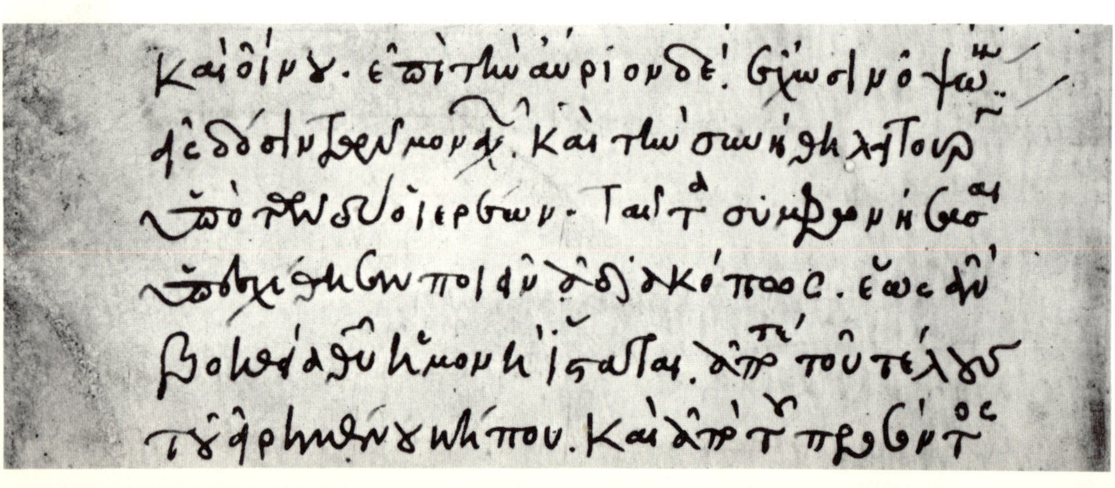

84

81 Between 15 August 1118 and 19 February 1133 (?)
In convent of the Theotokos *κεχαριτωμένη* (Constantinople)
Typikon of the convent
Parchment, 212 × 168 (140 × 107) mm
Paris, Bibliothèque nationale MS. grec 384 fol. 129^r-end

Fol. 1-128^v contain chapters 1-78 of the typikon, signed by the foundress Eirene Doukaina; fol. 129^r-end (ch. 79-80) were added after the death of her husband Alexios I Comnenos on 15 Aug. 1118, and before her own death on 19 Feb., probably in 1133.
Breathings (3). Accents (1). Diaeresis (3). Mute ι (2). Abbreviations (2), (5), occasionally (7). Ruling (3).
Another facsimile: Omont, *Plus anciens manuscrits*, pl. XLIX.

82 February 1186
Leon Gabalas, bishop of Nymphaion
O.T. Wisdom books
Parchment, 258 × 190 (*c.* 200×135) mm
Paris, Bibliothèque nationale MS. grec 11, pp.1-265

p.265 *ἐγρά[φη] ἡ παρου̃[σα] βίβλ(ος) χειρὶ ἐμου̃ του̃ εὐτελ[ου̃ς] ἐπϊσκ[ό]που νυμφαίου, λέοντ(ος) του̃ γαβαλ[ου̃]· μη[νὶ] φερου[άριω] (ἰνδικτιω̃νος) δ̅ ἔτ[ους] ϛχϥδ̅. ἐπὶ τ(ῆς) βα[σι]λ[είας] του̃ εὐσεβ(ου̃ς) ἀγγέλ[ου] κυ[ρου̃] ἰσαακί[ου].*
The bishop's hand is unlikely to be representative of a local school of writing in Nymphaion (the modern Nif, 15 miles E. of İzmir). Breathings (3). Accents (1), (2), (3), (4). Diaeresis (3). Abbreviations (2), (4), (6), but rarely used. No ruling.
Other facsimiles: Lake, V, MS.192, pl. 327-8; Omont, *Manuscrits datés*, pl. XLIX^II.

83 1278/9
Galaktion *μοναχός*
Euthymius Zigabenus
Parchment, 225 × 165 (150×105) mm
Oxford, Bodleian MS. Roe 7

Fol. 331^v *χεὶρ γαλακτΐωνος μοναχου̃ ἐν μοναχοι̃ς ἀναξΐου: ἔτους ϛφπζ (ινδικτιω̃νος) ζ.*
Not an extreme example of the flamboyant style with random variations in the sizes of letters. Breathings (3). Circumflex accent (1), and all sometimes (3) and (4). Diaeresis (3). Mute ι (2). Abbreviations (2), (4), (6), (8). Ruling (3).
Other facsimiles: New Pal. Soc. II.161.

84 11 February 1397
Demetrios Balsamon *διάκονος, σκευοφύλαξ* of S. Sophia, for convent of the Theotokos *τη̃ς βεβαίας ἐλπίδος* (Constantinople)
Typikon of the convent
Parchment, 235×170 (175×120) mm
Oxford, Lincoln College MS.Gr.35, fol. 161^r, line 2 - 162^r, line 6

Fol. 162^r *ἐγράφησαν ἐνταυ̃θα διὰ χειρὸς ἐμου̃ του̃ μ[ε]γ[ά]λ[ου] σκευοφύλακος τη̃ς ἁγιωτ[ά]τ[ης] του̃ ϑ(εο)υ̃ μ[ε]γ[α]λ[ης] ἐκκλη[σί](ας), διακόνου δημητρίου του̃ βαλσαμω̃ν· μη[νὶ] φερ[ουαρίω] ια′ (ἰνδικτιων)ος ε′. του̃ ἑξακισχϊλιοστου̃ ἐννακοσιοστου̃ ε^ου̃ ἔτους.*
Breathings (3). Accents (3) and (4). ι sometimes dotted. Abbreviations (2), (4), (6), (8). Ruling (2).

85 1112/13

Apophthegmata patrum etc. Parchment, 260×205 (175×140) mm

Milan, Ambrosiana MS.F.100 sup.

Fol. 186^{v} *Ἐτελειώθ[η] τὸ* ... [torn off] *ἀθανασίου αβᾶ* ... [torn off] *ουσ ϡχκα' ἰνδ[ικτιωνος]ϙ*.
Breathings (2). Circumflex accent sometimes (1) and (2). Diaeresis (1) and (2). Abbreviations (2), (4), and occasionally (5). Ruling (3).
Other facsimiles: Lake, III, MS.129, pl. 219-20.

86 1123/4 Basileios *νοτάριος ὁ Σκαλιδ-ρ--*, for Michael *ἱερεὺς τοῦ Φιλῆ*

John of Damascus Parchment, 215 × 170 (170/80 × 120/25) mm

Paris, Bibliothèque nationale MS. grec 1116, fol. 1^{r}-128^{v}

Fol. 128^{v} *Ἐγρά[φη] ἡ παρού[σα] θεῖα βί[βλος] δ[ι]ὰ συνεργεῖ(ας) μϊχα[ὴλ] ἱερέ[ως] τῶι τοῦ φϊλῆ· διὰ χειρ(ὸς) βασ[ι]λ[είου] νοτ[α]ρ[ίου] τοῦ σκαλιδ[']ρ[ου(?)]. ἐν ἔτ[ει] τῷ ϡχλβ ἰνδ[ικτίωνος]* [blank] *ἐπι τῆς βασιλ[είας] ιωάννου τοῦ κομνην[οὺ] καὶ πορφυρογ[εν]ν[ή]τ[ου]*. Phile has not been identified.
One of the earliest dated hands in which minuscule ν is evolving towards its modern form, losing its long downstroke; which also regularly uses ligatures reduced to their minimum shape. Breathings (2). Diaeresis (2) and (3). Mute ι (1). Abbreviations (2), (4), (6), (8). Ruling (3). Comparable hands are found in documents from S.Italy and Sicily, e.g. a will written in 1105 by Lukas bishop of Isola Capo Rizzuto, Calabria (Palermo, Museo nazionale, pergamena greca, reproduced in *Byzantion,* 34 (1964), 70).
Other facsimiles: Lake, V, MS. 185, pls. 315, 317; Omont, *Manuscrits datés,* pl. XLIV^{II}.

87 1408 Manuel Chrysoloras

Note in manuscript

of Ps. - Dionysius the Areopagite Parchment, 228 × 195 mm

Paris, Louvre, Ivoires A. 53, fol. 237^{v}

Fol. 237^{v} see transcription
Chrysoloras' hand here is unexpectedly plain and free from the flourished and contorted ligatures common at this time, perhaps deliberately so for the purpose of teaching non-Greeks. Breathings (3). Accents (3). Diaeresis (3). Abbreviations (5), (8).

88 1441 Palla Strozzi, a Florentine, in Padua

Simplicius on Aristotle Paper, 335 × 240 (215 × 155) mm

Paris, Bibliothèque nationale MS.grec 1908 Aristotle text

Fol. 213^{v} note by the late fifteenth-century scribe of Paris gr. 2038, Venice Marc. gr. 198 and other manuscripts: *ἐγράφη τοῦτο τὸ βιβλίον χειρὶ ἴω[άνν]ου ἀργυροπούλου γραικοῦ κωνσταντινουπολίτου ἐν τῷ παταουΐωι περὶ φιλοσοφί(αν) σπουδάζοντος χάριν πάλλαντος στρογίου φλωρεντίνου ἀξί(αν) ἵππικὴν ἔχοντος ἐν παταουΐω διατρίβοντος, ἔτει ἀπὸ τῆς ἐνσάρκου οἰκονομί(ας) τοῦ κ(υρίο)υ ἡμ(ῶν) ἰ(ησο)ῦ χ(ριστο)ῦ, ͵αυμα'. τὸ δὲ κείμενον χειρὶ πάλλαντος γέγραπται.*
Palla Strozzi was a pupil of Manuel Chrysoloras between 1397 and 1400, one of several who modelled their Greek hands on his. Breathings (3). Accents (4). Instead of diaeresis, a single dot (3). No ruling for marginalia.
He also copied Bodleian Laud Gr. 55, fol. 89 - end (Plutarch); Paris gr. 1906, fol. 1^{r}-10^{v} (Aristotle text only), fol. 11^{r} - end (text and commentary); 1909 (Simplicius on Aristotle); 1919, fol. 1^{r} -50^{r} (Psellos on Aristotle). Scholars who wrote Greek in a similar style include Giovanni Aurispa, Guarino Veronese, Leonardo Bruni Aretino, and Pier Candido Decembrio.

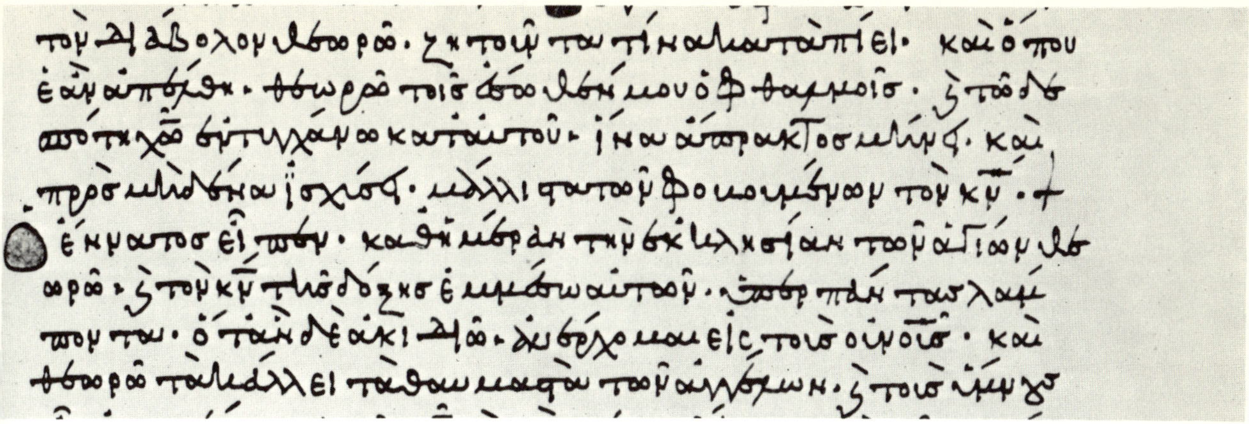

85

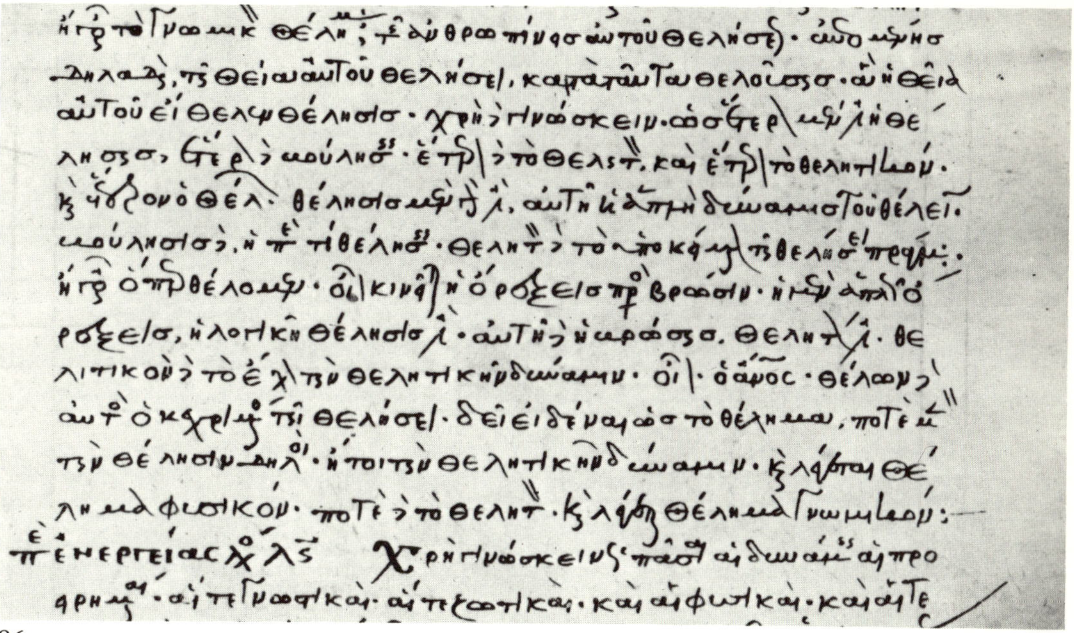

86

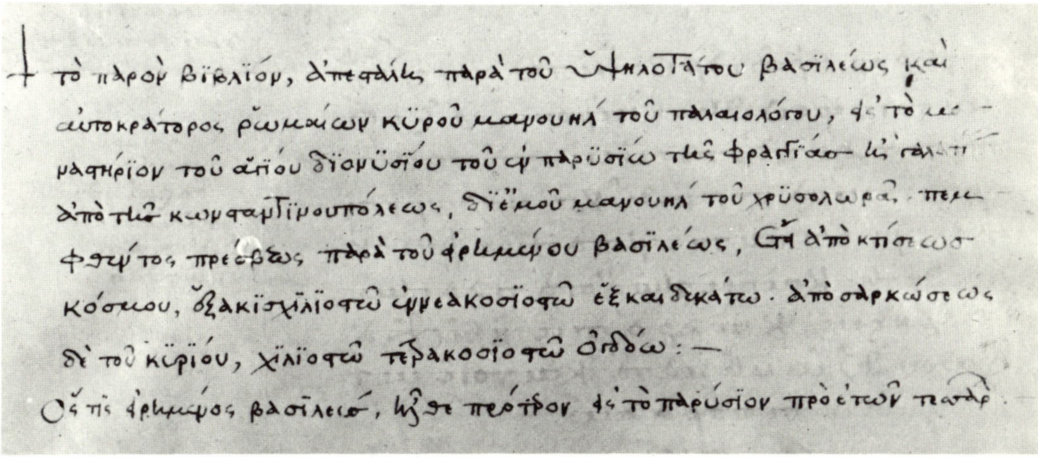
+ τὸ παρὸν βιβλίον, ἀπεστάλη παρὰ τοῦ ὑψηλοτάτου βασιλέως καὶ
αὐτοκράτορος ῥωμαίων κύρου μανουὴλ τοῦ παλαιολόγου, εἰς τὸ μο-
ναστήριον τοῦ ἁγίου διονυσίου τοῦ ἐν παρυσίῳ τῆς φραγγίας ἢ γαλλί-
ας ἀπὸ τῆς κωνσταντινουπόλεως, διʼ ἐμοῦ μανουὴλ τοῦ χρυσολωρᾶ πεμ-
φθέντος πρέσβεως παρὰ τοῦ εἰρημένου βασιλέως, ἔτει ἀπὸ κτίσεως
κόσμου, ἑξακισχιλιοστῷ ἐννεακοσιοστῷ ἓξ καὶ δεκάτῳ· ἀπὸ σαρκώσεως
δὲ τοῦ κυρίου, χιλιοστῷ τετρακοσιοστῷ ὀγδόῳ:—
Ὅστις εἰρημένος βασιλεύς, ἦλθε πρότερον εἰς τὸ παρύσιον πρὸ ἐτῶν τεσσάρ

87

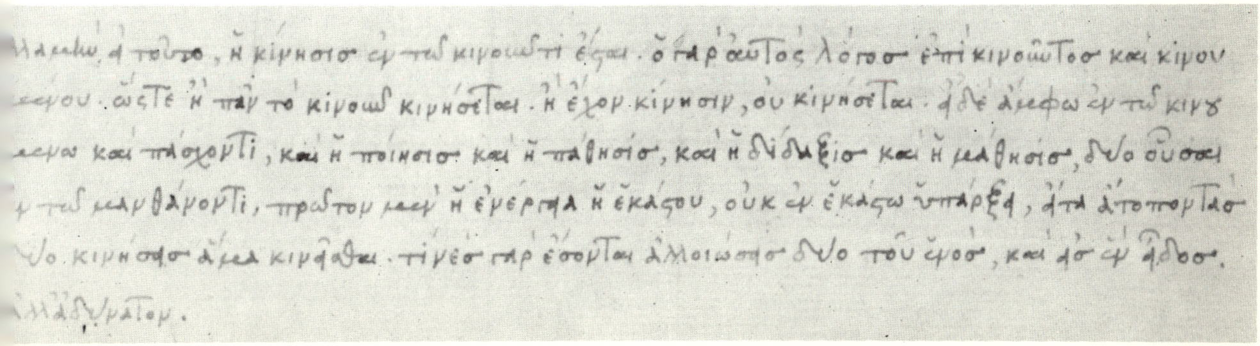

8

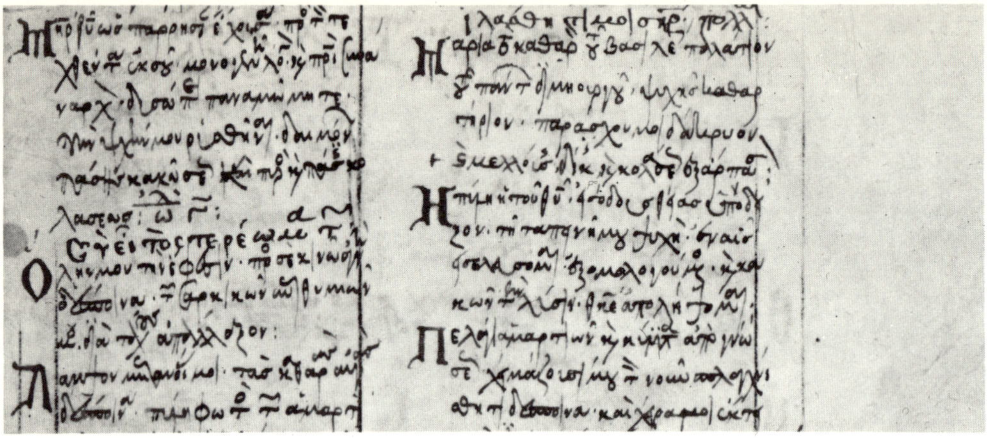

89

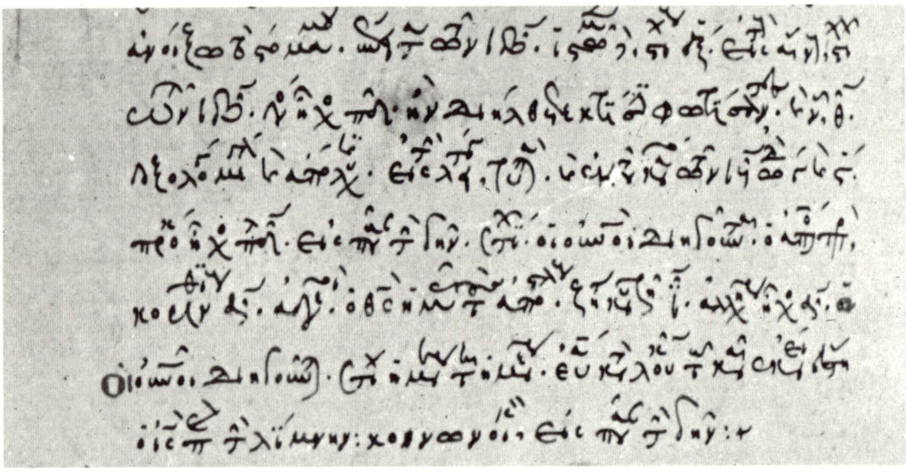

90

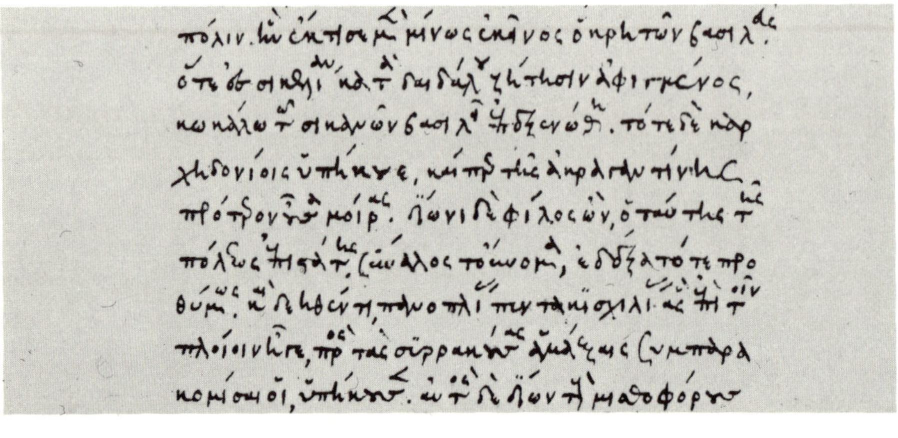

91

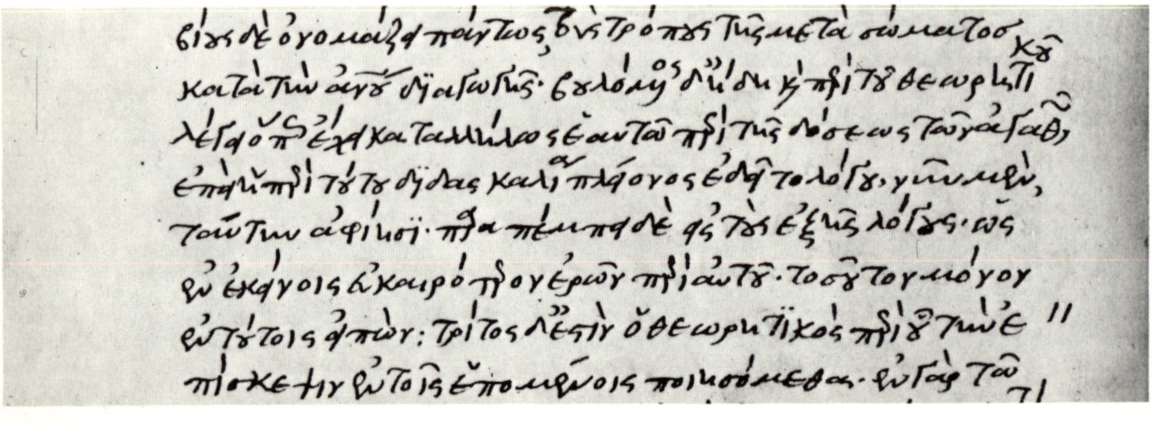

92

89 5 August 1291 — Romanos abbot of monastery *τοῦ ἁγίου Βενεδίκτου Οὐλλάνου,* at a metochion of S. Maria del Patire (Rossano)

Greco-Latin psalter — Parchment, 203×150 (150×95) mm

Vatican MS. Vat. gr. 1070

Fol 199^{v} *ἐγράφ[η] τὸ παρ(ὸν) ψαλτήρι(ον) δῐὰ χειρ(ὸς) τοῦ πολυημαρτήτου ῥωμανοῦ ἡγουμ[έν]ου ἀναξίου τοῦ ἁγίου βενεδικτου τοῦ οὐλλάνου τ(ῆς) βαθεί(ας) τοῦ γράτη ὄντ(ως) αὐτοῦ διωγμ[έν]ου δῐὰ τοὺς ἀθέους μουγαβάρους. καὶ καρτερ(ούν)τ(ος) εἰς τ[ὸ] μετοχ[ιον] τοῦ ἁγίου π(ατ)ρ(ο)ς τὸ λεγόμ[εν](ον) τοῦ ἁγίου σησύννίου μετὰ τοῦ ἁγιωτ[ά]τ[ου] αρχ[ι]μανδρίτ[ου] κ[υρο]ῦ νήφων(ος) σὺν τοῦ ἁγίου κοινοβ[ίου] αὐτοῦ: ἐτελειώθ[η] δὲ δῐὰ κόπ[ου] κ(αὶ) δαπάν(ης) (καὶ) προθυμίας τοῦ ἱερομονάχ[ου] μάρκου κ(αὶ) κ(α)τα τὴν ἡμεραν ἐκκλησιαρχ[ου] τ(ῆς) αὐτ(ῆς) ἁγί(ας) μον(ης) τοῦ π(ατ)ρ(ό)ς: Ἔτ(ους) δὲ ἀπο κτήσε(ως) κόσμου ϛψϥθ· ινδ[ι]κτ[ιῶνος] δ̄ μήν αὔγουστ[ος] εἰς τ[ὰς] ε̄:* The monastery must have been near the modern village of S. Benedetto Ullano in Calabria, 10 miles NW. of Cosenza; the dependent house of S. Sisinnios is likely to have been the unidentified oratory of that dedication mentioned in the life of S. Bartholomaeos, founder of S. Maria del Patire.

This is the more current hand of the scribe who copied the main Greek text in a formal hand. Breathings (3). Circumflex accents (1) and all accents sometimes (2). Diaeresis (3). Abbreviations (2), (4), (6), (8). Only lateral bounding lines are ruled.

Romanos also copied parts of Grottaferrata A.γ. II (Greco-Latin psalter); Vat. Barberin. gr. 541 (Greco-Latin gospels, 1291/2).

Other facsimiles: Follieri, tab. 57; Turyn, *Codices Vaticani,* tab. 45-6, 174a (with a full description).

90 2 October 1297 — Athanasios *ἀρχιμανδρίτης* of the monastery of S. Auxentios (Athos?), for Vatopedi

Typikon of S. Saba — Paper, 260×190 (160×100) mm.

Moscow, Historical Museum MS. 272

Fol. 13^{v} *Ἡ βίβλος αὕτη παρ ἐμοῦ πονηθεῖσα Τοῦ ἐν μοναχοῖς ἁμαρτωλοῦ ἐκ πόθου Ἀθανασίου τάλανος καὶ ἀχρείου Τοῦ καὶ χρηματῖσαντος ἀρχϊμανδρῖτου Μονῆς τῆς θείας καὶ βασιλεικοτάτης Ὄρους τῆ κλήσει ἁγῖου αὐξεντίου Ὡς εὐτελεῖ δῶρον τῆ πανάγνω παρθένω Μ(ητ)ρῖ τοῦ ... θ(εο)ῦ ... Μονῆς ... ἐτέθη βατοπεδῖου ... Προσετέθη δὲ δευτέρα ὀκτωμβρῖου ἐν ἔτει ἕκτω, ὀκτακοσϊοστῶ τὲ ἑξακϊσχϊλϊοστῶ ἐνδεκάτης ἰνδείκτου:-* No monastery dedicated to S. Auxentius is recorded on Athos; but a gift to Vatopedi is more likely to have come from nearby than from the holy mountain of S. Auxentius in Bithynia.

Breathings (3). Diaeresis (3). Mute ι (1). Abbreviations (2), (4), (6), (7), (8). No ruling.

Other facsimiles: Tsereteli and Sobolevski, I, pl. XXX [b].

91 Between *c.* 1400 and May 1452 — Georgios Gemistos Plethon

Plethon — Paper, 220×140 (160×80) mm

Venice, Marciana MS. gr. 406, fol. 2^{r} - 114^{r}, 122^{r}-140^{r}, corrections on 141^{r}-144^{v}

Fol. 140^{r} contemporary note *αὐτόχειρ κ(αὶ) τὸ πᾶν γέγραφ(εν) ... ὁ μέγιστος κατὰ σοφί(αν).* Bessarion (his pupil and lifelong friend), listing the books he gave to the Venetian Republic in 1468, notes this no. 333: 'Plethonis historica quaedam ... propriis litteris eius'. There is no certain evidence of when any of the many separate parts of this manuscript was written.

Breathings (3). Accents sometimes (2). Diaeresis (3). Abbreviations (6) and (8). No ruling.

On Pletho's autographs see A. Diller, 'The autographs of Georgius Gemistus Pletho', *Scriptorium,* 10 (1956), 27-41, and works cited therein.

Other facsimiles: Harlfinger, spec. 1; *Procli hymni,* ed E. Vogt (Klassisch-philologische Studien 18, Wiesbaden, 1957), Tab. II.

92 3 May 1495 — Ioannes Serbopoulos of Constantinople, in Reading

Eustratius of Nicaea on Aristotle — Parchment, 288×200 (195×115) mm

Oxford, Corpus Christi College MS. 106

Fol. 515^{v} *ἐτελειώθ[η] ἡ παροῦσα βίβλος δῐὰ χειρὸς ἐμοῦ ἰωάννου τοῦ σερβοπούλ[ου] κωνσταντϊνοπολίτου ἐν τῇ τῶν βρϊτανϊκ(ῶν) νήσῳ ἀγγλίᾳ. ἔν τϊνϊ κώμη καλουμένη ῥαδίνγ : μηνὶ μαΐω τῇ τρίτ[η] ἡμέρᾳ· ἔτους ἀπὸ τῆς τοῦ κ(υρίο)υ ἡμῶν ἰησοῦ χ(ριστο)ῦ σαρκώσεως χϊλϊοστῷ τετρα[κο]σϊοστῷ ἐνενηκοστῷ πέμπτῳ : ἤτοι α^{ῶ} υ^{ῶ} ϥ^{ῶ} ε^{ω}ʹ :—*

Breathings (3). Accents (1) and (3). Diaeresis (3). Mute ι (3). Abbreviations (2), (4), (6), (8). Ruling (3).

Other manuscripts copied by Serbopoulos include Cambridge, Trin. Coll. R. 9.22 (Theodore of Gaza, 1489); Dublin, Trin. Coll. K.3.8 (the same, 1484); Oxford, Bodl. Auct. D. 5.2 (Gospels), Gr. class. e. 96 (Theodore of Gaza), Seld. supra 19 (Moschopoulus), 29, fol. 38^{v}, 193^{r}, 204^{v} additions (Gospels); Corpus Christi 23-4 (Chrysostom, 1499-1500), 77, fol. 94 - end (Souda), 109 (Aristotle commentary); Linc. Coll. Gr. 18 (Gospels); New Coll. 68 (Gospels), 240-1, (Aristotle commentary, 1497), 254 (Theodore of Gaza, 1494).

93 September 1299 or 1301 — Maximos Planudes, in the monastery of Christ ἀκατάληπτος, Constantinople

Planudean Anthology etc. — Parchment, 270×205 (195×150) mm

Venice, Marciana MS. gr. 481 fol. 2r-16r, 19v, 22r, 23r, 24r - 123v (parts only of some pages)

Fol. 122v ἐγράφη ἡ μετάφρασΐς αὕτη τοῦ κ[α]τ[ὰ] ἰω[αν-νην] ἁγίου εὐαγγελίου. χειρὶ μαξίμου μοναχοῦ τοῦ πλα-νούδη. ἐντ(ὸς) κωνσταντινουπόλε(ως) κ[α]τ[ὰ] τ(ὴν) μο-ν(ὴν) τοῦ σ(ωτῆ)ρ(ο)ς χ(ριστο)ῦ. τ(ὴν) τοῦ ἀκαταλήπτου ἐπονομαζομ[έν]ην. μηνὶ σεπτ[εμβ]ρ[ιω]· (ινδικτιωνος) ιγ· ἔτους ϛω δεκάτ[ου]:

The Byzantine year 6810 was indiction 15; the year date was written over an erasure; perhaps the nearest indiction 13 (year 6808, A.D. 1299/1300) was the date when the Gospel paraphrase was finished, and only the year date was altered to 6810 (A.D. 1301/2) when the whole manuscript was completed.

One of the earliest dated hands to form uncial σ with a slight tail, foreshadowing the modern form. Breathings (3). Accents (1), sometimes (3) and (4). Diaeresis (3). Mute ι (3). Abbreviations (2), (6), (8). Ruling (3).

For Planudes' autographs see Turyn, op. cit. below. A similar style is found in the work of some of his collaborators and pupils.

Other facsimiles: Turyn, *Dated manuscripts in Italy,* pl. 71-4, 231c, with detailed description, bibliography, list of other facsimiles, and discussion of other autographs.

94 August 1308 — Demetrios Triklinios

Aphthonius and Hermogenes — Parchment, 248×175 (130×90) mm

Oxford, New College MS. 258

Fol. 250v ἐτελειώθη ἡ παροῦσα βίβλος δϊὰ χειρ(ὸς) δημητρ[ί]ου τοῦ τρϊκλίνη, ἐν μηνῒ αὐγούστω (ἰνδικτιῶ-ν)ος ϛ τοῦ ϛωι ϛ ἔτους.

Breathings (3), unlike in his later manuscripts where they are (1). Accents (1), (2), (4). Diaeresis (3). Mute ι (3). Abbreviations (4), (6), (8). Ruling (3).

On Triklinios' autographs see Turyn, *Dated manuscripts in Italy,* I. 123-7 and works cited therein.

Other facsimiles : *Greek manuscripts in the Bodleian,* pl. XI; W. J. W. Koster, *Autour d'un manuscrit d'Aristophane écrit par Démétrius Triclinius* (Groningen, 1957), pl. I; A. Turyn, *The Byzantine manuscript tradition of the tragedies of Euripides* (Illinois studies in language and literature 43, Urbana, 1957), pl. VI (b).

95 August 1464 — July 1465, or later up to *c.* 1468 — Georgios Scholarios (Gennadios II patriarch of Constantinople)

Scholarios — Paper, 203×145 (145×90) mm

Vatican MS. Vat. gr. 433, fol. I, 81r - 179v, 260r - 267v, notes on 1r, 4v, 7v

Fol. 81r ἰ(ησο)υ χ(ριστ)ε. ἐλέησόν με τ(ὸν) ἁμαρτωλ(ὸν) γεννάδιον. The summaries of Aquinas were made during his last period as patriarch.

Breathings (3). Accents sometimes (2) and (3). Diaeresis sometimes (3), but more often a single dot. Mute ι just a dot (3). Abbreviations (2), (4), and sometimes (6). No ruling.

On Scholarios' autographs see *Oeuvres complètes de Gennade Scholarios,* ed. L. Petit, X. A. Siderides, M. Jugie (Paris, 1928-36) pages indexed in VIII. 7*-8*; G. Mercati, 'Appunti Scolariani' I-III, *Bessarione,* 36 (1920), 109-33 (= *Opere minori* IV, Studi e Testi, 79, 1937, 72-97).

96 1441 — Ioannes Argyropoulos, in Padua

Paris, Bibliothèque nationale MS. grec 1908 text of Simplicius [for details see **88**]

Breathings (3). Accents (2), (3), (4). Instead of diaeresis a single dot (2) and (3). Abbreviations (4), (6), (8). Bounding lines only are ruled usually, ruling (2) occasionally.

Other manuscripts copied by Argyropoulos include Paris gr. 1906, fol. 1r-10v (Simplicius text).

Other facsimiles : Omont, *Manuscrits des XVe et XVIe siècles,* no. 24.

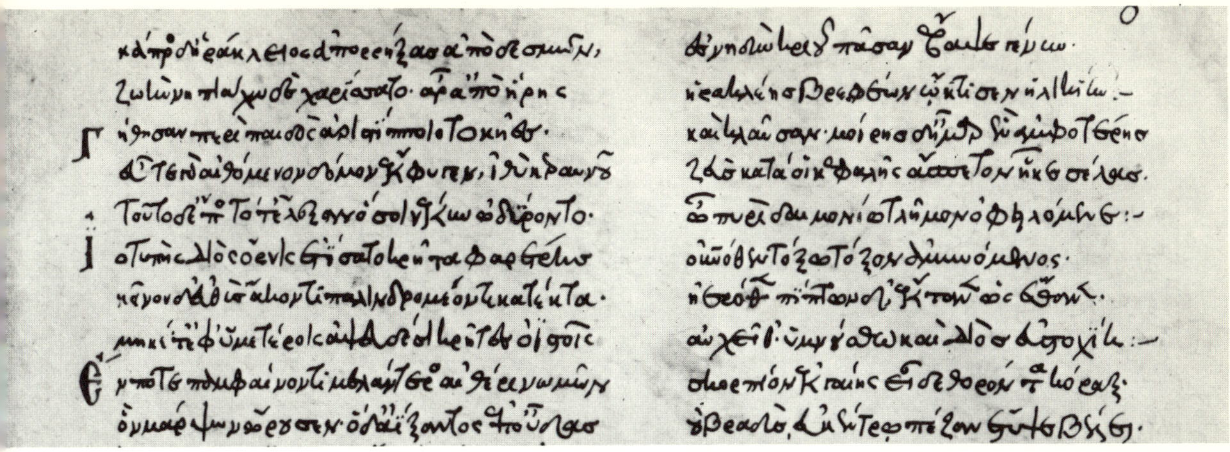

93

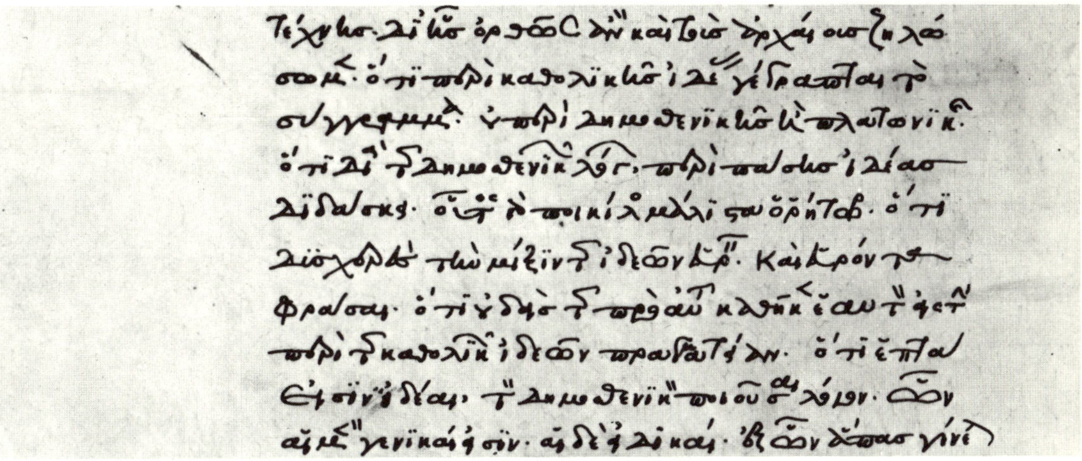

94

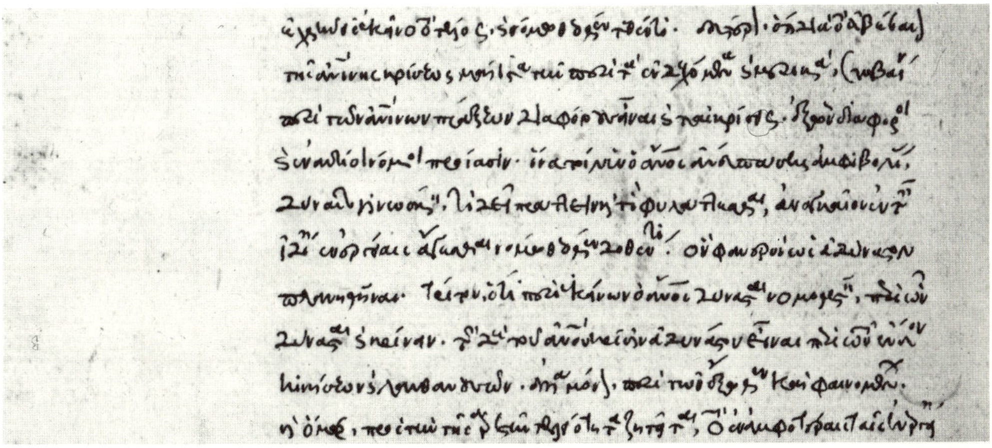

95

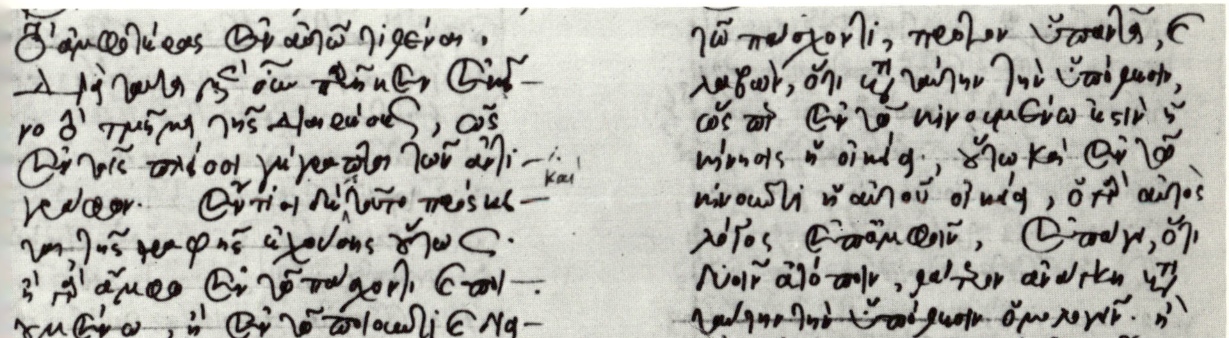

96

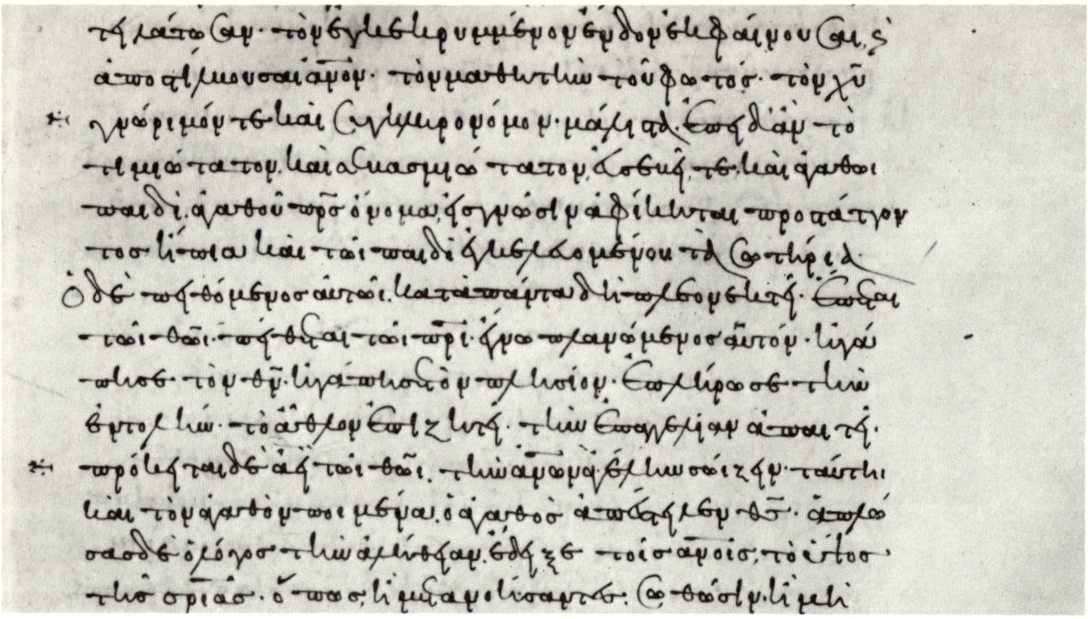

97

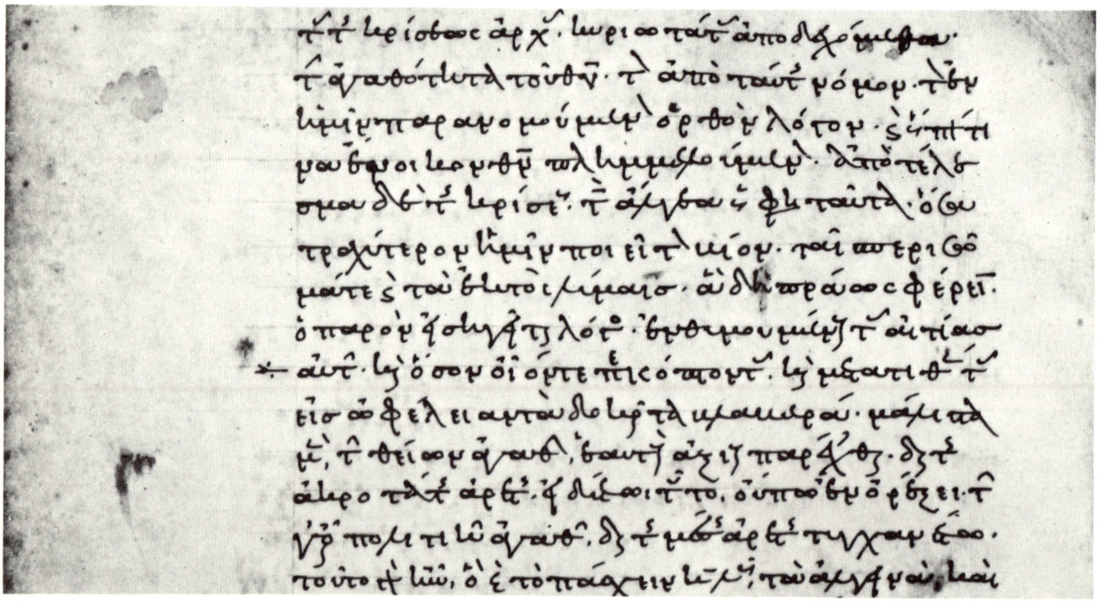

98

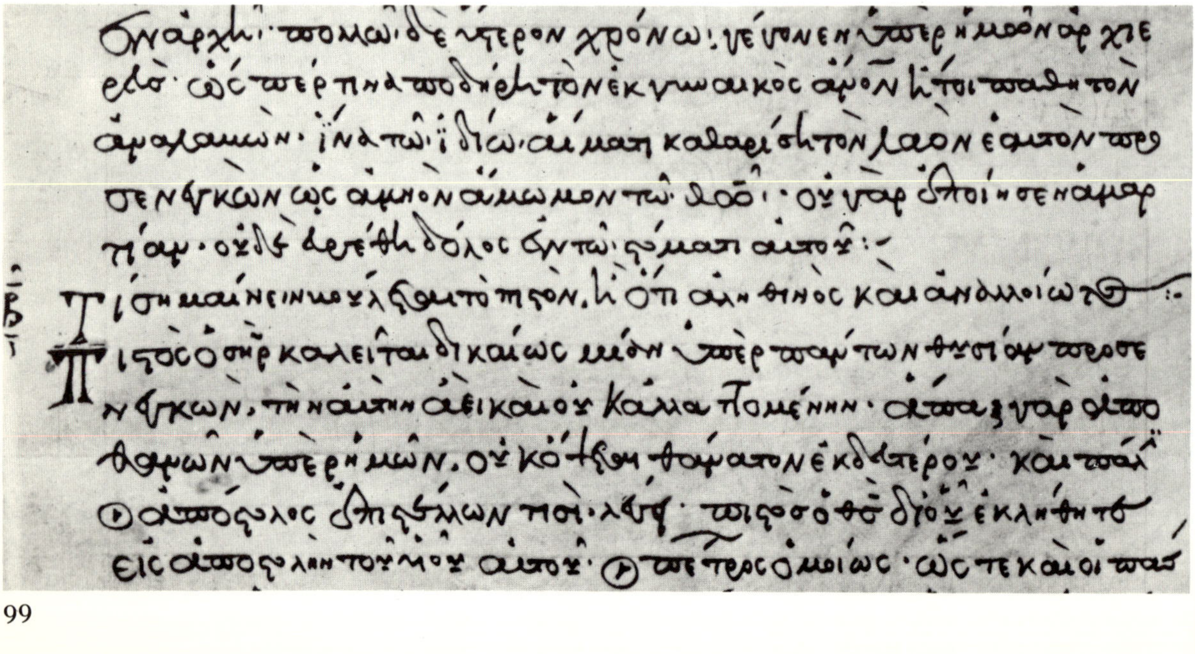

99

97 913/14 Baanes *νοτάριος*, for Arethas archbishop of Caesarea, Cappadocia
Clement of Alexandria etc. Parchment, 245×195 (*c.* 145×110/120) mm
Paris, Bibliothèque nationale MS. grec 451

Fol. 401^v *ἐγράφη χειρὶ βαάνους νοτ[αριου]. ἀρέθα αρχ[ι-]επισκ[ο]π[ω]. καισαρει(ας) καππαδοκι(ας). ἔτει κόσμου ςυκβ*. The manuscript was not necessarily copied in Caesarea or by a local scribe.
An individual, mannered hand, in advance of others of this date in some respects : uncial α, ζ, λ, ν, ξ, π, and σ are used; it is probably the earliest dated hand in which variation in the sizes of letters foreshadows the unevenness of later personal hands. Breathings, though mainly (1), have sometimes a tendency to roundness. Diaeresis (1). Mute ι (1). Abbreviations (1) and (4), very occasionally (2) but the accents may have been added later. Ruling (1). Baanes also copied B. M. Harl. 5694 (Lucian). Undated manuscripts with comparable script include Vat. gr. 218 (Pappus of Alexandria).
Other facsimiles: Lake, IV, MS. 136, pl. 230-1; Lefort and Cochez, pl. 18; Merkelbach and von Thiel, Abb. 16, pp. 49-54; Omont, *Manuscrits datés*, pl. II.

98 28 July 925 Ioannes *γραμματικός*
Philosophical collection Parchment, 195/8×150/5 (140/5×90/105) mm
Vienna, Nationalbibliothek MS. Phil. gr. 314, fol. 1^r-110^r

Fol. 110^r *ἐγράφη χειρὶ ἰωάννου γραμματικ(ου) ἀχρείου δούλου ι(ησο)υ χ(ριστο)υ μη[νι] ἰουλίωι εἰς τὰς εἰκοσιοκτ(ω) ἡμερα πέμπτη ινδ[ικτιωνος] ιγ: ἔτη κο[σμου] ςυλβ*. The year 6432 of the Constantinopolitan era was A.D. 923/4, but that was indiction 12 and 28 July was Wednesday; the Alexandrian year 6432 (A.D. 939/40) was indiction 13 but 28 July was Tuesday; since the combination of Thursday 28 July and indiction 13 is found in 924/5, it is most likely that the year date was, as often, incorrectly calculated.
Probably the earliest dated example of a scholarly hand used to copy the main text of a book, and therefore not unexpectedly in advance of contemporary conventional hands in several ways : it uses nearly all distinctively uncial forms of letter, although some very rarely, including η perhaps for the first time; it is one of the earliest dated hands to use completely open ε-ligatures (as in line 4), by a long way the earliest to use abbreviations freely thoughout the text, and the earliest in which the writing consistently hangs from the ruled lines. Breathings (1) but sometimes with a tendency to roundness. Diaeresis (1). Mute ι (1), sometimes slightly below the line. No feature of the manuscript suggests the S. Italian origin sometimes claimed for it; fairly strong contra-indications are the fluency of the hand, its advanced characteristics (even if the date were 940) in contrast to the backwardness characteristic of provincial products, and the date (if it be 925) considered in relation to events in S. Italy and Sicily.
Undated manuscripts with comparable script include Heidelberg Palat. gr. 23 + Paris suppl. gr. 384, fol. 453^r-517^r, 524^v-621^r (Palatine anthology); Bodleian Barocci 50 (grammatical and poetical collection) which also bears no signs of a S. Italian origin sometimes suggested for it; Paris gr. 1741, fol. 200^v-245^v, 294^r-298^v (Dionysius of Halicarnassus etc.).
Other facsimiles: Bick, Taf. I; Lake V, MS. 204, pl. 350-2; Lefort and Cochez, pl. 22.

99 4 December 1065 Theodosios *μοναχός*, probably in monastery of the Theotokos *ἡ εὐεργέτης* (Constantinople)
Cyril of Alexandria Parchment, 290×215 (235/40×150) mm
Paris, Bibliothèque nationale MS. Coislin 248, fol 5^r-6^v, 9^r-183^r

Fol. 183^r *Ἐτελειώθη ... ἡ βίβλος αὕτη ... μη[νὶ] δεκέ[μ-β]ρ[ιω] δ ἡμέρ[α] κυ[ριακη] ἰνδ[ικτιῶνος] δ ἔτους ςφοδ'· [ἐπὶ] τῆς κα[θ'ημᾶς] ἁγιωτά[της] [μονῆς] τῆς [ὑπερ]αγίας θεοτ[οκου] [τῆς εὐεργετιδος] του οσιωτάτου ἡμῶν π(α-τρο)ς τιμοθέου τοῦ δευτέρου κτήτορος, γραφεῖσα διὰ χειρὸς θεοδοσίου τοῦ ἁμαρτ[ω]λ[οῦ] (καὶ) σφαλματία [μον]αχ[ου]*. From *ἐπὶ* to *κτήτορος* has been erased and is difficult to read; *τῆς εὐεργέτιδος* cannot be seen, but *τιμοθέου τοῦ δευτέρου κτήτορος* is clear; a Timotheus was the second founder of the monastery of the Theotokos *ἡ εὐεργέτης* in Constantinople[1].
Breathings (2). Diaeresis (2). Mute ι (1) reaching only half way down the height of letters. Abbreviations (2), (4), (6). Ruling (3).
Undated manuscripts with comparable script include B.M. Add. 11727, fol. 2^r-7^v, 9^r-24^v, 34^r-39^v, 41^r- end (except parts of fol. 81^v-87^v).
Other facsimiles : Lake IV, MS. 171, pl. 293, 297; Omont, *Manuscrits datés*, pl. XXX.

[1]Professor Irigoin expounded this convincing hypothesis to me while we looked at the subscription in both ultra-violet and sun light.

100 1357/8

Stelianos Choumnos, for Ioannes Kontostephanos from Constantinople

Proclus

Paper, 240 × 170 (185 × 110) mm

Oxford, Bodleian MS. Laud Gr. 18

Fol. 288^{v} *στηλϊανὸς ἦν ὁ γράψας, ὁ καὶ τοῦ πείκλην χοῦμνος: - ἐτελειώθη δὲ χ(ριστο)ῦ χάριτϊ, ἐν ἔτη ͵ϛωξϛ*$^{\omega}$*: ἐξόδῳ πολλῷ τοῦ κυρ[οῦ] ἰω[αννο]σ͂υ τοῦ κωντοστεφάνου τοῦ ἀπὸ τὴν κωνσταντϊνούπ[ο]λ[ιν]:-* The last words suggest that the manuscript was not copied in Constantinople.

Breathings (3). Circumflex accent sometimes (1), and all accents sometimes (2) and (4). Diaeresis (2) and (3). Mute ι (3). Abbreviations (2), (4), (6), (8). Ruling (3).
Stelianos also copied Flor. Laur. conv. soppr. 103, fol. 287^{r}-408^{v} (Proclus).
Another facsimile: Wilson pl. 69.

101 2 May 1438

Ioannes

Euripides

Paper, 220 × 150 (150 × 75) mm

Oxford, Bodleian MS. Auct. T. 4.10 fol. 28^{r}-130^{v}

Fol. 130^{v} *τελειώθην τὸ παρ(ὸν) βϊβλί(ον) ... δϊὰ χειρὸς ἐμοῦ τὰ ταπεινοῦ ἰω[ά]ννου· κατὰ μῆνα μάϊον τῆ β̄ τοῦ αὐτοῦ ἡμέρα ϛ*$^{\eta}$*· ὥρ[α] ι*$^{\eta}$ *τῆς ἡμέρας: - [ε]τει ͵ϛ*$^{\omega}$ *ϡ*$^{\omega}$ *μ̄ζ̄ (ινδικτῶν)ος ᾱ:-* The Byzantine year 6947 (Sept. 1438-Aug, 1439) was indiction 2 and in it 2 May fell on Saturday; the combination of indiction 1 and Friday 2 May occurred in 1437/8, which is therefore more likely to be the correct year.
Breathings (3). Accents (1), (2), (3), (4). Diaeresis (3). Abbreviations (4), (6,), (8). Ruling (3).
The same Ioannes copied Flor. Laur. 31.17 (Euripides, 1431).

102 1491-2

Ianos Laskaris

Autograph notes

Paper, 162 × 113 mm (writing space varies)

Vatican MS. Vat. gr. 1412

The notebook contains lists of books collected for Lorenzo de Medici by Laskaris on journeys to Greek lands in 1491 and 1492, and epigrams with corrections which could only have been made by the author; Fulvio Orsini, the book's first owner (from Laskaris' death in 1535 until 1600) listed it in his inventory as 'scritto di mano di Gio. Lascari'.
Breathings (3). Accents (1), (2), (3), (4). Diaeresis (3). Abbreviations (4), (6), (8). No ruling.
Other manuscripts copied by J. Laskaris include Paris gr. 2061 (Aristotle scholia), 2891 (Anthology etc.); Vat. gr. 1413 and 1414 (notebooks). Many others are ascribed (not always correctly) to Laskaris in D.C.C. Young, 'A codicological inventory of Theognis manuscripts, *Scriptorium,* 7(1953), 3-36.
The manuscript is described in K.K. Müller, 'Neue Mittheilungen über Janos Laskaris und die Mediceische Bibliothek', *Centralblatt für Bibliothekswesen,* 1 (1884), 333-412.

103 Before July 1493

Probably Angelo Poliziano

Sophocles

Paper, 335 × 200 (310 × *c.* 60) mm

Oxford, Bodleian Auct. P. 2.2 (Ovid, pr. Parma 1477) Greek annotations

Fol. 482^{r} 'Contuli cu(m) ... codice ex medica libraria ... In Rusculo Fesulano. III. Kal. Octobr. 1493 ... Politianus'. Similar notes on fol. 274^{v}, 440^{r}, 487^{v} of collation with manuscripts in the Medici and S. Marco libraries in July and Sept. 1493 by Politian and helpers. All the Greek annotations in the book (although written at different times, and with various pens and inks and degrees of care) appear to be by the same hand, that of the signed autographs. All were already written in before the notes of variant readings from the Florence manuscripts were added in 1493.
Breathings (3). Accents (3) and (4). Diaeresis (3). Mute ι (3). Abbreviations very rare, occasionally (4) and (6). No ruling.
On Politian's autographs see I. Maïer, *Les manuscrits d' Ange Politien* (Travaux d'humanisme et Renaissance, 70) (Geneva, 1965).
Another facsimile: Wilson pl. 82.

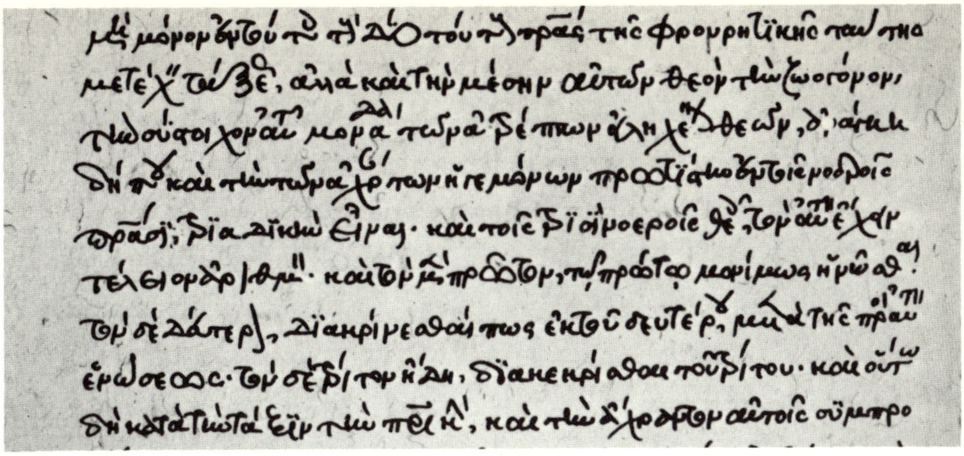

100

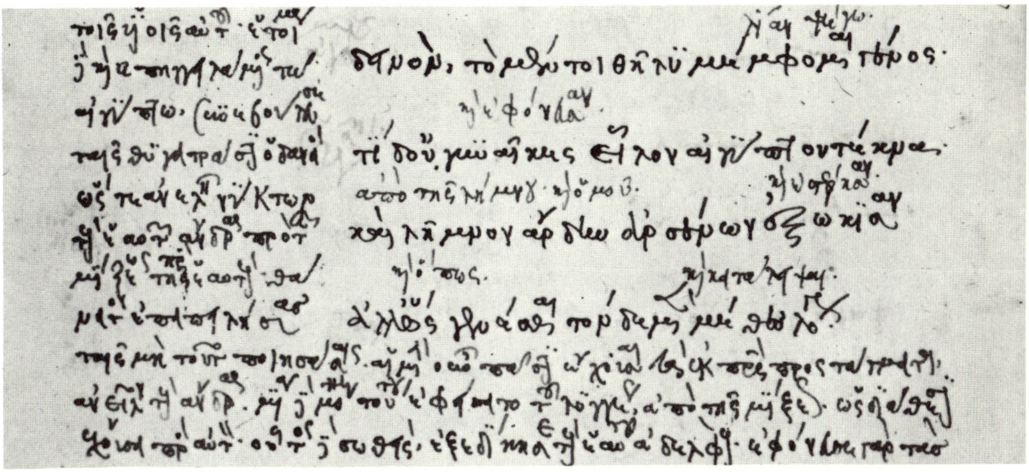

101

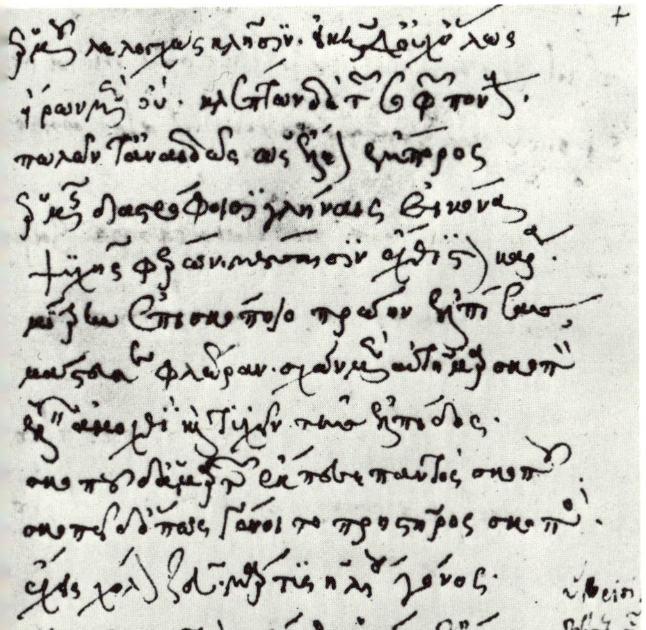

02

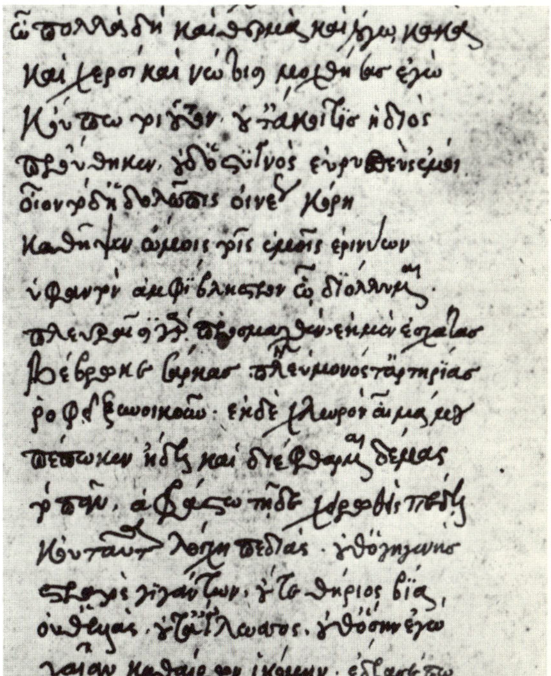

103

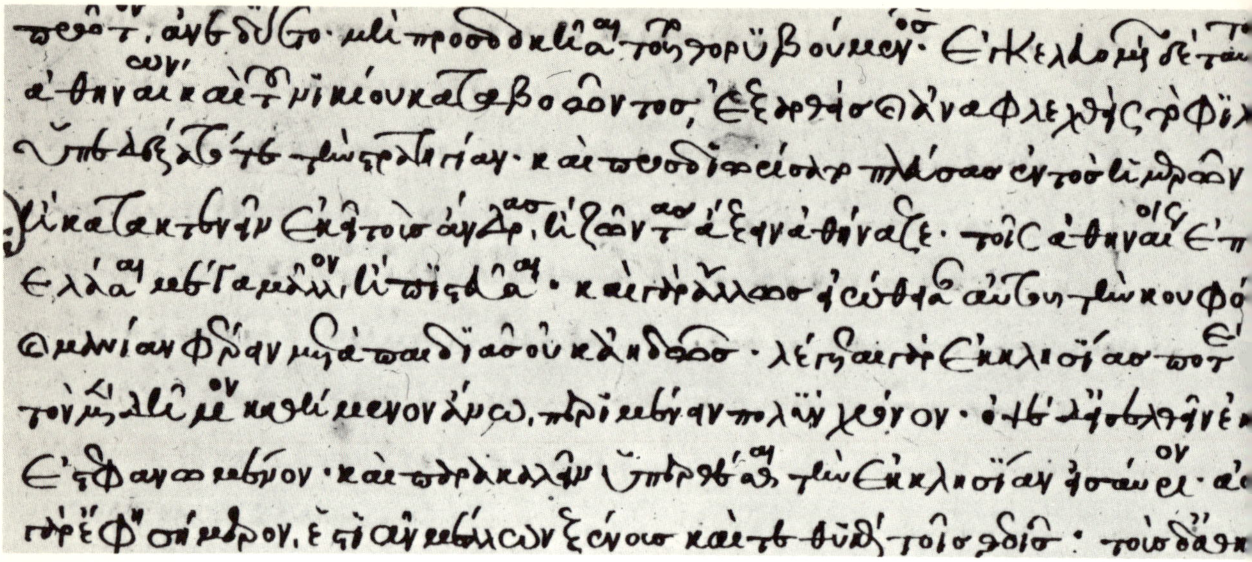

104

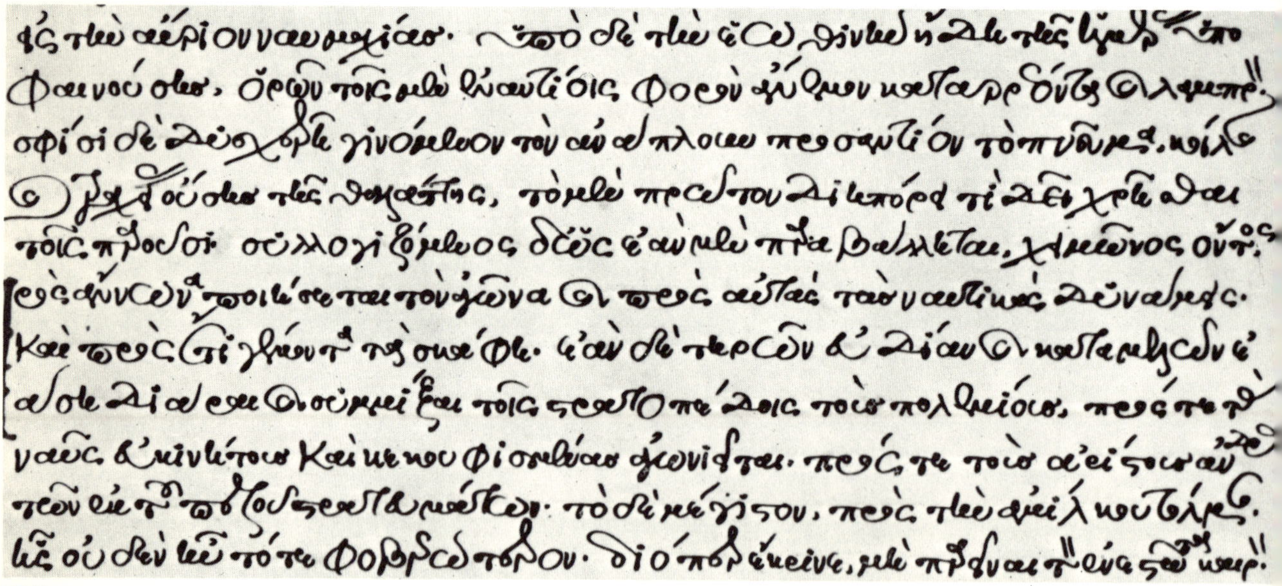

105

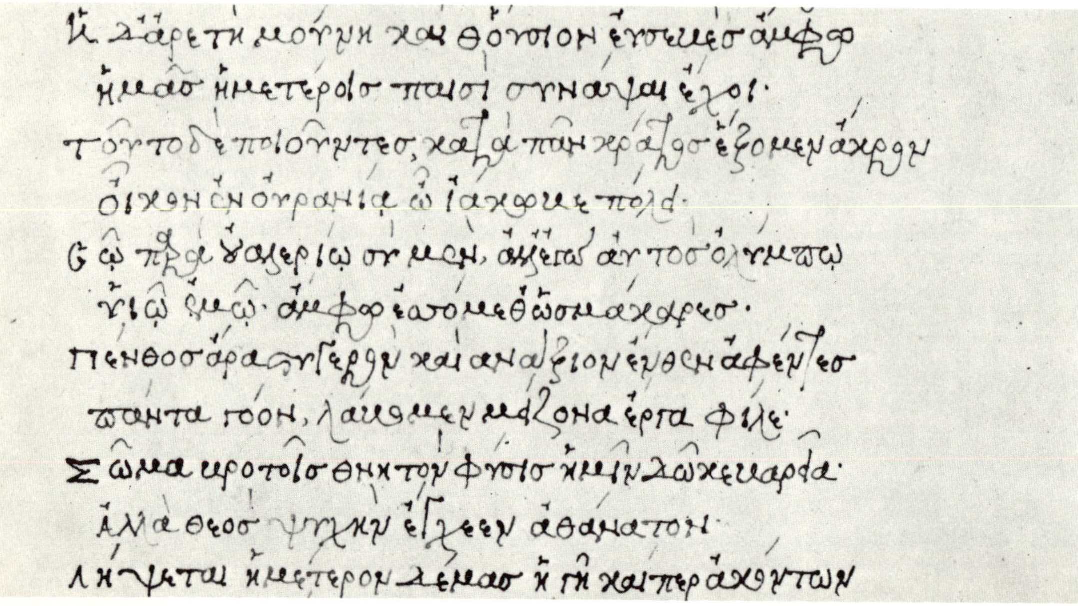

106

104 7 April 1362 — Manuel Tzykandyles, at Mistra
Plutarch — Paper, 380 × 280 (265 × 185) mm
Oxford, Bodleian MS. Canon. Gr. 93 + Milan, Ambrosiana MS. D 538 inf.

Milan D538 inf. fol. 305v *Εγράφη καὶ ἐτελειώθη ἡ βίβλος ἥδε, κατὰ τὴν πελοπόννησον· ἐν τῷ κάστρῳ μϊζϊθρᾶ· ἐξόδω τὲ (καὶ) σϋνδρομῆ (καὶ) σϋνεργΐαι κυρ[οῦ] δημητρϊ[ου] τοῦ κασανδρηνοῦ· κόπω δὲ (καὶ) γραφῆ μανουὴλ τοῦ τζϋκανδύλη· ἐν μηνΐ ἀπρϊλλΐῳ ζη· ἡμέρα πέμπτη· ἰνδϊκτιῶνος, πεντεκαιδεκάτης· τοῦ ϡοῦ ωοῦ ἑβδομηκοστοῦ ἔτους.*
Breathings (3). Circumflex sometimes (1), and all accents (2), (3), (4). Diaeresis (3). Mute ι occasionally (1), usually (3), sometimes just a dot. Abbreviations (4), (6), (8). Ruling (3).
On Tzykandyles' autographs see Turyn, *Codices Vaticani*, pp. 150-3, 162-3, 165-6, and *Dated manuscripts in Italy*, pp. XXV, 229-31, and works cited therein; to which **should be added Munich gr. 451 (Arrian, 1370).**
Other facsimiles: of Oxford MS., Wilson, pl. 70; of Milan MS., Steffens, Taf. 19; Turyn, *Dated manuscripts in Italy*, pl. 183-4, 243b.

105 2 October 1416 — Stephanos *ἱερομόναχος καὶ σκευοφύλαξ* of monastery of the Prodromos in Petra (Constantinople)
Polybius — Parchment, 380 × 270 (260 × 170) mm
London, British Museum MS. Add. 11728

Fol. 160v *ἐτελειώθη τὸ παρὸν βιβλΐον χειρὶ στεφάνου ἱερομονάχου κ(αὶ) σκευοφΰλ[α]κος τοῦ τιμΐου προδρ[ό]μ[ου] τ(ῆς) εὐλογημ[έν]ης πέτρ(ας)· μηνὶ ὀκτωβρ[ίω] β̄· **(ἰνδικτιῶνος) ι· τοῦ ϡοῦ λοῦ κε̄ ἔτους: -***
Breathings (3). Accents (1), (2), (3), (4). Diaeresis or more often a single dot (2) and (3). Mute ι (1).Abbreviations (4), (6), (8). Ruling (3).
On manuscripts attributed to Stephanos, who may later have been metropolitan of Medeia, see E.D. Kakoulides, **'Η βιβλιοθήκη τῆς μονῆς Προδρόμου - Πέτρας στὴν** *Κωνσταντινούπολη', Ἑλληνικά*, 21 (1968), pp. 26-8, εἰκ. 7-8.
Another facsimile: Pal. Soc. I.134.

106 25 December 1461 — Francesco Filelfo, in Milan
Filelfo — Paper, 233 × 167 (140 × 85/90) mm
Vatican MS. Vat. lat. 1790, fol. 155r-158r

Fol. 158r **ὁ αὐτὸς φιλέλφος τῇ ἰδίᾳ χειρί· Qui quidem** Franciscus Philelfus ... utrique consolationi et latinae et graecae extremam apposuit manum Mediolani octavo kalendas ianuarias anno a Christi natali die millesimo quadringentesimo sexagesimo primo.
One of the earlier Italian humanist hands apparently modelled on a curly Greek style similar to **105.** Breathings (1). Accents occasionally (4). Diaeresis (3). Mute ι (3).
Filelfo's Greek hand is found also in Milan, Trivulziana 873 (fair copies of his collected letters). For a study of his autographs see a forthcoming work by R. G. Adam. Among the few scholars who wrote in a similar style is Lapo da Castiglionchio il Giovane, one of his pupils; also the copyists of Bodl. Laud Gr. 13 (Pindar) and in some respects Paris gr. 2713, fol. 9r-16v (Euripides).

107 8 December 1523 — Zacharias Kallierges the Cretan, in Rome
Stobaeus — Parchment, 360 × 245 (235 × 130) mm
Oxford, New College MS. 270

Fol. 298[v] *Ἡ τοῦ ... στοβαίου αὕτη βίβλος, ... ἐπιμελῶς ἐν ῥώμῃ γραφεῖσα, ἤδη ... πέρας εἴληφεν· ἀναλώμασι μέν, τοῦ ... κυρίου ῥικάρδου, τοῦ πατίου ... πρεσβευτοῦ τοῦ ... βασιλέως, τῆς ... ἀγκλίας: χειρὶ δὲ ζα[χα]ρίου καλλιέργου τοῦ κρητός: Ἔτει τῷ ἀπὸ τῆς χ(ριστο)ῦ γεννήσεως, Χιλιοστῷ, πεντακοσιοστῷ, εἰκοστῷ τρίτῳ: Ποσειδεῶνος, ὀγδόῃ ἱσταμένου.*
Breathings (3). Diaeresis (1), (2), and (3) but more often a single dot. Mute ι (3). Abbreviations very rare, occasionally (4). Ruling (3).
Other manuscripts copied by Zacharias Kallierges (who also printed Greek in Venice 1499-1509 and in Rome 1515-23) include Bologna Bibl. Univ. 2302 (Aristotle); Oxford Bodleian Holkham Gr. 85, fol. 1-49, possibly the whole (Dionysius Periegetes etc.), Corpus Christi College 100, fol. 61[r]-164[v] (commentary on Ptolemy), New College 230, fol. 139[r]-end (Aristotle commentary), 236 (Aristotle commentary), 260 (Moschopoulus), 297, fol. 55[r]-end (Moschopoulus); Paris gr. 2202, fol. 1[r]-138[r] (medical works), 2811 (Euripides), 2823 (Aristophanes etc.), 2854 (Dionysius Periegetes); Rome Vallicelliana E. 36 (Iamblichus).
Another facsimile: *Greek manuscripts in the Bodleian*, pl. XX.

108 1564 — Nikolaos Tourrianos the Cretan, in Constantinople
Chrysostom — Paper, 375 × 265 (247 × 140) mm
Oxford, Bodleian MS. Auct. E. 2.7.

Fol. 195[v] *χειρὶ νικολάου τουῤῥιανοῦ τοῦ κρητός. ἐν κωνσταντινουπόλει, ἔτει ἀπὸ τ(ῆς) θεογονίας, ‚αφξδ.*
Breathings (3). Accents (2), (3), (4). ι is sometimes dotted. Mute ι (3). Abbreviations (2), (4), (6), (8), but rarely used. Ruling (2).
For a study of N. de la Torre, a list of manuscripts copied by him, and facsimiles of this one and others, see G. de Andres, *El Cretense Nicolas de la Torre* (Madrid, 1969).
A similar mannered style was practised by Angelos Bergekios (Vergecius) and others of his family, and used as a model for the 'grecs du roi' type cut in Paris in 1542.

109 29 July 1600 — Maximos *ἀρχιδιάκονος* of Alexandria, in Egypt
Nicolas Cabasilas — Paper, 210 × 140 (140 × 90) mm
Oxford, Bodleian MS. Canon. Gr. 52 fol. 1[v] -154a[r]

Fol. 154a[r] *ἐν αἰγύπτῳ· γ̄ φθίνοντος μεταγειτνιῶνος· ἤτοι ἰουλλίου· τοῦ ‚αχ^οῦ ἔτους τῆς ἐνσάρκου οἰκονομί(ας) τοῦ σ(ωτη)ρ(ο)ς ἡμῶν ἰ(ησο)υ χ(ριστο)υ:- χειρὶ μαξίμου, ἀρχιδιακόνου ἀλεξανδρεί(ας):-*
This style of writing continued in use in Greek lands from the sixteenth into the nineteenth century. Breathings (3). Accents (1), sometimes (3). Diaeresis (3). Mute ι (3). Abbreviations (2), (4), (6), (8). No ruling.
Other manuscripts copied by Maximos include Athos Iveron 353 (Meletios Pegas, 1603); Jerusalem Patr. 524 (M. Pegas, 1601); Leiden Vulcan. 62.I, fol. 36[r]-37[v] (letters, 1597, 1599).

110 24 July 1610 — Ioannes Sanctamauras the Cypriot, in the Vatican
Chrysostom — Paper, 345 × 240 (280 × 120) mm
Oxford, Bodleian MS. Auct. E. 3.7, pp. 936-1072

p. 1072 *Ἰωάννης ὁ Σαγκταμαύρ(ας), Κύπριος, ὁ τῶν ἑλληνικῶν τῆς οὐατικανῆς βιβλίων γραφεύς, ἀντέγραψα τὸ παρὸν βιβλίον, ὁ τῇ ἡλικίᾳ ὀγδοηκοντούτης δεόντων ἑπτὰ ἐτῶν· τῷ δὲ πόνῳ, τριακοντούτης ἐπὶ ἑπτά.* There follows a note by him in Italian describing the circumstances of the copying dated 24 July 1610.
Breathings (3). Accents (4). Diaeresis (3). Mute ι (3). Abbreviations (2), (4), (6), (8). No ruling.
A list of manuscripts ascribed to Sanctamauras is in H. Omont, 'Le dernier des copistes grecs en Italie, Jean de Sainte-Maure (1572-1612)', *Revue des études grecques*, 1 (1888), 177-91.

…ς πολλάκις αἰσθανομένους τῶν ἀγαθῶν τε καὶ τῶν κακῶν, ἐκπλήξασα ποι-
εῖν τὸ χεῖρον ἀντὶ τοῦ βελτίονος αἱρεῖσθαι; γίνεται τοῦτο ἔφη· σωφροσύ-
νης δὲ ὦ εὐθύδημε, τίνι ἂν φαίημεν ἧττον ἢ τῷ ἀκρατεῖ προσήκειν· αὐτὰ
γὰρ δήπου τὰ ἐναντία, σωφροσύνης καὶ ἀκρασίας ἔργα ἐστίν; ὁμολογῶ καὶ
τοῦτο ἔφη· τοῦ δὲ ἐπιμελεῖσθαι ὧν προσήκει, οἴει τι κωλυτικώτερον ἀκρα-
σίας εἶναι; οὔκουν ἔγωγε φημί· τοῦ δὲ ἀντὶ τῶν ὠφελούντων
τὰ βλάπτοντα προαιρεῖσθαι ποιοῦντος, καὶ τούτων μὲν ἐπιμελεῖσθαι, ἐκεί-
νων δὲ ἀμελεῖν πείθοντος, καὶ τοῖς σωφρονοῦσι τὰ ἐναντία ποιεῖν ἀναγκά-
ζοντος, οἴει τι ἀνθρώπῳ κάκιον εἶναι; οὐδὲν ἔφη· οὔκουν τὴν ἐγ-

107

τάξει δεσποίνης ὀφείλουσαν προκαθῆσθαι καὶ ἐπὶ τὸ πλεῖον καταβιβάσασαν τοῦ
ἀπὸ τοῦ θρόνου, τῷ ὑπακούειν ταῖς τῆς σαρκὸς ἡδοναῖς καταναγκάζομεν, ἀγνο-
οῦντες αὐτῆς τὴν εὐγένειαν, καὶ ὅση ταύτης ἡ προεδρεία τυγχάνει. ἐννόησον
ἔχων τὴν τάξιν τῆς διαπλάσεως, ἐλογίζου πρὸ τοῦ ἐμφυσήματος τοῦ δεσπότου.
τί ἦν αὐτὰρ γέγονεν; εἰς πνοὴν ζωῆς. ἐγένετο εἰς ψυχὴν ζῶσαν. τί ἦν ὁ πλασθείς,
ἁπλῶς εἰκὼν ἄψυχος καὶ ἀνενέργητος, καὶ εἰς οὐδὲν χρήσιμος. ὥστε τὸ πᾶν καὶ
τὸ εἰς τοσαύτην τιμὴν αὐτὸν ἀγαγόν, ἐκεῖνό ἐστι τὸ παρὰ τοῦ θεοῦ γενόμενος εἰς αὐ-

108

ἢ ἐπὶ προσώπων μελλήσει τὴν ἀξίαν πι-
ζων, ὡς [illegible] ἡλικιώτας καὶ [illegible]
οἷς δὲ περιπεσεῖν· ταύτην δὲ τὴν λύπην, ἀπο-
[illegible] θανατοῦν μετὰ φανερῶς [illegible]
ἢ πρὸς ἄλλην ἀγωγήν· τὴν μετ' [illegible] ἀπάθειαν ἢ
ὁ πολλοῦ τινος ἡμᾶς ἀξιοῦν· τὴν ἐθέλειν
δέ, ὁ [illegible] φίλον ἢ [illegible]

109

ξίαν μου. ὁ καταναλώσας πᾶσαν τὴν πατρικὴν οὐσίαν
καὶ τῷ λιμῷ ζῶν. ἔχομεν οὖν πατρικὴν οὐσίαν καὶ ἡμεῖς,
ποίαν δὴ ταύτην; ἀπήλλαξεν ἡμᾶς τῶν ἁμαρτημάτων.
ἐχαρίσατο ἡμῖν δύναμιν. τὴν πρὸς τὴν τῆς ἀρετῆς ἐργασίαν.
ἐχαρίσατο ἡμῖν προθυμίαν. ὑπομονήν. ἐχαρίσατο ἡμῖν τὸ
τῷ βαπτίσματι πνεῦμα ἅγιον. ὅταν ταῦτα καταναλώσωμεν,

110

TRANSCRIPTIONS

and references to published texts

1

Plate from fol. 465[r]. Anonymous paraphrase of Oppian, *Halieutica*, IV. 404-21, ed. in *Incerti auctoris in Oppiani Halieutica paraphrasis*, ed. I. Gualandri (Milan, 1968) p. 52, §10, lines 14-24. *Τοις ιπ'πουροις δε φιλη μεν εστιν τρο ... λιψανα· δρομος δε εσπουδασμενος ... θαλασσης διαρηξιεν ζαλη· καὶ τας διεσπ ... σιν των σανιδων· και προς αυταις ραδι ... τις επελ'θων αλιευοι αλ'λα τον μεν τω ... δυνον ο θαλατ'τιος αποκυλωοι θεος ... δια των κυματων φαιρομεναι τους φ ... ζοιεν· τους ιπ'πουρους δε και κατ αλλ ... θηραν· και τι κατ αυτων τοιονδε ἕξη ... τινας φακελ'λους συνδησαντες επα ... σιν· λιθον τοῖς καλαμοις ενθεντες·*

2

Plate from fol. 47[r]. *τὰ ἀπο διοκ͡λητιανôυ ἔτη κατεχων ἐν τῆ χειρι σου. αφαιρεσον ἐξ αυτῶν εν. τα λοιπὰ μερισον παρα τον δεκα εννεα· και τα λοιπα πολυπλασιασον επι τον ιθ̄· και ριψον τριακοντάδας. και τα καταλειπόμενα λεγε επακτὰς ειναι· υποδειγματος χαριν εστω ετ[η] σλθ̄ αφ ων ᾱ λ[οι]π[α] σλη̄. παρα τον ιθ̄ δεκα δεκα εννεα δις δεκα εννεα λ[οι]π[α] ῑ ταυτα ἐπι τον ενδεκα γινεται δεκα δεκα εννεα ρῑ ριπτομεν τρις τριακοντα λοιπαι κατα ταυτας λεγομεν ἐπακτάς:*

3

Plate from fol. 144[v]. Luke 4: 16,18. *ἦλθεν ὁ ι(ησου)ς εἰς τὴ(ν) ναζαρὲθ· οὗ ἦν τεθραμμένος καὶ εἰσῆλθε κατὰ τὸ εἰωθὸς αὐτῶ· ἐν τῆ ἡμέρα τῶ(ν) σαββάτων εἰς τὴ(ν) . . . ἰάσασθαι τοὺς συ(ν)τετριμμένους τὴν καρδίαν κηρύξαι· αἰχμαλώτοις ἄφεσιν καὶ τυφλοῖς ἀνάβλεψιν ἀποστεῖ*

4

Plate from lines 3-16. Ed. Milne, op. cit., p.70. *ε χαρῖτων ... ερωτα ... ηελιωνι ... α ουκ'ετ' αειρω ... ν ολβιστηρων ... χον εγγυς ανακτων ... δρον ἰκᾱνης ... παντοθεν οικτρω ... ν εγγυαλιξη ... βιον εκτος ανῑης ... νι δυσμενεεσσιν ... αμηφιν εᾱων ... ουσαν αριστην ... ηματα πασχω*

5

Plate from fol. 316[v]. Letter 102, ed. *PG* 37 193 B.10 - C. 5. *[Ε]πειδὴ πολλοὶ προσϊόντες τη σῆ εὐλαβεία πληροφορίαν ζητοῦσι περὶ πίστεως. καὶ διὰ τοῦτο ἀπήτησας ἡμᾶς ἀγαπητικῶς. σύντομον ὅρον τινὰ καὶ κανόνα τοῦ ἡμετέρου φρονήματος. διὰ τοῦτο ἐγράψαμεν τῆ σῆ ἐυλαβεια. δ καὶ πρὸ τῶν γραμμάτων ἐγνώριζες· ὅτι ἡμεῖς τῆς κατὰ νίκαιαν πίστεως, τῆς τῶ(ν) ἁγίων πατέρων τῶν ἐκεῖ συνελθόνιων ἐπὶ καθαιρέσει τῆς ἀρειανῆς αἱρέσεως. οὐδὲν οὔτε προετιμήσαμε(ν)*

6

Plate from fol. 122[v]. Scholia in *Element.* VII ad def. 1, 6 sq., §8, ed. J.L. Heiberg (Leipzig, 1883-1916), V. 362, 365-6. *Μον(ας) λέγετ(αι) κ(αὶ) ἐν τ(οις) θε(οις)· λέγετ(αι) κ(αὶ) ἐν φυσικ(οις)· ... λέγομ(εν) τ(ον) ἐκ(ασ)τ(ῆς) σειρ(ας) ἄρχ(ον)τα· οὐχ (οτι) (ἔστι) μον(ας). ἀλλ ... τ(ον) αὐτ(ὸν) τρόπ(ον) κ(αὶ) αὐτ(ος) εξάρχει τ(ης) σειρ(ας). ἡ δε φυ ... οι(ον) ὁ εἷς ἵππ(ος) μον(ας) (εστι) φυσική. (ὅτι) τ(ης) μαθηματικ(ης) ... θὴν μετέχ(ον)τα τα φυσικὰ λέγετ(αι) ἕν· τ(ης) μο ... γ(αρ) κ(αὶ) μετέχοντ[α] τα φυσικ(α) λέγετ(αι) ἕν· κ(αὶ) ἀριθμ ... 'Αρτιάκ(ις) ἄρτιος ἀριθμ(ος) (ἐστιν), ὁ υπο ἀρτιου αριθ ... μεν τὸ μόν(ως) υπ ἀρτι(ου) ἀριθμ(ου) μετρεῖσθ(αι) κ[α]τ[α] ἄρτι(ον) ἀ ... μοναδ[ος] δίχα δ(ια)[ι]ρ(ου)μεν(ον). οι(ον) ὁ ὀκτ(ω)· υπ[ο] ἀρτι(ου) ἀριθμ(ου) ... ἀρτιάκ(ις) ἄρτιος, καθὸ μετρεῖτ(αι) μ(εν) κ(αὶ) υπ ἀρτι(ου) κ ... τέσσαρα· ἀρτιάκ(ις) δὲ περισσ(ον) λέγει. τ(ον) υπ ἀρ ... Περισσάρτι(ος) δὲ ὁ δεκαδύο. υπ[ο] γ(αρ) τ(ου) τρι(α) μετρεῖτ(αι) ... θέσει, κατ' εκεῖνο λέγομ(εν) μετρεῖσθ(αι) τ(ον) ἀριθμ(ον)· ... ρείων ου[τ](ως) καλ(ου)μεν(ον) τ(ον) πλείον(ας) δ(ια)[ι]ρεσεις δεχό ... κ[α]τ[α] τ(ην) δ(ια)[ι]ρεσ(ιν). οἶδ(εν) κ(αὶ) αὐτ(ος) κ(αὶ) μέμνητ(αι) αὐτ(ου) ἐν τ(ω) ἐ ... ἀρτιοπέρισσ(ον). τῆι απ[ο]φάσει τ(ων) δύο ἄκρ(ων) αὐτ(ον) σημ ... ὄνομ(α) τ(ην) σημασι(αν) εὑρίσκομ(εν) τῆι απ[ο]φάσει λέγ(ον)τ(ες) τ(ων)*

7

Plate from p. 190. *Quaestiones ad Thalassium* qn. 39, schol. 3, ed. *PG* 90 393. *σχο[λιον] Λύχνός ἐστιν κατ[α] ταυτὸν ὁμοῦ καὶ φῶς ὁ τοῦ θ(εο)υ λόγος· καὶ (ὡς) φωτίζων τοὺς κατὰ φύσιν λογισμοὺς τῶν πιστῶν. καὶ ὡς καίων τοὺς παρὰ φύσιν· κ(αι) ὡς λύων τὸν ζόφον τῆς κατ' αἴσθησιν ζωῆς τοῖς διὰ τῶν ἐντολῶν πρὸς τὴν ἐλπιζομένην ἐπειγομένοις ζωὴν· και ὡς κολάζων τῆ καύσει τῆς κρίσεως τοὺς ταύτης τῆς σκοτεινῆς τοῦ βίου νυκτὸς κατὰ γνώμην διὰ φιληδονίαν σαρκὸς ἀντεχομένους.*

8

Plate from col. V, lines 141-8. Ed. Schmidt and Schubart, op. cit., p. 73. *μαλλον δε θεοπρεπως εαυτον απ ... θεισης εξ ημων δι ημας εμψυχου ... τη προς αυτην του λογου οικειωσει ... τιρρητως το ασυγχυτον. τουτεστιν ... αδιασπαστον θεοτητος τε φημι κ ... και διαιρεσεως εξω καθεστηκοτα· . . . δυο φυσεσιν αυτον ϋποβαλλομενο . . . τον αριθμον τη αγια περιποιειται τ*

9

Plate from fol. 123[v]. List of questions in *Short Rules*, qns. 110-16 ed. *PG* 31 1061 A.14 - B 13. *ρῑ εἰ χρὴ ἐξομολογουμένης ἀδελφῆς τῶ πρεσβυτέρω. καὶ τὴν πρεσβυτέραν παρεῖναι· ρῑᾱ εἰ τοῦ πρεσβυτέρου γενέσθαί τι προστάξαντος ἐν ταῖς ἀδελφαῖς παρὰ γνώμην τῆς πρεσβυτέρας.*

εὐλόγως ἀγανακτεῖ ἡ πρεσβυτέρα· ριβ ἐάν τις προσέλθῃ τῷ κατὰ θ(εὸ)ν βίω. εἰ ἀκόλουθόν ἐστι τὸν προεστῶτα ἄνευ γνώμης τῶν ἀδελφῶν τὸν τοιοῦτον προσδέχεσθαι: ριγ εἰ δύναται ὁ φροντίδα ψυχῶ(ν) ἐγκεχειρισμένος φυλάξαι. τὸ ἐὰν μὴ στραφῆτε καὶ γένησθε ὡς τὰ παιδία: ριδ τοῦ οὖν κ(υρίο)υ προστάσσοντ(ος). ἐάν τις σε ἀγγαρεύσῃ μίλιον ἓν ὕπαγε με τ'αὐτοῦ δύο. εἰ δεῖ παντὶ τῷ ἐπιτάσσοντι καὶ ὡδηποτοῦν ὑπακούειν: ριε πῶς ὑπακούειν ἀλλήλοις χρή: ριϛ μέχρι πόσου ὑπακούειν χρὴ ἐν τῷ κανόνι:

10

Plate shows fol. 6v. Verses on the Psalter printed in [T. Gaisford,] *Catalogus . . . manuscriptorum qui a E.D. Clarke comparati in Bibliotheca Bodleiana adservantur* (Oxford, 1812-15) Pt. 1, p.59, lines 16-23. καὶ πυρπολοῦσαν δυσμενεῖς ἄρδην πέριξ· ἀλλ' ὦ προφῆτα καὶ βασιλεῦ καὶ τόκου καπνοῦ προπάτορ· ὡς ἔχων παρρησίαν λιτὴν κινοίης πρὸς τὸν ἐκ σῆς ὀσφύος σ(ωτῆ)ρα χ(ριστό)ν τὸν δότην τῶν λωιόνων, κ' αμοὶ γενέσθαι βρωτὸν ἡδὺ καὶ πόμα· ῥύψιν τε νύκτωρ δεμνίων ἄσης πλέ(ων), καθημερινὸν ἁγνὸν ἐκ ψυχῆς δάκρυ·

11

Plate from lines 14-19. Edited ibid., p. 273. τε διοικησαντος την ανω χωραν περιεχον του μειναι υμας ... μων συντελουντας μεντοι τα διαγραφα υμων και επιβεβαιων ... λλιν τω παροντι σιγιλλιω εχρησαμην δι ου επιτρεπων υμιν ... τη ταυτοτητι εις τον τοπον υμων και λογον εχειν του μη ... ε παρελθειν δι υμων τινα ; υμων μεντοι φυλαττοντων ... υμων καταστασιν και συντελουντων το διαγραφον υμων

12

Plate shows fol. 344r. Obits of Plato, Theodoros, and Ioseph, printed in Allen, 'The origin', p.3. ετελειωθη εν κ(υρι)ω ο οσιος (και) θεοφορος π(ατ)ηρ ημων πλατων ο του χ(ριστο)υ ομολογητης ο μεγας της οικουμενης φωστηρ μ[ηνι] απριλλιω δ ινδ[ικτιωνος] ζ ημε[ρα] δ ετελειωθη ο εν αγιοις θεοδωρος ο κοινος π(ατ)ηρ ημων (και) νέος του χ(ριστο)υ ομολογ[ητης] πολλους δρομους (και) αγωνας διανοίσας εν τη αμωμητω (και) αληθινη των χριστιανων πιστει· πολλους τε φωτισας (καὶ) οδηγησας εις επιγνωσιν ευσεβει(ας) (και) σ(ωτη)ριας μ(ην)[ι] νοεμβριω ια ἰνδ[ικτιωνος] ε ημε[ρα] α ετους δε απο κτισεως κοσμου ϛτλε· ετελειωθ[η] ο εν αγιοις π(ατ)ηρ ημω[ν] ἰωσηφ ο αγιωτατος αρχ[ι]επισκ[ο]π[ος] θεσσαλονικης (και) νεος του χ(ριστο)υ ομολογητης εν καλη ὁμολογια (και) μαρτυρία θανων ϋπερ της αληθειας μ(ην)[ι] ἰουλιω ιε ἰνδ[ικτιωνος]ι ετους δε κοσμου ϛτμ.

13

Plate shows fol. 161v. Luke 1:6-13. ἄμεμπτοι· κ(αὶ) οὐκ' ἦν αὐτοῖς τέκνον, καθότι ἡ ελισάβετ ἦν στείρα. κ(αὶ) ἀμφότεροι προβεβηκότες ἐν ταῖς ἡμέραις αὐτῶν ἦσαν· ἐγένετο δὲ ἐν τῷ ἱερατεύειν αὐτὸν. ἐν τῇ τάξει τῆς ἐφημερίας αὐτοῦ ἔναντι τοῦ θ(εο)ῦ. κατὰ τὸ ἔθος τῆς ἱερατείας, ἔλαχε τοῦ θυμϊάσαι εἰσελθὼν εἰς τὸν ναὸν τοῦ κ(υρίο)υ. (καὶ) πᾶν τὸ πλῆθος ἦν τοῦ λαοῦ προσευχόμενον ἔξω τῇ ὥρα τοῦ θυμϊάματος· ὤφθη δὲ αὐτῷ ἄγγελος κ(υρίο)υ ἑστὼς ἐκ δεξιῶν τοῦ θυσιαστηρίου τοῦ θυμιάματος. κ(αὶ) ἐταράχθη ζαχαρίας ἰδὼν, (καὶ) φόβος ἐπέπεσεν ἐπ' αὐτόν· εἶπε δὲ πρὸς αὐτὸν ὁ ἄγγελος. μὴ φοβοῦ ζαχαρία. διότι εἰσηκούσθη ἡ δέησίς σου. κ(αὶ) ἡ γυνή σου ελισάβετ γεννήσει υἱόν σοι. (καὶ) καλέ

14

Plate from fol. 175v. Homily 62 on Matthew, ed. *PG* 58 604, lines 5-12. δίκην δῶμεν. (καὶ) ἐκεῖ κολασθῶμεν ἀπέρ αντ ... γενώμεθα τῆς ἀρετῆς ἐρασταί· οὕτω γὰρ ... πρὸ τῆς βασιλείας τὰ μέγιστα ἐνταῦθα κ ... ποσώμεθα καλά. (καὶ) ἀπελθόντες ἐκεῖ, τω ... αἰωνίων μεθέξωμεν ἀγαθῶν· ὧν, γένοιτ ... πάντας ἡμᾶς ἐπιτυχεῖν· ἐν χ(ριστ)ω ι(ησο)υ τῷ κ(υρι)ω ἡμῶν· ὦ, ἡ δόξα εἰς τοὺς αἰῶνας τῶν αἰώνω

15

Plate from fol. 200r. Life of S. Calliopius (*BHG* 290), ed. *Acta Sanctorum Aprilis*, I (Antwerp, 1675), [Suppl. Graec.] p. LXXXV D. 11-15. λαβοῦσα δὲ ἡ μ(ητ)ηρ αὐτοῦ τὸ λείψανον τοῦ ἁγιωτάτου (καὶ) τρισμακαρίστου υἱοὺ αὐτῆς, περιεπλάκη περι τὸν τράχηλον αὐτοῦ δοξάζουσα τὸν χ(ριστό)ν· καὶ εὐθέως καὶ αὐτὴ ἀπέδωκεν τὴν ψυχήν· (καὶ) ἐλθόντες οἱ ἀδελφοὶ

16

Plate from fol. 17r. Life of S. Irene (*BHG* 953), ed. A. Wirth, *Danae in christlichen Legenden* (Vienna etc., 1892) p. 144, lines 903-10. ρωσε τὴν ἀθλοφόρον μάρτυρα· ἰδῶν δὲ ἅπαν τὸ πλῆθος ὅτι οὐκ ἐκυρίευσεν αὐτῆς τὸ πῦρ. ἀνέκραξαν πάντες λέγοντες· ἐλέησον ἡμᾶς ὁ θ(εὸ)ς κατὰ τὸ μέγα ἔλεός σου· σὺ γὰρ εἶ ὁ θ(εὸ)ς μόνος ὁ διὰ εἰρήνης ποιήσας ἔνδοξα σημεῖα· ἦσαν δὲ οἱ λέγοντες ταῦτα. ὡσεὶ δέκα μυριάδες· οἵτινες (καὶ) ἐπίστευσαν τῷ κ(υρι)ω ἐν φόβω πολλῶ· ὑπελείπετο δὲ (καὶ) ἕτερον πλῆθος ἦσαν γὰρ συνηθροισμένοι ἐκ πάσης τῆς περιχώρου δίκην μελισσῶν· γνοὺς δὲ ὁ βασιλεὺς ὅτι περπολλοὶ ἐπίστευσαν τῷ κ(υρι)ω. ἤρξατο ἰσχυρῶς βλασφημεῖν τὴν παρθένο(ν)

17

Plate from Lake pl. 32 (p. 314). Oration 5 ed. *PG* 35 677 A. 6-B.7. παρείκοι βάλλουσα καὶ τοξεύουσα· καὶ τὰ καίρια τῆς διόδου προκαταλαμβάνουσα. ῥαδίως εἶργε τοῦ πρόσω· τηνικαῦτα ἐν απορία τε ἦν ἤδη πολλῆ καὶ οὐκ ἔχων ὅποι τράπηται, λύσιν εὑρίσκει πονηρὰν τοῦ βουλεύματος· [Ἀ]νὴρ γάρ τις τῶν οὐκ αδοκίμων ἐν πέρσαις· τῶν ἐπι βαβυλῶνι πρόσκαιρον ζώπυρον μιμησάμενος. ὡς δή τι τῶι περσῶν βασιλεῖ· μᾶλλον δὲ μέγιστα (καὶ) ἐπι μεγιστοις προσκεκρουκῶς. καὶ δύσνους μὲν τοῖς ἐκείνου μάλιστα εὔνους δὲ τοῖς ῥωμαίων πράγμασι. διὰ τοῦτο τυγχάνων καὶ τὸ

18

Plate from fol. 288^r. *Elementa* XI, 23 demonstratio altera, ed. J. L. Heiberg (Leipzig, 1883-1916) IV. 352, lines 9-20. *ξομεν ὅτι κ(αι) ἡ ὑπο ΗΘΚ γωνία τῆς ὑπο ΟΞΡ μείζων εστίν· συνεστάτω δη προς τηι ΛΞ εὐθείαι και τῶι προς αὐτῆι σημείωι τῶι Ξ. τῆι μεν ὑπο ΑΒΓ γωνιαι ἴση ἡ ὑπο ΛΞΣ· τῆι δε ὑπο ΘΗΚ ἴση ἡ ὑπο ΛΞΤ· και κείσθω εκατερα τῶν ΞΣ ΞΤ ἡ ΟΞ ἴση· και ἐπεζέυχθωσαν αἱ ΟΣ ΟΤ ΣΤ· και ἐπεὶ δύο αἱ ΑΒ ΒΓ δύο ταῖς ΟΞ ΞΣ ἴσαι εισιν. κ(αι) γωνία ἡ ὑπο ΑΒΓ γωνίαι τῆι ὑπο ΟΞΣ ἴση· βασις αρα ἡ ΑΓ τουτ' ἔστιν ἡ ΛΜ βάσει τῆι ΟΣ εστιν ἴση· δια τα αὐτα δη κ(αι) ἡ ΛΝ τῆι ΟΤ ἴση εστιν· κ(αι) επεὶ δύο αἱ ΜΛ ΛΝ δύο ταις ΟΣ ΟΤ ἴσαι εἰσιν. κ(αι) γωνια ἡ ὑπο*

δ(ια) το Δ' τ(ου) Α'

δ(ια) το Κ'Δ τ(ου) Α'.

19

Plate from fol 69^r. *Scala* gradus 7, ed. *PG* 88 808 A. 2-5, 11-14. *ἄχρις οὗ ὑποχωρήσῃ· πολλὴ γὰρ ἡ ἰσχὺς τούτου ὑπερ τὴν τοῦ ἐξ ἡμετέρας σπουδῆς. και ἐπινοίας προσγινομένου· Οὐχ' ὅτε βούλεται ὁ πενθῶν. οὗτος ... ὀδύνη ψυχῆς· μηδεμίαν ἑαυτῇ παρηγορίαν παρέχουσα. μόνην δὲ τὴν ἑαυτῆς ἀνάλυσιν. καθ' ὥραν φανταζομένη· (καὶ) τὴν τοῦ παρακα*

20

Plate from fol. 132^r. Commentary on Isaiah 6: 11-13, ed. *PG* 30 444 D.10 - 445 A.6. *Τάχα δὲ καὶ διὰ τὸ ἐκπεπτωκέναι τῆς ἰουδαϊκῆς χώρας. καὶ ἐν τῇ διασπορᾷ γεγενῆσθαι, βαλάνῳ παρεικάζεται ἐκπιπτούσῃ ἐκ τῆς θήκης αὐτῆς· τὸ δὲ σπέρμα ἅγιον τὸ στήλωμα αὐτῆς· ἐκ τῶν θεοδοτίωνος πρόσκειται· μὴ κείμενον παρὰ τοῖς ἑβδομήκοντα· ἀξιόλογον νοῦν. ὡς πρὸς τὴν τῶν προαποδεδομένων ἀκολουθίαν ἔχον·*

21

Plate from fol. 63^r. Mark 16: 9-14. *'Αναστὰς δὲ πρωΐ πρώτηι σαββάτων. ἐφάνη πρῶτον μαρίαι τηῖ μαγδαληνῆι· ἀφ' ἧς, ἐκβεβλήκει ἑπτὰ δαιμόνια: ἐκείΝη πορευθεῖσα ἀπήγγειλεν τοῖς μετ' αὐτοῦ γενομένοις. πενθοῦσιν καὶ κλαίουσιν· κακεῖνοι ἀκούσαντες ὅτι ζῆι· καὶ ἐθεάθη ὑπ' αὐτῆς. ἠπίστησαν: μετὰ δὲ ταῦτα δυΣὶν ἐξ' αὐτῶν περὶπατοῦσιν. ἐφανερώθη ἐν' ἑτέρα μορφῆι. πορευομένοις εἰς ἀγρόν: κακείνοι ἀπελθόντες ἀπήγγειλαν τοῖς λοιποῖς· οὐδε ἐκείνοις ἐπίστευσαν: ὕστερον*

22

Plate from fol. 200^v. Anonymous *λόγος ἀσκητικός* beginning *τί θέλει εἶναι ὁ μονάζων* as in Vat. gr. 735 fols. 286^v-288. *τὸς πειρασμοῦ, ἵνα μὴ προσευχόμενος ὀχλεῖται ὑπ' αὐτῶν· ἐὰν γαρ μη λύσῃ μάτ(ην) πρὸσεῦχετ(αι)· ὁ νοὺς γὰρ περὶ ἐκείνου ρεύμμετ(αι)· καὶ δῆθεν πρὸσεῦχεται· καὶ ἡ πρὸσευχῆ αὐτοῦ πρὸς τὸν θ(εό)ν οὐκ ἀναβαίνει· ἐὰν γὰρ μὴ καθαρὰν πρὸσεὐχὴν πεπληροφορουμένην εν πίστει πρὸσεύξηται, οὐ προσδέχεται ὁ θ(εός)· ὁ γὰρ μονάζων ἀφ' αἰαὑτοῦ οὐδὲν ἰσχύει οὔται δύναται· οὔτε τῶ διαβόλω ἀντιστῆν(αι), οὔται τοὺς λόγισμοὺς τῆς ἁμαρτίας ῥίψαι ἀφ' ἑαυτοῦ*

23

Plate from fol. 91^r. *Quaestiones ad Thalassium* qn. 56, ed. *PG* 90 577 A. 10 - B. 9. *τῶν κακῶς πεπραγμένων λεγόμενος· ἐξομολόγησις γὰρ λέγεται. καὶ ἡ παρὰ τῶ(ν) εὖ πεπονθότων μετ εὐχαριστίας τῶν θείων εὐεργεσιῶ(ν) ἀπαρίθμησις· καὶ ἡ τῶν κακῶς πεπραγμένων παρὰ τῶν ὑπαιτίων ἐξαγόρευσις· ἀμφότερα δὲ, ταπεινώσεως ὑπάρχει ποιητικά· ὅ τε γὰρ ἐπ' ἀγαθοῖς εὐχαριστῶν ὁμοῦ καὶ ὁ ἐπ εγκλήμασιν ἐταζόμενος, ταπεινοῦται· ὁ μὲν ἑαυτὸν κρίνων, ἀνάξιον τῶν δοθέντων καλῶν, ὁ δὲ λαβεῖν ἄφεσιν τῶ(ν) πλημμεληθέντων δεόμενος· βενιαμὶν δὲ, πένθος ἢ στεναγμὸς μ(ητ)ρ(ο)ς· ἢ μέτρον μ(ητ)ρ(ο)ς· ἢ ὑ(ιὸ)ς δεξιᾶς· ἢ οἰκοδομῆ λαοῦ· κατὰ τὴν ἀπο*

24

Plate from fol. 212^r. Long catechesis, sermon 61, ed. in *Nova patrum bibliotheca*, ed. A. Mai and G. Cozza-Luzi (Rome, 1852-1905) IX. 2, p. 172, lines 26-35. *ρὰν καὶ ζωὴν· τὸ ἐμὸν αὔχημα καὶ στεφάνωμα· τὸ περὶ ἐμὲ κλέος καὶ ἐγκώμϊον· οὕτως ὡς ἐξεζητήσατε· οὕτως ὡς ἠρνήσασθε· οὕτως ὡς προεπολιτεύσασθε παλαιοί τε καὶ νέοι· οἱ ἑτερόποιμνοι καὶ αὐτόχθονες. ἀλλ' οὖν πάντες νῦν τῆς αὐτῆς ἀγέλης καὶ τῆς αὐτῆς ποίμνης καὶ τῆς αὐτῆς αὐλῆς. καὶ τοῦ αὐτοῦ ποιμένος καὶ θρέμματα καὶ γεννήματα· ἐάσθω γὰρ τὰ ἀσύμφορα ἐπινοεῖν· οὕτως καὶ ἐπιβϊώσατε· καὶ ἐπείχθητε καὶ τε*

25

Plate from fol. 161^r. Luke 19: 33-7. *τοῦ πρὸς αὐτούς· τί λύετε τὸν πῶλον· οἱ δὲ, εἶπον· ὁ κ(ύριο)ς, αὐτοῦ χρείαν ἔχει· καὶ ἤγαγον αὐτὸν πρὸς τὸν ἰ(ησοῦ)ν· (καὶ) ἐπιρρίψαντες ἑαυτῶν τὰ ἱμάτια ἐπὶ τὸν πῶλον, ἐπεβίβασαν τὸν ἰ(ησοῦ)ν· πορευομένου δὲ αὐτοῦ, ὑπεστρώννυον τὰ ἱμάτια αὐτῶν ἐν τῇ ὁδῶ· 'Εγγίζοντος δὲ αὐτοῦ ἤδη πρὸς τῇ καταβάσει τοῦ ὄρους τῶν ἐλαιῶν, ἤρξαντο ἅπαν τὸ πλῆθος τῶν μα*

26

Plate from fol. 99^v. Timotheus Constantinopolitanus presbyter, *De receptione haereticorum*, ed. *PG* 86 40 B.2-13. *ποκειμένων ἀρρήτων ἀγαθῶν τοῖς ἁγίοις. εἰς πολλὴν ταπεινότητα κατάγειν· τουτέστιν εἰς τὰ ἰουδαϊκά· θυσιας παλιν τοιαύτας ἐπιτελεῖν ἐν τῶι ναῶι· ἔτι λέγει τὸν θ(εο)ν λόγον ἐπαγόμενον σάρκα ἐκείνην ἣν ἔχων ἐν οὐρανοῖς ἐτύγχανε· προαιώνιόν τινα καὶ συνουσιωμένην· καὶ τὸ πάθος δὲ. τηῖ ἰδίαι αὐτοῦ θεότητι δέξασθαι· καὶ ἐν τηῖ τριημέρωι ἐκείνηι νεκρώσει τοῦ σώματος. (καὶ) τὴν θεότητα συναπονεκρωθῆναι τῶι σώματι. καὶ οὕτως παρὰ τοῦ π(ατ)ρ(ο)ς πάλιν ἀπὸ τοῦ θανάτου διαναστῆναι· ταῦτα ὁ ἅγιος γρηγόριος ὁ ἐπίσκοπος ναζιανζοῦ γράφει πρὸς νεκτάριον τὸν γενόμενον πατριάρχην*

27

Plate from fol. 73^r. Ecclesiastical hierarchy IV, 4-5 ed. *PG* 3 480 A.6 - B.4. *τους ἀτμούς· ἐφ' οἷς οἱ νόες εὐπαθῶς ἡδόμενοι· καὶ τῶν ἱερῶν ἀντιλήψεων ἀποπληρούμενοι. τροφῆι νοητῆι χρῶνται τῆι πρὸς τὸ νοερὸν αὐτῶν εἰσδύσει τῶν κατὰ θεῖαν μέθεξιν εὐώδων διαδόσεων· ἔστι δὲ ὡς οἶμαι δῆλον. ὅτι ταῖς ὑπερ ἡμᾶς οὐσίαις ὡς θειοτέραις ἡ τῆς πηγαίας εὐωδίας ἀνάδοσις. ἐγγυτέρα πῶς ἐστι καὶ μᾶλλον ἑαυτὴν ἐκφαίνει καὶ διαδίδωσιν εἰς τὸ*

28

Plate from fol. 151[r]. *Scala* gradus 22, ed. *PG* 88 953 C.14 - D.2, D.8-11. *κάθειντο· καὶ ὁ μὲν ἔνυττέν μου τὴν πλευρὰν τῶι δακτύλωι αὐτοῦ τῶι κενοδόξωι. προτρεπόμενός με λέγειν τινὰ θεωρίαν ἢ εργασίαν ἣν πεποίηκα ἐν τῆι ἐρήμωι· ὡς δὲ τοῦτο(ν)... ἐγὼ εὐθυβόλως τὸ ἑξῆς τοῦ στίχου ἀναλαβὼν εἴρηκα· ἀποστραφήτωσαν παραυτίκα αἰσχυνόμενοι. οἱ λέγοντές μοι εὖγε εὖγε πεποίηκας· ἐρωτησαντί μοι τὸν αὐτὸ(ν)*

29

Plate from fol. 161[r]. 2 Thessalonians 1: 3-5, 2: 2-4. *περὶ ὑμῶν ἀδελφοὶ καθὼς ἄξιόν ἐστίν· ὅτι ὑπεραυξάνει ἡ πίστις ὑμῶν. καὶ πλεονάζει ἡ ἀγάπη ἑνὸς ἑκάστου πάντων ὑμῶν εἰς ἀλλήλους· ὥστε ἡμᾶς αὐτοὺς ἐν ὑμῖν καυχᾶσθαι ἐν ταῖς ἐκκλησίαις τοῦ θ(εο)υ ὑπὲρ τῆς ὑπὸ μονῆς ὑμῶν καὶ πίστεως. ἐν πάσιν τοῖς διωγ'μοῖς ὑμῶν καὶ ταῖς θλήψεσιν αἷς ἀνέχεσθαι. ἔνδειγμα τῆς δικαίας κρίσε... ἐνέστηκεν ἡ ἡμέρα τοῦ... ὑμᾶς ἐξἀπατήση κατ... τρόπον ὅτι ἐὰν μὴ ἔλ... στασία πρῶτον. καὶ ἀ... φθῆ ὁ ἄν(θρωπ)ος τῆς ἁμαρ... τῆς ἀπωλείας ὁ ἀντικ... ὑπεραιρόμενος ἐπὶ π... μενον θ(εο)ν ἢ σέβασμα.... εἰς τὸν ναὸν τοῦ θ(εο)υ ὡς θ(εο)ν...*

30

Plate from fol. 238[v]. Apocalypse IV. 9-10, V. 5-7. *ξαν καὶ τιμὴν τῶ καθημένω ἐπὶ τῶ θρόνω τῶ ζῶντι εἰς τοὺς αἰῶνας τῶν αἰώνων. πεσοῦνται οἱ εἴκοσι τέσσαρις πρεσβύτεροι ἐνώπιον τοῦ καθημένου ἐπὶ τοῦ θρόνου. (καὶ) προσκυνήσουσιν τῶ ζῶντι εἰς τοὺς αἰῶνας τῶν αἰώνων· καὶ βάλουσιν τοὺς... ζα δα(υει)δ· ἀνοίξαι τὸ βιβλίον καὶ τὰς ἑπτὰ σφραγίδας αὐτοῦ· καὶ ἴδον ἐν μέσω τοῦ θρόνου (καὶ) τῶν τεσσάρων ζῶων. καὶ ἐν μέσω τῶν πρεσβυτέρων. ἀρνῖον ἑστικῶς ἐσφαγμένον. ἔχων κέρατα ἑπτὰ· ἅ εἰσὶν τὰ πν(ευμ)ατα τοῦ θ(εο)υ ἀπεσταλμένα εἰς πᾶσαν τὴν γῆν· (καὶ)*

31

Plate from Leningrad 355, fol.2[v]. part of ode 9 for 26 Aug. ed. *Μηναῖα* (Rome, 1888-1901), VI. 510. *Λαμπὰς· θεόφωτος ἄστρα φαίνοντα· λύχνοι ἡμῖν. τὸ φῶς τῆς εὐσεβείας πυρσέβοντες. τοῦ ἡλίου τῆς δόξης αὐγάσματα. τέκνα τῆς ἀνεσπέρου. μακαριότητος· μάρτυρες ἐδείχθητε χ(ριστο)ῦ· σεβασμιώτατοι: Πηγὴ ναμάτων πλήρης τοῦ πν(εύματο)ς· καὶ ποταμός· ἐνθέων χαρισμάτων πληρούμενος· καὶ κρατὴρ ἀθλήσεως· προχέων κρουνούς· πέλαγος σ(ωτη)ρίας· μάρτυρες ὤφθητε· ζάλης πειρασμῶν*

32

Plate from fol. 45[r]. Hebrews 11:39 - 12:1. *αν τοῦ θ(εο)ῦ περι ἡμῶν, κρίττον τι πρὸβλεψαμένου, ἵνα μὴ χωρὶς ἡμῶν τελιῶθῶσιν· τί γὰρ οὖν καὶ οἱμοῖς· τὸσούτον ἔχωσιν περικείμενον ἡμὶν νέφ(ος) μαρτύρον· ὄγκον ἀπὸθέμενοι πάντα καὶ τὴν εὐπερίστατον ἁμαρτί(αν)· δι ἠπομονῆς τρέχωμεν· τὸν πρὸκεί*

33

Plate from fol. 186[v]. Ammonius of Egypt, letter to Theophilus (*BHG* 1397), §13-14, ed. in *S. Pachomii vitae Graecae*, ed. F. Halkin (Subsidia Hagiographica 19, Brussels, 1932), pp. 103, line 38 - 104, line 6. *τὴν ἐκκλησίαν τοῦ θ(εο)υ σπουδάζοντες· ἐμοὶ δὲ τὸ πν(ευμ)α τὸ ἅγιον εἶπεν, ὅτι στύλον αὐτὸν (καὶ) λύχνον ἤγειρα τῆ ἐκκλησία· (καὶ) ὅτι θλίψεις πολλαὶ (καὶ) συκοφαντίαι ἀν(θρωπ)ων ἕνεκεν τῆς εἰς χ(ριστο)ν εὐσεβείας μένουσιν αὐτόν· (καὶ) πάντα νικήσας πειρασμὸν, μέχρι τέλους ὑπ' αὐτοῦ δυναμούμενος. τὴν ἀλήθειαν τοῦ εὐαγγελίου ταῖς ἐκκλησίαις κηρύξει· μετὰ δὲ ταῦτα, θεόδωρος*

34

Plate from Lake, pl. 19 (fol. no. unknown). Mark 2:24-5, 3:1-3. *βάσιν δ οὐκ ἔξεστϊ καὶ αὐτὸς ἔλεγεν αὐτοῖς οὐδέποτε ἀνέγνωτε τί ἐποίησε δα(υει)δ· ὅτε χρείαν ἔσχε καὶ ἐπείνασεν αὐτὸς καὶ οἱ με... ραμμένην ἔχων τὴ(ν) χεῖρα καὶ παρετήρουν αὐτὸν εἰ τοῖς σάββασι θεραπεύση αὐτόν, ἵνα κατηγορήσωσϊν αὐτοῦ καὶ λέγει τῶ ἀν(θρώπ)ω τῶ ἐξηρα*

35

Plate from fol. 168[r]. Commentary on Luke 4:22-30, ed. *PG* 123 752 B. 8-12, D. 1-5. *ὁ σύρ(ος)· καὶ ἐπλήσ... τες θυμοῦ ἐν τῆ συ... τοντες ταῦτα· καὶ ...ς ἐξέβαλον αὐτὸν... καὶ ἤγαγον αὐτὸν... ς τοῦ ὄρους· ἐφ οὗ... κοδόμητο· εἰς τὸ... ται (καὶ) τὰ ἐξαίρετα τῶν πραγμάτων ὅταν μὴ σπάνια εἴη ἀλλὰ κοινὰ (καὶ) συνήθη· (καὶ) πάντες οὐ θέλουσιν ἀπολαυεῖν αὐτῶν· εἰ γὰρ εἰώθαμεν οἱ ἄν(θρωπ)οι τ(ῶν) μὲν ξένων καὶ σπανίων φροντίζειν (καὶ) θαυμάζειν· τῶν*

36

Plate from Leningrad 431, fol. 1[v]. Part of stichera for 6 Feb., ed. *Μηναῖα* (Rome, 1888-1901), III. 513. *Ο ποιητὴς τῶν ἀπάντων, καὶ λυτρωτὴς ἡμῶν· ὑπὸ μ(ητ)ρ(ὸ)ς παρθένου, τῶ ναῶ προσηνέχθη· ὅθεν ὁ πρεσβύτης· τοῦτον λαβὼν· μετὰ χαρὰς ἀνεκραύγαζε· νῦν ἀπολύεις τὸν δοῦλον σου ἀγαθέ· ἐν εἰρήνη ὡς ηὐδόκησας: Ὁ συμεὼν ἐν ἀγκάλαις, ἐκ τῆς παρθένου λαβὼν· τὸν πρὸ πάντων αἰώνων· γεννηθέντα σ(ωτῆ)ρα· εἶδον ἀνὲβόα· τὸν φωτϊσμὸν· τῆς σῆς*

37

Plate from fol. 150[r]. *Politicus* 285 c9-286 b4 *ἐρωτηθῆι τίνων ἐστι γραμμάτων πότερο... σθαι τὴν ζήτησιν ἑνὸς ἕνεκα μᾶλλον τοῦ... πάντα τὰ προβαλλόμενα γραμματικωτ... τι τοῦ περὶ ἅπαντα: τί δ' αὖ νῦν ἡμῖν ἡ πε... ἕνεκα αὐτοῦ τούτου προβέβληται μᾶλλον... κωτέροις γίγνεσθαι: καὶ τοῦτο δῆλον ὅ... τὸν τῆς ὑφαντικῆς γε λόγον αυτῆς ταύ... δεὶς ἂν ἐθελήσειεν νοῦν ἔχων. ἀλλ' οἶμα... ὅτι τοῖς μὲν τῶν ὄντων ῥαιδίως καταμα... μοιότητες πεφύκασιν ἃς οὐδὲν χαλεπ... βουληθῆι τῶι λόγον αἰτοῦντι περὶ τοῦ μὴ... χωρὶς λόγου ῥαιδίως ἐνδείξασθαι· ... καὶ τιμιωτάτοις. οὐκ ἔστιν εἴδωλον οὐδὲ... εἰργασμένον ἐναργῶς οὐ δειχθέντος... ψυχὴν ὁ βουλόμενος ἀποπληρῶσαι π... προσαρμόττων ἱκανῶς πληρώσει· δι ... στου δυνατὸν εἶναι δοῦναι καὶ δέξασθαι· ... ὄντα καὶ μέγιστα. λόγωι μόνον ἄλλωι δὲ ὀ... τούτων δὲ ἕνεκα πάντ' ἐστι τὰ νῦν λεγόμε... λάττοσιν ἡ μελέτη παντὸς πέρι μᾶλλον... στ' εἶπες: ὧν τοίνυν χάριν ἅπανθ' ἡμῖν τα*

38

Plate from fol. 36r. *Didascalia* 10.104-5, ed. in Dorothée de Gaza, *Oeuvres spirituelles,* ed. L. Regnault and J. de Préville (Paris, 1963) pp. 336-8. *Ἑαυτούς· βάλωμεν ἀρχήν· θελήσωμεν τέως τὸ καλόν· κἂν γὰρ οὔπω ἐν τελειώτητι ἐσμὲν. ἀλλ αὐτὸ τὸ θέλειν ἀρχὴ σ(ωτη)ριας ἡμῖν ἐστίν· ἐκ τοῦ γὰρ θέλειν, ἀρχόμεθα σὺν θ(ε)ω (καὶ) εἰς τὸ ἀγωνίσασθαι· βοηθεῖταί τις. εἰς τὸ κτήσασθαι τὰς ἀρετάς· διὰ τοῦτό τις τῶν π(ατε)ρων λέγει· δὸς αἷμα (καὶ) λάβε πν(ευμ)α· τοῦτ ἐστιν· ἀγώνησαι. (καὶ) γίνη ἐν ἕξει τῆς ἀρετῆς: ὅτε ἀνεγίνωσκον εἰς τὴν ἔξω παιδείαν. ἐκοπίων ἐξ ἀρχῆς πάνυ· (καὶ) ὅτε ἠρχόμην λαβειν τὸ βιβλίον· οὕτως ἤμην. ὡς τίς ποτε ὑπάγων ἅψασθαι θηρίου· ὡς οὖν ἔμεινα βιαζόμενος ἑαυτὸν. ἐβοήθισεν ὁ θ(εο)ς· (καὶ) οὕτως ἐγενόμην ἐν ἕξει τοῦ πράγματος. ὥστε μήτε εἰδέναι με τί ἔτρογον ἢ τί ἔπινον. ἢ πῶς ἐκοιμώμην ἐκ τῆς καύσεως τῶν ἀναγνωσμάτων· οὐδέποτε δὲ ἑλκύσθην εἰς ἄριστον μετά τινος τῶν φίλων μου. ἀλλ οὐδὲ εἰς συντυχείαν ἠρχόμην μετ αὐτῶν ἐν τῷ καιρῷ τοῦ ἀναγνώσματος· καίτοι φιλοσυνήθης ὤν, (καὶ) ἀγαπῶν τοὺς ἑτέρους·*

39

Plate from fol. 37r. Mark 15: 26-32. **ἰουδαίων: (καὶ) συν** *αυτῷ στ(αυ)ροῦσιν δύο λῃστάς· ἕνα ἐκ δεξιῶν. (καὶ) ἕνα ἐξ ευωνύμων αὐτοῦ: (καὶ) οἱ παραπορευόμενοι ἐβλασφή*-**μουν αὐτὸν. κινοῦντες τὰς κεφαλὰς αὐτῶν, (καὶ) λέγοντες: οὐᾶ· ὁ καταλύων τὸν ναὸν, (καὶ) ἐν τρισσὶν ἡμέραις** *οἰκοδομῶν. σῶσον σεαυτὸν (καὶ) κατάβηθι ἀπὸ τοῦ* **στ(αυ)ρου: ὁμοίως δὲ (καὶ) οἱ ἀρχϊερεῖς, ἐμπαίζοντες** *πρὸς ἀλλήλους, μετὰ τῶν γραμματέων, ἔλεγον· ἄλλους* **ἔσωσεν. ἑαυτὸν οὐ δύναται σῶσαι; ὁ χ(ριστο)ς ὁ βασι**

40

Plate from fol. 106v. *De baptismo* II, qn. 4, ed. *PG* 31 1588 A.12-B. 11. *μέρει, ἕνεκε τῆς ὑπερβαλλούσης δόξης· ἐι γὰρ τὸ καταργούμενον διὰ δόξης, πολλω μᾶλλον τὸ μένον ἐν δόξῃ· οὕτως εἰ καὶ ἐκ τῶν εἰρημένων ἐπαιδεύθημεν τὰ ἐν τῷ εὐαγγελίῳ εἰρημένα· ἐν πίστει ἀδιακρίτω βεβαιώτερα γνωρίσαι καὶ ὁμολογεῖν· ὅμως πάλιν αὐτοῦ τοῦ κ(υριο)υ μνημονεύσωμεν λέγοντος· ὁ οὐ(ρα)νὸς καὶ ἡ γῆ παρελεύσεται, οἱ δὲ λόγοι μου οὐ μὴ παρέλθωσιν· ἤρκει μὲν οὖν τὰ τοῦ κ(υριο)υ ῥήματα, πλέον πάντων ἐν πν(ευματ)ι ἁγίω καὶ ἡγεμονικῶ, στηρίξαι τὰς καρδίας ἡμῶν· ἀδιστάκτως καὶ ἀραρότως ἔχειν περὶ παντ(ὸς) ῥήματος ἐκπορευομένου διὰ στόματος θ(εο)ῦ· ἵνα δὲ καὶ τῇ τινῶν ἀσθενεία βοηθήσωμεν, ἀκόλουθον ἂν εἴη, καὶ μαρτυρίαν ἑνὸς ἢ δευτέρου ἐκ πολλῶν παραθέσθαι· ὁ μὲν οὖν δα(υει)δ φή[σι]· πισταὶ πᾶ*

41

Plate from fol. 163r. Homily 22 on I Corinthians, ed. *PG* 61 181. 6-16. *Πολλὴν ποιεῖτε σπουδὴν ὥστε δεῖξαι μὴ κεκωλυμένον τὸ λαμβάνειν· δι' ὅπερ τοσαῦτα εἰπὼν ἔμπροσθεν, οὐκ ἠρκέσθη· ἀλλὰ καὶ ἐπὶ τὸν νόμο(ν) χωρεῖ· οἰκειότερον τοῦ προτέρου. παρέχων ὑπόδειγμα· οὐδὲ γὰρ ἦν ἴσον τοὺς βοῦς παραγαγεῖν εἰς μέσον. καὶ ῥητῶς περὶ ἱερέων νόμον ἐπι τούτω κείμενον ἀναγνῶναι· σκόπει δέ μοι κ ἂν τούτω τὴν σύνεσιν τὴν παύλου. πῶς μέμνηται τοῦ πράγματος μεγαλοπρεπῶς· οὐδὲ γὰρ εἶπεν οἱ τὰ ἱερὰ ἐργαζόμενοι ἐκ των προσφερόντων λαμβάνουσιν· ἀλλὰ τί, ἐκ τοῦ ἱεροῦ ἐσθίουσιν· ἵνα*

42

Plate from fol. 101r. Homily 21 on St. John, ed. *PG* 59 132. 51-9· *χάνοντες· παρακαλούμενοι πρὸς ἀρετὴν. τὸ αὐτὸ δὴ τοῦτο προβάλλονται λέγοντες· ὁ π(ατ)ηρ ὁ ἐμὸς καὶ ὁ πάππος. καὶ ἐπίπαππος· σφόδρα εὐσεβεῖς καὶ σπουδαῖοι ἐτύγχανον ὄντες· τοῦτο γάρ σε κατακρίνει μάλιστα· ὅτι τοιούτων ὢν ἔκγονος. ἀνάξια τῆς οἰκείας* **ἔπραξας ῥίζης· ἄκουσον καὶ ὁ προφήτης τὶ φη[σι]** *πρ(ὸς) τοὺς ἰουδαίους· ἐδούλευσ(εν) ἰ(σρα)ηλ ἐν γυναικὶ· καὶ ἐν γυναικὶ ἐφυλάξατο· καὶ πά*

43

Plate shows fol. 13r. Acts 5: 4-10. *ἐν τῇ καρδίᾳ σου τὸ πρᾶγμα τοῦτο· οὐκ ἐψεύσω ἀν(θρώπ)οις. ἀλλὰ τῷ θ(ε)ῷι· ἀκούων δὲ ἀνανίας τοὺς λόγους τούτους. πεσὼν ἐξέψυξε· καὶ ἐγένετο φόβος μέγας. ἐπὶ πάντας τοὺς ἀκούοντας ταῦτα· ἀναστάντες δὲ οἱ νεώτεροι· συνέστει*-**λαν αὐτὸν. καὶ ἐξενέγκαντες ἔθαψαν· ἐγένεΤο δὲ ὡς** *ὡρῶν τριῶν διάστημα. κ(αὶ) ἡ γυνὴ αὐτοῦ μὴ εἰδυῖα τὸ γεγονὸς· εἰσῆλθεν· ἀπεκρίθη ὁ πέτρος εἰπέ μοι εἰ τοσούτου τὸ χωρίον ἀπέδοσθε· ἡ δὲ εἶπεν· ναὶ τοσούτου· ὁ δὲ πέτρος εἶπε πρὸς αὐτήν· τί ὅτι συνεφωνήθη ὑμῖν· πειράσαι τὸ πν(ευμ)α κ(υρίο)υ· ἰδοὺ οἱ πόδες τῶν θαψάντων τὸν ἄνδρα σου ἐπὶ τῇ θύρα. καὶ ἐξοίσουσί σε· ἔπεσε*

44

Plate from fol. 62v. Parts of odes 3 and 6 of canon for *ὄρθρος* on 18 Oct., ed. in *Μηναῖα* (Rome, 1888-1901), I. 456, 458, and of another ode ed. in *Gli inni sacri di S. Bartolomeo juniore,* ed. G. Giovanelli (Innografi italogreci 3, Grottaferrata, 1955) p. 44. *οὗ τὸ εὐαγγέλιον· λουκᾶ θεσπέσιε ἂν ... ἐπισκεψαμένην· τοὺς ἀν(θρωπ)ους παρίστ ... ράξεις ἐνθεώτατα· διαπραττώμενος ... σεβῶς· τὰς τῶν ἀποστόλων· γραφικῶ ... αὖλος ὁ μακάριος· τῶν ἐγκωμίων σοιὲ ... παρχὰς· καὶ τοὺς σοὺς ἐπαίνους· ἐ ... ἐ νῦν μακαρίζομεν· ὡς προεφήτ ... αἱ γενεαὶ· πᾶσαι τῶν ἀν(θρωπ)ων· καὶ δια ... Καθ[ισμα] ηχ[ος] πλ[αγιος] α̅ πρ[ος το] τὸν συνάναρχον ... ἧς σοφίας τὸν μέγαν ἱεροφάντορα· ... εὐθέτως καλλιγραφήσαντα· τὸν ἀπόστ ... ἄσωμεν· ὅτι ἐκήρυξεν ἡμῖν· ... τοῦ· ἀκέστωρ μέγας δὲ ὤφθη· ψυχῶν ὁμ ... των· τῇ χειρουργία. δια τῆς χάριτος ... ἄλλ(ον) ηχ[ος] δ̅ πρ[ος το] ἐπεφάνης σήμερον ... αθητὴς γενόμενος· τοῦ θείου λόγου· σ ... ἅπασαν· ἐφωταγώγησας τὴν γῆν ... πεδίωξας· τὸ θεῖον γράψας θ(εο)υ εὐαγγέλ*

45

Plate from fol. 195r. Chrysostom. Letter 2, ed. *PG* 52 561 23-31. *ἐξετάσειεν· ὅτι ἐν ἀώρ(ω) ἡλικία ταῦτα κατορθοῦτο· καὶ τὴν ἐρημί(αν) τῶν διδαξό(ν)των· καὶ τὸ πλῆθος τῶν σκανδαλϊζόντων· καὶ ὅτι ἐν ψυχῇ ἐξ ἀσεβοῦς οἴκου νῦν αὐτομολ(αί)σαση πρὸς τὴν ἀλήθειαν· καὶ ὅτι ἐν σώματι γυναικείω τε (καὶ) ἄλλως ἀπολῶ διὰ τὴν τῶν προγόνων περιφανεί(αν) καὶ τὴν τρυφὴν, πόσα πελάγει θαυμάτων εὑρήσει καθ' ἕκαστον τούτων ἀνοιγόμενα· διά τοι τ(οῦ)το, ἄλλων οὐδὲ ἐπιμνησθήσομαι· τῆς ταπεινοφρούνης· τῆς ἀγάπ(ης) τῶν λοιπῶν ἀρετῶν·*

46

Plate from Lake, pl. 645 (fol. no. unknown). On baptism, ed. *PG* 31 1580 B. 5-12. *νατον· ἵν' ὥσπερ ἠγέρθη ... ἐκ νεκρῶν διὰ τῆς δόξης ... π(ατ)ρ(ὸ)ς, οὕτω καὶ ἡμεῖς ἐν κ ... νότητι ζωῆς περιπατ ... μεν, (καὶ) τὰ ἑξῆς· καὶ ἐν ... ρω τόπῳ ἐντρεπτικώτερ ... καὶ σαφέστερον ἡμῖν παρ ... δωσι τοιοῦτον δόγμα, εἰπ ... ὅσοι εἰς χ(ριστὸ)ν ἐβαπτίσθητε χ ... ἐνεδύσασθε· οὐκ ἔνι ἰου ... ος οὐδὲ ἕλλην· οὐκ ἔνι δο ... οὐδὲ ἐλεύθερος· οὐκ ἔνι ... σεν καὶ θῆλυ· πάντες γὰ*

47

Plate from fol. 238^{r}. Synopsis Basilicorum major P.I. 5-11, ed. in *Jus Graecoromanum*, ed. J. and P. Zepos (Athens, 1931) V. 495-6. *μέγϊστον τῆς θαλάσσης ἐκτρέχει κῦμα· τὸ αὐτὸ καὶ ἐπὶ λίμνης· εἰ μὴ ἄρα πᾶσα ἰδιωτϊκή ἐστϊ· ἐν δὲ τῷ σλ͞γ κε[φαλαίῳ] ἀκοντϊον λέγεται οὐ μόνον τὸ ἀπὸ* **τόξου, ἀλλὰ καὶ τὸ ὁπωσοῦν βαλλόμενον· ἐν δὲ τῶι σλ͞δ κε[φαλαίῳ] τῶι ὀνόματϊ τῆς βαλάνου, πάντες οἱ καρποὶ** *δηλοῦνται· ἐπεὶ καὶ τῷ ὀνόματϊ τῶν ἀκροδρύων, πάντα* **τὰ δένδρα· ἐν δὲ τῷ σμ͞α κε[φαλαίῳ] ἀκάρδιος καὶ ἄνυσσος λέγεται, ὁ μὴ ἔχων καρδίαν ἢ ὑγείαν· ἐν δὲ τῷ ϟε͞ κε[φαλαίῳ] ἀναδοῦναι, καὶ τὴν δόσϊν λαβεῖν· ἐν δὲ τῷ ρλ͞γ κε[φαλαίῳ] οὐ λέγεται γεννῆσαι ἢ μετὰ τὸ θανεῖν ἀνατμηθεῖσα· ἐν δὲ τῷ**

48

Plate from fol. 130^{v}. Commentary on Luke 10: 29-37, ed. *PG* 123 849 C.1 - D.3. *οἷον τί λέγω· ὁ κ(ύριο)ς τὰ μ(ὲν), ἀν(θρωπ)ίνως ἐνήργει· τὰ δέ, θεϊκ(ῶς)· τὸ μ(ὲν) γ(ὰρ) ἐσθί(ειν) καὶ πίν(ειν) κ(αὶ) τ(ὸν) ἄνετον βί(ον) μεταδιώκ(ειν) ἀλλ' οὐχὶ σκληραγωγί(αν) ἐνδείκνυσθαι ὥσπερ ὁ ἰω[άννης], τοῦτο ἐστὶ τὸ ἔλαι(ον)· ἡ δὲ ξένη νηστεία· ὁ ἐν θαλάσσῃ περίπατ(ος)· καὶ ὅσα ἄλλα τ(ῆς) θεί(ας)* **δυνάμε(ως), ταῦτα (ἔστιν) ὁ οἶν(ος)· οἴνῳ γ(ὰρ) ἀπεικαστέ(ον) τ(ὴν) θεότητα· ἣν ἄκρατ(ον) ὑπενεγκ(εῖν) οὐδεὶς ἂν ἠδυνήθη, εἰ μὴ καὶ τὸ ἔλαι(ον) ἦν· τουτέστιν, ἡ κ[α]τὰ ἀν(θρωπ)ον δϊαγωγή· ἐπεὶ οὖν δϊ' ἀμφοτέρ(ων) ἔσωσ(εν) ἡμ(ᾶς), θεότητός φημϊ καὶ ἀνθρωπότητ(ος), δια τοῦτο λέγεται οἶν(ον) καὶ ἔλαι(ον) ἐπϊχέαι· καὶ καθ ἑκάστ(ην) (δὲ) οἱ βαπτϊζόμ[εν]οι τ(ῶν) τραυμ[ά]τ(ων) ἀπαλλάττονται, ἐλαίῳ μ(ὲν) τ(οῦ) μύρου χριόμ[εν]οι· εὐθὺς δὲ κοινωνοῦντ(ες), καὶ τ(οῦ) θείου αἵμ[α]τ(ος) μεταλαμβάνοντ(ες)· ἀνεβίβασε δὲ ὁ κ(ύριο)ς τ(ὴν) τραυμ[α]τϊσθεῖσ(αν) ἡμ(ῶν) φύσ(ιν), ἐπὶ τὸ ἴδϊ(ον) ὑποζύγϊον·**

49

Plate from fol. 158^{r}. *Topica* VIII. 1.155 b 6-18. *πρὸς ἑαυτὸν· τὸ δὲ λοιπὸν καὶ τρίτον, εἰπεῖν ταῦτα ἤδη πρὸς ἕτερο(ν)· μέχρι μὲν οὖν τοῦ εὑρεῖν τὸν τόπον, ὁμοίως τοῦ φιλοσόφου καὶ τοῦ διαλεκτικοῦ ἡ σκέψις· τὸ δ' ἤδη ταῦτα τάττειν καὶ ἐρωτηματίζειν, ἴδιον τοῦ διαλεκτικοῦ· πρὸς ἕτερον γὰρ πᾶν τὸ τοιοῦτον· τῶι δὲ φιλοσόφωι καὶ ζητοῦντι καθ' ἑαυτὸν, οὐδὲν μέλλει ἐὰν ἀληθῆ μὲν ἦι καὶ γνώριμα δι' ὧν ὁ συλλογισμ(ός). μὴ θῆι δὲ αὐτὰ ἀποκρινόμενος διὰ τὸ σύνεγγυς εἶναι τοῦ ἐξ ἀρχῆς, καὶ προορᾶν τὸ συμβησόμενον· ἀλλ' ἴσως ἂν σπουδάσειεν ὅτι μάλιστα γνώριμα, καὶ σύνεγγυς εἶναι τὰ ἀξιώματα. ἐκ τούτων γὰρ οἱ ἐπιστημονικοὶ συλλογισμοί· τοὺς μὲν οὖν τόπους ὅθεν δεῖ λαμβάνειν, εἴρηται πρότερον· περὶ τάξε*

50

Plate from fol. 143^{r}. Commentary on Zechariah 8: 1-6, ed. *PG* 81 1912 B. 14-C. 10. *καὶ τὸ ὄρος κ(υρίο)υ παντοκράτορος. ὄρος ἅγιον· ταῦτα Τυπικῶς μετὰ τὴν τοῦ ζοροβάβελ οἰκοδομίαν ἐγένετο· τὴν δὲ ἀλήθειαν τῆς προφητείας. μετὰ τὴν τοῦ σ(ωτη)ρ(ο)ς ἡμῶν ἐνανθρώπησιν δι' ἔγνωσαν ἅπαντες· πρὸς τούτοις. ὑπισχνεῖται καὶ πλῆθος οἰκητόρων παρέξειν τῇ πόλει· καὶ εἰς γῆρας αὐτοὺς ἐλάσειν βαθὺ, ὥστε καὶ βακτηρίαις σκηριπτομένους κατὰ τὴν ἀγορὰν ἰέναι· καὶ ἐν τοῖς συνήθεσι συλλόγοις καθῆσθ(αι)· καὶ μειρακίων παιζόντων πληροῦσθαι τὰς ἀγυιάς. ὅπερ ἐν ταῖς πολυανθρώποις εἴωθε γίνεσθαι πό*

51

Plate from Holy Cross 43, fol. 103^{v}. Hebrews 2: 11-14. *δελφοὶ· ὁ ἁγιάζων καὶ οἱ ἁγιαζόμενοι· ἐξ ἑνὸς πάντες· δι' ἣν αἰτίαν οὐκ ἐπαισχύνεται· ἀδελφοὺς αὐτοὺς καλεῖν λέγων· ἀπαγγελῶ τὸ ὄνομά σου τοῖς ἀδελφοῖς μου· ἐν μέσῳ ἐκκλησίας ὑμνήσω σε· καὶ πάλιν· ἐγὼ ἔσομαι πεποιθὼς επ'αυτῶ· καὶ πάλιν· ἰδοὺ ἐγὼ καὶ τὰ παιδεία ἅ μοι ἔδωκεν ὁ θ(εό)ς· ἐπεὶ οὖν τὰ παιδία κεκοινώνηκε σαρκὸς καὶ αἵματος· καὶ*

52

Plate from fol. 75^{r}. Life by Nicephoros Ouranos (*BHG* 1690), ed. *PG*. 86 3108 A. 10 - B. 2. *χ(ριστ)ε βασιλεῦ χρηστότητος, εὑρίσκει τοῦτον, σίτου σαφ(ῶς) ὑποπεπλησμένον· καρπῶν ἀμόχθων ὄντως καὶ ἀσπόρων καὶ ἀνηρότων· μόνης εὐχῆς γεωργίων, (καὶ) τῆς ἐντεῦθεν πιότητος· ἔργον χειρὸς ἀκριβῶς ἐκείνης, ἧς τὸ κατὰ τοὺς ἄρτους θαῦμα· καὶ ἡ ἐν ἐρήμῳ τράπεζα· τό,τε ἐξ οὐ(ρα)νου μάννα· καὶ ἡ ἀπὸ στερεᾶς πέτρας οὐχ ὕδατος μόνον, ἀλλὰ καὶ αὐτοῦ*

53

Plate from Lake, pl. 160 (fol. no. unknown). Homily 86 on John, ed. *PG* 59 473. 3 - 474 5. *καὶ τοὺς ἱερέας αὐτοῦ ἐντίμως ἔχωμεν, πᾶσαν αὐτοῖς ἀπονέμοντες τιμήν· ἵνα καὶ ὑπὲρ τῶν οἰκείων κατορθωμάτων· καὶ ὑπὲρ τῆς εἰς ἐκείνους θεραπείας, πολλὴν λάβωμεν παρὰ τοῦ θ(εο)υ τὴν ἀμοιβήν· χάριτι καὶ φιλαν(θρωπ)ια τοῦ κ(υριο)υ ἡμῶν ι(ησο)υ χ(ριστο)υ· μεθ' οὗ τῷ π(ατ)ρι ἅμα τῷ ἁγίῳ πν(ευματ)ι, δόξα κράτος τιμή· νῦν καὶ ἀεὶ καὶ εἰς τοὺς αἰῶνας τῶν αἰώνων·*

54

Plate from fol. 61^{v}. Questions and answers no. 10 (end), ed. *PG*. 89 436 A. 2-13. *λέγει ῥήματα· ἀπολαύσω τῶν ... τέως, καὶ τότε σκέψομαι περ ... δίδου μοι τὴν σήμερον. καὶ ... ριον· καὶ τί τράγων ἢ χοίρων οἱ ... τες διαφέρουσιν: τοῦ αὐτοῦ ἐκ τῆς τῶν πρά ... Οἱ πολλὰ πταίοντες καὶ μὴ κο ... φοβεῖσθαι πολλὰ καὶ τρέμει ... αὔξεται γὰρ αὐτοῖς τὰ τῆς τιμ ... διὰ τῆς ἀτιμωρισίας καὶ μα ... τοῦ θ(εο)υ· καὶ γὰρ ὅσω ἂν ὦμεν ... νοι μεγάλα, τοσοῦτο μᾶλλον κο ... μειζόνως· ὅτἂν ἀνάξιοι τῆς ... φανῶμεν:*

55

Plate from fol. 241^{r}. Anonymous work *περὶ τῶν ἁγίων καὶ οἰκουμενικῶν ἐξ συνόδων* (*BHG* 2341 b). *ὃν καθελοῦσα ἀνεθεμάτισε. σὺν τοῖς ὁμόφροσιν αὐτοῦ· τό(ν) δὲ υἱὸν ὁμοούσιον καὶ συνάναρχον τῷ π(ατ)ρὶ. καὶ θ(εὸ)ν ἀληθινό(ν) καὶ κτίστην πάντω(ν). ὀρθοδόξως ἐδογμάτισεν· ἐτύπωσε δὲ καὶ τὸ ἅγιον πάσχα ἑορτάζειν ἡμᾶς κατὰ τὴν* **κρατοῦσα(ν) συνήθειαν· δευτέρα [Σ]ύνοδος γέγονεν ἐν** *κωνσταντινουπόλει.*

56

Plate from fol. 5r. Commentary on Matthew, preface, ed. *PG* 123 145 A. 9 - B. 1, 6-9 *τῶν ἀποκτενόντων τὸ σῶμα, τὴν δὲ ψυχὴν μὴ δυναμένων ἀποκτεῖναι· τὴν δὲ φρόνησϊν, ὅταν παραινῆ· γίνεσθε φρόνιμοι ὡσεὶ ὄφεις, καὶ ἀκέραιοι ὡς αἱ περιστεραί· τὴν ((δὲ)*added) *δικαιοσύνην, ὅταν διδάσκῃ· καθὼς θέλετε ἵνα ποιῶσιν ὑμῖν οἱ ἄν(θρωπ)οι, καὶ ὑμεῖς ποιεῖτε αὐτοῖς· ὁμοίως δὲ τὴν σωφροσύνην, ὅταν ἀποφαίνηται, ὁ ἐμβλέψας γυναῖκι* (corr. to *κα) πρὸς τὸ ἐπιθυμῆσαι αὐτῆς, ἤδη ἐμοίχευσ(εν) αὐτὴν ἐν τῇ καρδίᾳ αὐτοῦ: - [Κ]αὶ ἄλλως δέ εἰσι τέσσαρα* (*εἰσὶ* added) *τὰ εὐαγγέλϊα· ὡς ἂν δηλώσῃ, ὅτι τέσσαρα ταῦτα περιέχῃ· δόγματα· ἐντολάς· ἀπειλὰς, καὶ ἐπαγγελί(ας)· καὶ τοῖς μὲν πιστεύσασϊ τοῖς δόγ*

57

Plate from fol. 463r. Nonnus abbas, commentary on Oration 39, ed. *PG* 36 1065 C. 6 - D.3 *κτύπον τινὰ ἐν ταῖς ἀσπῖσιν ἐποίουν οὗτοι, πρ(ὸς) τὸ ὑπερηχ ... τὸν κλαυθμὸν τοῦ παιδίου· κρητ(ῶν) δὲ τυράννου εἶπεν· ὅτι οἱ ... θεολόγοι τ(ῶν) ἑλλήνων, θεὸν λέγουσι γενέσθ(αι), καὶ τ(ὸν) κρόνον (καὶ) τὸν ... ἡ δὲ ἱστορία ἡ δημώδης· ἦν καὶ τίθεται ὁ θεῖος γρηγόριος, λέγ ... ὅτι ὁ ζεὺς οὗτ(ος), τύραννος ἦν κρήτης· καὶ θέλοντες αὐτ(ὸν) θερα ... οἱ ὑπήκοοι. ἐμυθολόγουν, ὡς ἐκ κρόνου θεοῦ καὶ ῥέας ἔχειν ... γέννησιν· ἐπεὶ ἄν(θρωπ)ος ἦν. διὸ ἐπήγαγε. κὰν ἕλληνες ἀπαρέσκω ... οἱ γὰρ ἕλληνες, οὐ θέλουσιν αὐτὸν εἶναι ἄν(θρωπ)ον καὶ τύραννον κρητ*

58

Plate from fol. 58v. Oration 24, ed. *PG* 35 1188 B. 15 - C. 4, D. 3 - 1189 A. 4. *Καταφρονεῖν μὲν ξιφῶ(ν) ἀνέπειθε· ψυχρὸν δὲ νομίζειν τὸ πῦρ· ἡμέρους δὲ οἴεσθαι, θηρ(ῶν) τοὺς ἀγριωτάτους· λιμὸν δὲ ὑπολαμβάν(ειν), τὴν ἀνωτάτω τρυφή(ν)· δάκρυα δὲ τῶν οἰκεί ... μισθὸν τούτων κομίζετ(αι), ὡς δαψιλῆ καὶ φιλότιμον. μάρτυς ἐπὶ πᾶσι(ν) οἷς προέπεμψε γίνεται· ξίφει τὴν κεφαλὴν τμηθείς· καὶ ταῖς πολλαῖς βασάνοις, ταύτην ἐπιτίθησι κορω*

59

Plate from fol. 240v. Part of prayer for Pentecost vespers, ed. *Πεντεκοστάριον* (Rome, 1883), pp. 411-12. *ἁμαρτωλοῦ τὰ χείλη· καὶ δίδαξόν με πῶς δεῖ καὶ ὑπὲρ ὧν χρὴ προσεύχεσθαι· σὺ γὰρ εἶ ὁ γϊνώσκων τὸ πολὺ τῶν ἁμαρτιῶν μου πλῆθος· ἀλλ' ἡ σὴ εὐσπλαγχνία, νϊκήσει τούτων τὸ ἄμετρον· ἰδοὺ γὰρ φόβω παρίσταμαί σοι· εἰς τὸ πέλαγος τοῦ ἐλέους σου, τὴν ἀπόγνωσιν ἐπιρρίψας*

60

Plate from fol. 35v. Homily 12, ed. *PG* 31 400 A. 14-B.5 *σοφϊσματώδεις καὶ ἀπατηλοὶ. τῖνες δὲ οἱ περῒ τῶν κατὰ τὸν βῖον πρακτέων τὰ βέλτϊστα ἡμῖν ϋποτϊθέμενοι· καὶ ὡς δοκϊμος τραπεζῖτης. τὸ μὲν δοκϊμον καθέξει. ἀπὸ δὲ παντὸς εἴδους πονηροῦ ἀφέξεται· αὕτη ἡ φρόνησΐς χαρῒζεται τῷ οἰκοδομοῦντϊ τὴν ἑαυτοῦ οἰκῖαν, τὸν θεμέλϊον αὐτοῦ*

61

Plate from fol. 289r. *Topica* II.4.111 a 22-31. *φαύλη καὶ σπουδαία· ἡ γὰρ διάθεσις τῆς ἐπιστήμης γένος· ὁ μὲν οὖν πρότερος τόπος ψευδής ἐστι πρὸς τὸ κατασκευάσαι· ὁ δὲ δεύτερος ἀληθής· οὐ γὰρ ἀναγκαῖον ὅσα τῶι γένει ὑπάρχει καὶ τῶι εἴδει ὑπάρχειν· ζῶιον μὲν γάρ ἐστι πτηνὸν καὶ τετράπουν· ἄν(θρωπ)ος δ' οὔ· ὅσα δὲ τῶι εἴδει ὑπάρχει, ἀναγκαῖον καὶ τῶι γένει· εἰ γάρ ἐστιν ἄνθρωπος σπουδαῖος. καὶ ζῶιον ἐστὶ σπουδαῖον· πρὸς δὲ τὸ ἀνασκευάζειν ὁ μὲν πρότερος ἀληθής· ὁ δὲ ὕστερος ψευδής· ὅσα γὰρ τῶι γένει οὐχ' ὑπάρχει, οὐδὲ τῶι εἴδει· ὅσα δὲ τῶι εἴδει μὴ ὑπάρχηι, οὐκ ἀνάγκη*

62

Plate from fol. 171r. Luke 3: 4-5, 7 *βοῶντος ἐν τῇ ἐρήμω ἑτοιμάσατε· τὴν ὁδὸν κ(υριο)υ· εὐθείας ποιεῖτε· τὰς τρίβους αὐτοῦ πᾶσα φάραξ· ... ὄχλοις· βαπ ... σθῆναι ὑπ' ἀ ... γεννήματα ... δνῶν· τίς ὑπ ... δειξεν ὑμῖν φ ... ἀπὸ τῆς μελλ ... σης ὀργῆς*

63

Plate from fol. 31v. 'Constantinopolitan' creed, ed. E. Schwartz in *Acta Conciliorum Oecumenicorum*, II: *Concilium universale Chalcedonense*, I.2 (Berlin, 1933), Actio V, §33, p. 128 [324], lines 10-12. *τὸ ἅγιον τὸ κύριον καὶ ζωοποιὸν. τὸ ἐκ τοῦ π(ατ)ρ(ο)ς ἐκπορευόμενον. τὸ σὺν π(ατ)ρι καὶ ὑιῶ συμπροσκυνούμενον καὶ συνδοξαζόμενον*

64

Plate from fol. 101r. Stichera idiomela for 9 Mar., ed. *Μηναῖα* (Rome, 1888-1901), IV. 58. *αγιαζων και φωτιζων τας ψυχας ημων: - ἦχ(ος) β̄'' Αληθειας κρατηρα· εξ οικειων αιματων· τω πυρι των βασανων· τη του υδατος πιξει τοις πιστοις κατηρδευσαν· τετραριθμω γαρ αδαντες δεκαδι τω σωτηρι· εις μεν ουν τοις απασιν· εν σωμασι δε πλειους προσηνεχθησαν χριστω· και θεονυμφος μητηρ·*

65

Plate from fol. 84v. Matthew 19: 3,5. *σαίοι τῶ ι(ησο)υ πειράζοντες αὐτὸν καὶ λέγοντες αὐτῶ εἰ ἔξεστιν ἀν(θρωπ)ω ἀπολύ ... τὰ λήψει αν(θρωπ)ος τὸν π(ατε)ρα αὐτοῦ καὶ τὴν μ(ητε)ρα· καὶ προσκολληθήσεται τῇ γυναι*

66

Plate from fol. 47v. Kontakion for 8 Sept. ed. *Μηναῖα* (Rome, 1888-1901), I.99. *ααααατων λυτρωθηηηηναι τουουου κρααααεζειειειν σοιοιιι η στειρα· τιιικτει την θεοτοοοοοοοοοοκοον (και) τροφω.*

67

Plate from fol. 112r. Part of ode 6 for 18 Nov. ed. *Μηναῖα* (Rome, 1888-1901), II.189. *Τῶ τῆς ψυχῆς νοερῶ· τῇ εὐπρεπεία τοῦ κτήσαντος· ἐνατενίζων ἀεὶ· καὶ κατοπτριζόμενος· τὸ κάλλος τὸ ἄρρητον· τῆς τῶν ὁρωμένων· εὐτελείας κατεφρόνησας: — Ὡς ἔμψυχος κιβωτὸς. τὸν νομοδότην ἐχώρησας· ὡς ἅγιος δὲ ναὸς· ἐδέξω τὸν ἅγιον· γενόμενον ἄν(θρωπ)ον· ἐπ' εὐεργεσία· τῶν ἀν(θρώπ)ων*

68

Plate from fol. 67r Proverbs 31: 24-8. *ἀπέδω τῆς φύνηξιν· περιζώματα δὲ τοῖς χαναναίοις· ἴσχὺν (καὶ) εὐπρέπειαν ἐνεδύσατο· (καὶ) ηὐφράνθη ἐν ημέραις ἐσχάταις· στόμα δὲ αὐτῆς διήνοιξεν προσεχόντως· (καὶ) τάξιν ἐστείλατο τῇ γλώσσῃ αὐτῆς· στεναὶ διατριβαὶ οἴκων αὐτῆς· σίτα δὲ ὀκνιρὰ οὐκ ἔφαγεν· στόμα δὲ αὐτῆς, ἀνοίγει σοφῶς (καὶ) νόμοθέμ(ως)· ἡ δὲ ἐλεημοσύνη αὐτῆς, ἀνέστησεν τὰ τέκνα αὐτῆς,*

69

Plate from fol. 104r. Part of ode 9 for 23 Nov., ed. *Μηναῖα* (Rome, 1888-1901), II. 259. *νως ἰάσεις πηγάζουσα· προσέλθωμ(εν) βρύει γὰρ ἡμῖν· ἡ γρηγορίου θήκη· φωτισμ(ὸν) ἀένναον· καὶ ἀθανασίαν: — Ὡς ποταμὸς πεπλήρωσαι· τῶν ναμάτων τοῦ χ(ριστο)ῦ· ὡς ἐλαία· ἔλαιον πηγάζεις ζωῆς· ὡς φοῖνιξ ὑψώθης γρηγόριε· ὡς ἄμπελος βότρυας ἡμῖν· τῶν ἀρετῶν σου φέρεις· ἐξ ὧν ποτιζόμεθα· οἶνον ἀφθαρσίας:-*

70

Plate from fol. 16r. Matthew 5: 29-30. *σκανδαλίζει σε, ἔξελε αὐτὸν καὶ βάλε ἀπὸ σοῦ· συμφέρει γάρ σοι ἵνα ἀπόληται ἓν τῶν μελῶν σου. καὶ μὴ ὅλον τὸ σῶμα σου βληθῇ εἰς γέενναν· καὶ εἰ ἡ δεξιά σου χεὶρ σκανΔαλίζει σε, ἔκκοψον αὐτὴν. καὶ βάλε ἀπὸ σοῦ· συμφέρει γάρ σοι ἵνα ἀπόληται ἓν τῶν μελῶν σου. καὶ*

71

Plate from fol. 113r. *Bis accusatus* 23 (822), ed. C. Jacobitz (Leipzig, 1896-7), III, p. 18, lines 5-11. *τὼ δεῖνα μέντοι μὴ λαμβανέτωσαν οὗτοι τὸ δικαστικὸν αδίκαστος γὰρ ἡ δίκη μεμένηκεν αὐτοῖς: μάτην οὖν ανεληλυθότες ὦσι γέρ(ον)τες ἄνδρες οὕτω μ(α)κρὰν τὴν ἀνάβασιν ἱκανὸν εἰ τριτημόριον λάβοιεν· ἄπιτε μὴ ἀγανακῆτε αὖθις δικάσετε:*

72

Plate from fol. 22v. Scholion on Oration 44, ch. 4 *γενόμ[εν](ος) φη[σιν] ἄν(θρωπ)ος ὁ θ(εο)ς. ἀλλ οὐ καθὸ θ(εο)ς πάσχει· τῶ ἡμετέρω (δὲ). ἤτοι τ(ῶ) ἀν(θρωπ)ω ἢ τ(ῶ) ἀν(θρωπ)ίνω πάθει ἀν(θρωπ)ινον φη[σιν] (ὅτι) τὸ οὕτ(ω) πάσχ(ειν)· γενόμ[εν](ος) οὖν ἄν(θρωπ)ος. πάθει ἀν(θρωπ)ίνω πάσχει· ἐπειδὴ (δὲ) θεοϋπόστατ(ος) ἄν-(θρωπ)ος. ἀλλ' οὐχ ἁπλ(ῶς) ἄν(θρωπ)ος. θ(εο)υ (καὶ) τὸ πάθ(ος)· ἀπαθ(ῶς) αὐτ(οῦ) εἰς ἑαυτ(ὸν) ἀναδεχομ[έ-ν](ου) (καὶ) οἰκειουμ[έν](ου) τὸ πάθ(ος). κατὰ τὸν πολ-λάκις ῥηθέντα τρόπον τῆς ἀντιδόσεως:-*

73

Plate shows fol. 35r. Nonnus abbas, Commentary on Oratio 1, ed. *PG* 36 1020 D. 11 - 1021 B.6. *δέδωκε δὲ καὶ ποιμέσι πιεῖν· οἱ δε ποιμέν(ες) μεθυσθέντ(ες) δ(ια) τὸ ἐκ π(αρα)δόξ(ου) πρῶτον πιεῖν οἶν(ον)· νομίσ(αν)τ(ες) φαρμαχθῆν(αι) π(αρα) τοῦ ἰκαρίου, ἀποκτείν(ου)σιν αὐτ(όν)· ἡ δε ἠριγόνη ἡ τούτου θυγάτηρ δ(ια) τ(ῆς) κυν(ὸς) τ(οῦ) ἰκάρ(ου) γνοῦσα ὅτι ἐποτνιάτο καὶ ἦσχαλ-λ(εν). καὶ καθὼς μυθεύουσιν οἱ πλαν(ώ)μ[εν]οι ἕλλη-ν(ες). ταύτ(ην) ἐλεήσαντ(ες) φη[σιν] οἱ θεοὶ δ(ια) τὸ πάθ(ος), μετέθηκαν αὐτ(ὴν) εἰς τ(ὸν) οὐ(ρα)νόν· (καὶ) νῦν (εστιν) ἐν τ(οῖς) ἄστρ(οις) ἡ ἠριγόνη. τὸ (δὲ) λέγειν μυστήρι(ον) ἡμῖν ἐποίησ(εν) αἰσχρὸν· ταῦτα οὐ πε(ρι) τοῦ ἰκαρίου λέγει ἀλλὰ πε(ρι) τ(ῆς) κατὰ τ(ὴν) δημήτραν μυθολογίας λέγετ(αι) (δὲ) αὕτη οὐ μόν(ον) δεδωκέν(αι) αὐτοῖς τὰ σπέρματα, ἀλλα καὶ θεσμ(όν) τινα μυστηρίων ἐδίδαξ(εν). ἅτινα τελοῦντ(αι) παρ ἕλλησιν· ὡς γ(ὰρ) π(αρα) τοῖς θεοδιδάκτ(οις) χριστιανοῖς (εστι) τὸ ἁγίον φώτισμα, οὕτω παρ εκείνοις ἡ τοιαύτη ἑορτή· λέγετ(αι) μ(ὲν) (οὖν) μυστήρια. καλοῦντ(αι) (δὲ) καὶ δημήτρια: — ἡ κατ[α] τὸ θρησκεύειν καὶ μυεῖσθ(αι): — Λέγετ(αι) ὁ ὀρφεὺς θρᾶξ ὢν τὸ γένος καὶ θεολογήσ(ας) τὰ ἑλλήν(ων) μυστήρια. ἐδίδαξ(εν) πῶς τε (καὶ) δεῖ τιμᾶν τ(οὺς) θεούς· τοῦτο (οὖν) τὸ τιμᾶν θεοὺς ἐκάλεσ(εν) θρησκεύειν· ὡς θρακίας οὔσ(ης) τ(ῆς) εὑρέσε(ως). ἄλλοι (δὲ) ἠιτυμολόγησ(αν) ὅτι τὸ θρησκεύειν ἀπὸ τοῦ οἱονεὶ*

74

Plate from fol. 254v. Beginning of *λόγος ιθ* as in Vat. gr 694, fol. 138v-143r. *κ(υριο)ς ἡμῶν ι(ησου)ς χ(ριστο)ς προσευ ... τοὺς ἑαυτοῦ μαθητὰς ... λεσάντων αὐτὸν διδά ... προσεύχεσθαι· οὕτως ... λέγεται π(ατ)ερ ἡμῶν ὁ ἐν ... ἁγιασθήτω τὸ ὄνομά ... ἡ βασιλεῖα σου· γενη ... λημα σου· ὡς ἐν οὐ(ρα)ν ... γῆς· τὸν ἄρτον ἡμῶ ... σιον δὸς ἡμῖν σήμε ... φες ἡμῖν τὰ ὀφειλ ... τὴν εὐχὴν ταύτην ἐδί ... χεσθαι τοὺς ἀκμὴν ζ ... φεσιν ὀφλημάτων· ... δοῦλος δεσπότου ἄχε ... λὰ ἁμαρτίσας καὶ φυ ... δὲ πολλὺν χρόνον ἐπ ... πρὸς ἀποστέλλει τῶ ... τη ἀξιῶτας πρὸς τὸ κ ... αὐτῶ τὸν ἀγαθὸν δεσπ*

75

Plate from fol. 79r. Didache X. 2-7, ed. in *Die Apostolischen Väter*, ed. F.X. Funk and K.Bihlmeyer (Tübingen, 1956) I. 6. *ἧς ἐγνώρισ(ας) ἡμῖν διὰ ἰ(ησο)ῦ τοῦ π(αι)δ(ός) σου σοὶ ἡ δόξα εἰς τ[οὺς] αἰῶν(ας)· σὺ δέσποτ[α] παντοκράτορ ἔκτισ(ας) τὰ π(άν)τ(α) ἕνεκεν τοῦ ὀνόμα-τ(ός) σου· τροφήν τε καὶ ποτ(ὸν) ἔδωκ(ας) τ(οῖς) ἀν-(θρώπ)οις εἰς ἀπόλαυσ(ιν)· ἵνα σοι εὐχαριστήσωσιν· ἡμῖν (δὲ) ἐχαρίσω πν(ευματ)ικὴν τροφὴν (καὶ) ποτ(ὸν) (καὶ) ζωὴν αἰώνι(ον) διὰ τ(οῦ) π(αι)δ(ός) σου· πρὸ π(άν)τ(ων) εὐχαριστοῦμ(εν) σοι ὅτι δυνατ(ὸς) εἶ σὺ ἡ δόξα εἰς τ[οὺς] αἰῶν(ας)· μνήσθητι κ(υρι)ε τ(ῆ)ς ἐκ-κλη[σιας] σου τοῦ ῥύσασθ(αι) αὐτ(ὴν) ἀπὸ π(αν)τ(ὸς) πονηροῦ. (καὶ) τελει(ῶ)σ(αι) αὐτ(ὴν) ἐν τῆ ἀγάπη σου· (καὶ) σύναξ(ον) αὐτ(ὴν) ἀπὸ τ(ῶν) τεσσάρ(ων) ἀνέμ(ων)· τὴν ἁγιασθεῖσ(αν) εἰς τ(ὴν) σὴν βασιλείαν· ἣν ἡτοίμασ(ας) αὐτῆ· ὅτι σοῦ (ἐστιν) ἡ δύναμ(ις) καὶ ἡ δόξα εἰς τ[οὺς] αἰῶν(ας)· ἐλθέτω χάρ(ις). (καὶ) παρελ-θέτω ὁ κόσμ(ος) οὗτ(ος)· (ὡς)ἀννὰ τ(ῶ) θ(ε)ῶ δα(υεί)δ· εἴ τις ἅγιος ἐστὶν ἐρχέσθω· εἴ τ(ις) οὐκ ἔστι μετανοείτω· μαραν αθά ἀμήν· τ(οῖς) (δὲ) προφήτ(αις) ἐπιτρέπετε εὐχαρι*

76

Plate from fol. 276v. Confession of faith resembling that in J.B. Pitra, *Iuris ecclesiastici Graecorum historia et monumenta* (Rome, 1864-8) II. 272 and 357 n.2. *ἕνα θ(εὸ)ν ὁμολογοῦμεν (καὶ) οὐχὶ τρ(εῖς)· οὐ γ(ὰρ) κεχ(α)ρισμ[έ-ν]οι εἰσ(ιν) ἀπ ἀλλήλ(ων)· ὥσπερ οἱ ἄν(θρωπ)οι. ἀλλ'ἅ-μ(α) π(ατ)ὴρ καὶ υἱὸς· καὶ ἅγι(ον) πν(ευμ)ᾶ. (καὶ) ἐν ἀλλήλοις ἀσυγχύτ(ως)· καὶ ἀδιαίρετ(ως)· περιχ(ω)ροῦσι· ἕκατ(ον) πρόσωπ[ον] φυλάττον τὸ ἴδιον· ὁ μ(ὲν) τὴν πατρότ[ητα]· ὁ (δὲ) τὴν υἱότ[ητα]· τὸ (δὲ) τ(ὴν) ἐκπόρευσ(ιν)· εἰ (οὖν) ἔροιτό σοι τ(ίς). τί (ἐστι) π(ατ)ὴρ. ἀποκρίθ[ητι] πρ(ὸς) αὐτ(ὸν). ὅπερ (ἐστὶ) υ(ἱὸ)ς κ(αὶ) τὸ πν(ευμ)ᾶ τὸ ἅγιον· μέν(ον) π(ατ)ήρ. εἰ (δὲ) λέγοι τί (ἐστι) υἱός, ἀπόκριν(αι)· ὅπερ ἐστὶν ὁ π(ατ)ὴρ καὶ τὸ πν(ευμ)ᾶ τὸ ἅγιον μέν(ων) υἱός· ὡσαύ-τ(ως) καὶ ἐπὶ τοῦ πν(ευμάτο)ς τοῦ ἁγίου· τοῦτο γ(άρ) ἐστιν ὁ π(ατ)ὴρ καὶ ὁ υἱὸς μένον πν(ευ)μᾶ· ἡ γ(ὰρ) ἰδιότ(ης) ἀκίνητ(ος)· π(ῶς) γ(ὰρ) ἂν ἰδιότ(ης) μείνη· κινουμ[έν]η (καὶ) μεταπίπτουσα· (ἐστίν) (οὖν) ἡ θεό-τ(ης) εἰ δεῖ συντόμ(ως) εἰπ(εῖν). ἀμέριστ(ος) ἐν μεμερισμ[έν](οις)· τὸ μ(ὲν) τῆ φύ[σει]· τὸ (δὲ) τ(αῖς) ὑποστάσεσιν· οἷον ἐν ἡλίοις τρισ(ὶν) ἐχομ[έν](οις) ἀλλήλων· μία τοῦ φωτ(ὸς) σύγκρασις· πλ(ὴν) κατὰ τ(ὸν) εἰπόντ[α] πίστ(ις) ἡγείσθω καὶ μὴ ἀπόδειξ(ις)· χρὴ (δὲ) πάντα ἄν(θρωπ)ον διὰ καθαρ(ὰς) κ(αὶ) θεολαμπ(οῦς) πρ(ά)ξεως ὁδηγ(ῶν) τῶ πν(ευματ)ί χρ(ώ)μ[εν](ον). ἵνα φωτὶ καταλαμβάν[ο]ντ[α] φῶς πιστεύ(ειν) εἰλικριν(ως)· εἰς π(ατέ)ρα*

77

Plate from fol. 135^{v}. Commentary on *Odyssey* IX. 34 and 19, ed. Rom. § 1613, ed. Leipzig (1825), p.319, line 42 - p.320, line 10. πόπλ(ουν) ἔπαθε: ση[μείωσαι] (δὲ) κἀνταῦθα συνήθ(ως) τὸ ποιητ[ικ](ὸν) διήγημα, ἐξ ὑπαρ[κ]τ[ικ]οῦ ἀρξάμ[εν](ον) ῥήμ[α]τ(ος) τοῦ, εἰ ... πασε τοὺς φαίακ(ας) ὁ ξεῖν(ος) εἰς ἑαυτ(όν)· ἔχοντ(ες) γ(ὰρ) ἤδη ἐκ τοῦ δημοδόκου τὸ τοῦ ὀδυσσέ(ως) ὄνομα ... ἤειδε, γῖ[νον]τ(αι) ὅλοι τ(ῆς) τούτου ξενῖ(ας). (καὶ) νῦν μ(ὲν), ἡδέ(ως) αὐτοῦ ἀκροάσοντ[αι] ὕστερ(ον) δὲ, (καὶ) πλείω δῶρα ... πιθήσουσϊ· (καὶ) μάλιστα, ὅτϊ θαρρήσ(ας), εἶπε τὸ, κλέ(ος) αὐτῶ οὐ(ρα)νῖον εἶναι: ἰστε(όν) (δὲ) (ὅτι) τοῦ εἰμῖ τουτέστ(ιν) ... κοινοτ[έ]ρ(ον); ἡρακλείδ(ης) λέ[γ]ει περῖ αὐτοῦ ὡς ἔνϊοι τῶν αἰολ[ικ](ῶν) μετατϊθέντ(ες) ἐν πρώτη (καὶ) δευτ[έ]ρα συζυ ... σϊ ῥήμ[α]τα εἰς μ̅ι̅ πλεονασμῶ τ(ῆς) μ̅ι̅ συλλα[β](ῆς) ἐπὶ τέλους· οὕτω φα[σὶ] (καὶ) ἀπὸ τοῦ φῶ, τὸ αἰολ[ικ](ὸν) φ ... νῖων, φῆμϊ γράφει βαρυτ[ό]ν(ως) αἰολϊκώτ[ε]ρ(ον)· οἶον φῆμϊ γ(ὰρ) οὖν κ[α]τανεῦσαι. οὐκοῦν (καὶ) ἀπὸ τοῦ ὦ ἤγου ... ἦμϊ· (καὶ) βοιωτ[ικ]ῆ μεταθέ[σ]ει τοῦ η̅ εἰς τ(ὴν) ε̅ι̅ δ[ί]φ[θογγ](ον), εἰμῖ· ἡμαρτημ[έν](ον) ὂν τῶ τόνω καθὰ ἑτέρωθϊ λέ[γ]ει ἁ ... βαρύνοντ[αι]· τοῦ δὲ τοιούτου βοιωτῖ ἦμϊ, τὸ δεύτ[ε]ρ(ον) εἶς· οἶον τ(ίς) ποθ(εν) εἶς ἀνδρ(ῶν). λέ[γ]ει δὲ ὁ αὐτ(ὸς),... τέλευτ(ον) ὂν τ(ῆς) πρώτ(ης) τ(ῶν) εἰς μ̅ι̅ μετατϊθέντ(ες) εἰς τ(ὴν) ε̅ι̅ δ[ί]φ[θογγ](ον), πολλάκ(ις) (καὶ) ἀναδϊπλοῦσ(ιν)· οἶον ... ὅσα τῶν εἰς μ̅ι̅ τῆ α̅ι̅ δ[ι]φ[θόγγ]ω π(αρα)λή[γον]τ[αι] οἶον τὸ γέλαιμϊ (καὶ) τὰ λοιπὰ, αἰολ[ικ]ὰ ὄντα, τ(ῆς) λεσβϊ(ων) ἔχοντ[αι]

78

Plate from fol. 134^{v}. Letter to Philip 78.6 - 80.3 (Steph. 97e - 98b). τὴν ἀλήθειαν· ἴσως δ' ὑπολαμβάν(εις) μικροψυχίαν εἶναι· τὸ τ(ῶν) βλασφημούντ(ων)· (καὶ) φλυαρούντ(ων)· (καὶ) τ(ῶν) πειθομέν(ων) τούτοις φροντῖζειν· ἄλλως θ'ὅταν (καὶ) μηδὲν σαυτῶ συνῖδης ἐξαμαρτάνων· χρὴ δὲ· μὴ καταφρονεῖν τοῦ πλήθους· μὴδὲ παρὰ μικρὸν ἡγεῖσθ(αι) τὸ παραπᾶσ(ιν) εὐδοκιμεῖν· ἀλλὰ τότε νομῖζειν καλὴν ἔχειν· (καὶ) μεγάλην τὴν δόξαν· καὶ πρέπουσαν. καὶ σοὶ· (καὶ) τοῖς προγόνοις. (καὶ) τοῖς ὑφ' ὑμῶν πεπραγμένοις, ὅτἂν οὕτω διαθῆς τοὺς ἕλληνας ὥσπερ ὁρᾶς λακεδαιμονίους τὲ πρὸς τοὺς ἑαυτ(ῶν) βασιλέας ἔχοντας· τούς τε ἑταίρους τοὺς σοὺς πρὸς σὲ διακειμένους· ἔστι δὲ

79

Plate from fol. of unknown number. *Scala* gradus 25, ed. *PG* 88 1000 D.5-1001 A.4. κτίσει. μϊκρὸν (καὶ) μέγα πῦρ θεάσασθαι τῆ φύσει· (καὶ) οὐκ ἔστιν ἐν τῆ ἀνοθεύτω ταπεινοφροσύνη. ὕλης εἶδ(ος) ἐνἀπομεῖναι τὸ σύνολον· ἕως οὗ ἑκουσίως πταίομεν. τοῦτο ἐν ἡμῖν οὐ πρόσἐστιν· (καὶ) τοῦτο τὸ σημεῖον τῆς παρουσίας αὐτοῦ γϊνώσκων ὁ δεσπότης. τῆ ἔξωθε διαγωγὴ συσχηματίζεσθαι τὴν τῆς ψυχῆς ἀρετὴ(ν). λαβὼν λέντιον, ὑπέδειξεν ἡμῖν μέθοδον ὁδοῦ ταπεινώσεως· τοῖς γὰρ ἐπϊτηδεύμασιν ἐξόμοιοῦται ἡ ψυχὴ, (καὶ) πρὸς ἃ πράττει τυποῦται. (καὶ) πρὸς αὐτὰ σχηματίζεται· ἀρχὴ ἀγγέλων τινὶ. γέγονεν ὑψηλοφρο

80

Plate from fol. 1^{v}. Part of synaxarion and ode 7 for Sunday after Easter, ed. *Πεντεκοστάριον* (Venice, 1837), p.34, col. 1, line 43 - col. 2, line 11, p.35, col. 1, lines 6-21. ἀκούων; βάλε τὴν χεῖρα σου εἰς τὴν πλευράν μου· δηλοῖ δὲ, καὶ ὅτϊ εὐρεῖα ἦν ἡ καταπλευρᾶς πληγῆ. ὡς καὶ χεῖρα εἴσω χωρεῖν· ὁ δὲ θωμᾶς ἀκρϊβῶς δϊἐρευνησάμενος. (καὶ) τὴν πῖστιν λαβὼν διἀφ'ῆς, σϋνεχωρεῖτο ταὐθ'ὁρᾶν. καὶ ποιεῖν ἐκεῖνον· κἂν ἐν ἀφθάρτῳ καὶ τεθεωμένω ἄκρως τῷ σώματϊ δϊ ἀσφαλεί(αν) ἔκραξεν. ὁ κ(υριό)ς μου, καὶ ὁ θ(εό)ς μου. τὸ μὲν, διὰ τ(ὴν) θεότητα· καὶ ὁ χ(ριστὸ)ς πρὸς αὐτόν λέγει· ὅτϊ ἰδών με ἐπῖστευσας; μακάρϊοι οἱ μὴ ἰδόντες, καὶ πϊστεύσαντες. δίδϋμος δὲ λέγετ(αι) ὁ θωμᾶς, ἢ ὅτϊ μεθ' ἑτέρου γεγένητ(αι); ἢ καὶ δϊὰ τὸ δϊστάσαι, τῇ ἀναστάσει. ἢ ὅτϊ οὕτως ἐκ φῦσεως κεκολλημένοι ἦσαν αὐτοῦ οἱ δύο τῆς ...... βεργετήσας ἡμᾶς. θωμα ... λύει μὲν. τὴν ζοφώδη ἄγν ... σϊ πέρασϊ. τῇ πϊστῇ ἀπιστ ... τὸν στέφανον πλέκει σαφῶ ... εἶ κ(υριό)ς. ὁ ϋπερυψούμενος ... Οὐ μάτην δϊστάσας, ὁ θωμᾶς ... σου οὐ κατέθετο· ἀλλ'ἀνα ... σπευδεν. ἀπὸδεῖξε ταύτη ... σιν ἔθνεσϊν. ὅθεν δϊ ἀπι ... σάμενος πάντας ἐδίδαξ ... εἶ κ(υριό)ς, ὁ ϋπὲρυφοῦμενος τῶ ... Ἐμφόβως τὴν χεῖρα, ὁ θωμ ... ρᾶ σου τῇ ζωηφόρω χ(ριστ)ὲ. ἐν ... τρομος ἤσθετο· ἐνἐργείας σ(ωτ)ὲρ

81

Plate from fol. 136^{v}. Typikon ch. 80, ed. in *Acta et diplomata graeca medii aevi*, ed. F. Miklosich and J. Müller (Vienna, 1860-90), V, p.386, lines 15-18. Ἐπεὶ δὲ ἀπαραίτητον ἦν· καί τινα παρ' ἐμοῦ καταστῆναι ὥστε ἀντϊλαμβάνεσθαι τῆς μονῆς· καὶ σπουδάζειν ἐν ἅπασϊν ἀπαράθραυστα τηρεῖσθαι τὰ ἐν τῷ τυπϊκῶ δϊηγορευμένα· καὶ μέντοι καὶ διωρῖσατο ἡ βασϊλεία μου ἐν τῷ περῖ τῶν ὀφειλόντων ἀντϊλαμβάνεσθαι τῆς

82

Plate from p.250. Ecclesiasticus 43: 19-25. σκολόπων ἄκρα· ψυχρὸς ἄνεμος βορέας πνεύσει (καὶ) παγήσεται κρύσταλλος ἐφ ὑδατος· ἐπὶ πᾶσαν συναγωγὴν ὕδατος καταλαμβάνει· καὶ ὡς θώρακα ἐνδύσεται τὸ ὕδωρ· καταφάγεται ὄρη· ὡς ἔρημον ἐκκαύσει· καὶ ἀποσβέσει χλόην ὡς πῦρ· ἴασις πάντων κατὰ σπουδὴν ὁμίχλη· δρόσος ἀπαντῶσα ἀπὸ καύσων(ος) ἱλαρώσει· λογϊσμῶ αὐτοῦ ἐκόπασεν ἄβυσσον· καὶ ἐφύτευσεν αὐτῆ νήσους· οἱ πλέοντες τὴν θάλασσαν διηγήσονται τὸν κῖνδυνον αὐτῆς· καὶ ἀκοαῖς ὠτίων ἡμῶν θαυμάζομεν καὶ ἐκεῖ τὰ παράδοξα καὶ τὰ θαυμάσια· ἔργα ποικιλῖα

83

Plate from fol. 168^{v}. Commentary on Psalm 68:37, ed. *PG* 128 705 D.11 - 708 A.14. λαμβάνουσϊν· ἀπηλλοτρϊώθην τῶν ἀδελφῶν μου· μὴ, συγχωρούμ[ε]ν(ος) σὺνδϊάγειν αὐτοῖς· ἅτε δϊαφόροις δεσπόταις δουλευόντ(ων)· (καὶ) ὅτϊ ὁ νόμ(ος), οὐκ οἶδε δούλ(ων) συγγένειαν· τὸ αὐτὸ δὲ καὶ ὁ ἐφἐξῆς δϊέξεισϊ στίχ(ος)· ἀναλογϊζόμ[εν](ος) δὲ (καὶ) τὴν ἐρήμωσϊν τοῦ ναοῦ δαπανῶμαι τῆ λύπη· (καὶ) τοὺς σοὺς ὀνειδϊσμοὺς οὓς ὀνειδῖζει παρὰ τῶν βαβϋλωνῖων· ὡς μὴ δυνάμ[εν](ός) μοι βοηθεῖν, οἰκείους λελόγϊσμαι· δϊὸ (καὶ) μὴ προσϊέμ[εν](ος) τροφὴν ἐτάκην· οἱ δὲ μᾶλλον μ(ὲν), ὠνἠδϊζον ὡς μάτην νηστεύοντ[α]· (καὶ) ἐνεδυσάμην σάκκ(ον) σῦμβολον θλῖψε(ως)· δῆλα δὲ τὰ ἐξ ἧς εἶτα προσηυχόμην λέγων· ὅτϊ καιρ(ὸς) ἀγαθοθελείας· εἴτουν ἐλεημοσύνης· τὰ δὲ ἐντεύθεν, ὡς προηρμηνεύσαμ(εν)· πλὴν, ὅτϊ παῖδα, οὐ τὸν φύσει ἀλλὰ τὸν θέσει λέγουσϊν· υἱὸς γάρ φη[σι] πρωτότοκός μου ἰ(σρα)ὴλ· ἢ

84

Plate from fol. 161^v. Typikon ch. 157, ed. H. Delehaye, *Deux typica byzantins de l'époque des Paléologues* (Académie royale de Belgique. Classe des lettres et des sciences morales et politiques. Mémoires, collection in-8°, 2^{e}série, tome 13, mémoire 4; Brussels, 1921), p.103, lines 11-15. *καὶ οἶνου. ἐπὶ τὴν αὔριον δὲ. ἔχωσιν ὀψών[ιον] εἰς δόσιν τῶν μοναχ(ῶν). καὶ τὴν συνήθη λειτουργ[ῖαν] ὑπὸ τῶν δύο ἱερέων· ταῦτα σύμφωνήσασαι ὑπεσχέθησαν ποιεῖν ἀδιακόπως. ἕως ἂν βοηθεία θ(εο)ῦ ἡ μονὴ ἵσταται. ἀπό τε τοῦ τέλους τοῦ εἰρημένου κήπου. καὶ ἀπὸ τοῦ προσόντος*

85

Plate from fol. 133^r. Sayings of twelve anchorites (*BHG* 1448r), ed. *PL* 73 1063 D.4-12. *τὸν διάβολον θεωρῶ. ζητοῦντα τίνα καταπίει· καὶ ὅπου ἐὰν ἀπέλθη. θεωρῶ τοῖς ἔσωθέν μου ὀφθαλμοῖς. (καὶ) τῷ δεσπότη χ(ριστ)ῷ ἐντυγχάνω κατ' αὐτοῦ. ἵνα ἄπρακτος μήνει, καὶ πρὸς μηδένα ἰσχύσει· μάλλιστα τῶν φοβουμένων τὸν κ(υριό)ν. Ὁ ἔννατος εἶπεν· καθ' ἡμέραν τὴν ἐκκλησίαν τῶν ἁγίων θεωρῶ, (καὶ) τὸν κ(ύριο)ν τῆς δόξης ἐμ μέσω αὐτῶν, ὑπερ πάντας λάμποντα· ὅτ' ἂν δὲ ἀκιδιῶ, ἀνέρχομαι εἰς τοὺς οὐ(ρα)νοῦς· καὶ θεωρῶ τὰ κάλλει τὰ θαυμαστὰ τῶν ἀγγέλων, (καὶ) τοὺς ὕμνους*

86

Plate from fol. 60^r. *De fide orthodoxa* II.22, ed. *PG* 94 948 C. 1 - 949 A.10. *ἦγ(οῦν) τὸ γνωμικ(ὸν) θέλημ(α), τ(ῆς) ἀνθρωπίνεις αὐτοῦ θελήσε(ως)· ἑπομένης δηλαδὴ, τῇ θεία αὐτοῦ θελήσει, κατὰ ταῦτα θελοῦσης· ἃ ἡ θεῖα αὐτοῦ εἴθελεν θέλησις· χρὴ (δὲ) γινώσκειν. ὡς ἕτερ(ον) μέν (ἐστιν) ἡ θέλησης, ἕτερ(ον) (δὲ) βούλησ(εις)· ἕτερ(ον) (δὲ) τὸ θελητ(όν), καὶ ἕτερ(ον) τὸ θελητικόν. κ(αὶ) ἕτερον ὁ θέλ(ων). θέλησις μὲν γ(ὰρ) (ἐστὶν), αὐτῆ ἡ ἁπλὴ δύναμις τοῦ θέλει(ν). βούλησις (δὲ), ἡ πε(ρὶ) τί θέλησ(εις)· θελητ(ὸν) (δὲ) τὸ ὑποκείμ[εν](ον) τῇ θελήσει πράγμ(α). ἦγ(οῦν) ὅπερ θέλομεν· οἷ(ον) κινεῖτ(αι) ἡ ὄρεξεις πρ(ὸς) βρώσιν· ἡ μὲν ἁπλ(ῶς) ὄρεξεις, ἡ λογικῆ θέλησις (ἐστὶ)· αὐτῆ (δὲ) ἡ βρώσης, θελητ[ική] (ἐστι)· θελιτικὸν (δὲ) τὸ ἔχ(ον) τὴν θελητικῆν δύναμιν· οἷ(ον)· ὁ ἄν(θρωπ)ος· θέλων (δὲ) αὐτ(ὸς) ὁ κεχριμ[έν](ος) τῆι θελήσει· δεῖ εἰδέναι ὡς τὸ θέλημα, ποτὲ μ(ὲν) τὴν θέλησιν δηλοί. ἤτοι τὴν θελητικῆν δύναμιν. κ(αὶ) λέγεται θέλημα φυσικόν· ποτὲ (δὲ) τὸ θελητ(όν). κ(αὶ) λέγετ(αι) θέλημα γνωμικόν: - πε(ρὶ) ἐνεργείας λό[γος] λ ϙ Χρὴ γινώσκειν (ὡς) πᾶσαι αἱ δυνάμ(εις) αἱ προειρημ[έν]αι· αἵ τε γνωστικαὶ· αἵ τε ζωτικαὶ· καὶ αἱ φυσικαὶ· καὶ αἱ τε*

87

Plate shows note on fol. 237^v. *τὸ παρὸν βῖβλῖον, ἀπεστάλη παρὰ τοῦ ὑψηλοτάτου βασιλέως καὶ αὐτοκράτορος ῥωμαίων κὺροῦ μανουὴλ τοῦ παλαιολόγου, εἰς τὸ μοναστήρῖον τοῦ ἁγΐου δϊονΰσΐου τοῦ ἐν παρΰσΐω τῆς φραγγΐας ἢ γαλατί(ας) ἀπὸ τῆς κωνσταντϊνουπόλεως, δϊ' ἐμοῦ μανουὴλ τοῦ χρΰσολωρᾶ πεμφθέντος πρέσβεως παρὰ τοῦ εἰρημένου βασϊλέως, ἔτει ἀπὸ κτίσεως κόσμου, ἑξακϊσχϊλϊοστῶ ἐννεακοσϊοστῶ ἑξκαιδεκάτω. ἀπὸ σαρκώσεως δὲ τοῦ κυρΐου, χϊλϊοστῶ τετρακοσϊοστῶ ὀγδόω: - Ὅστῒς εἰρημένος βασΐλεὺς, ἦλθε πρότερον εἰς τὸ παρυσϊον πρὸ ἐτῶν τεσσάρ(ων).*

88

Plate from fol. 179^r. *Physics* III. 3.202 a 28-36. *ἀλλα μὴν εἰ τοῦτο, ἡ κίνησις ἐν τῷ κινοῦντι ἔσται. ὁ γὰρ αὐτὸς λόγος ἐπὶ κινοῦντος καὶ κινουμένου. ὥστε ἢ πᾶν τὸ κινοῦν κινήσεται. ἢ ἔχον κίνησιν, οὐ κινήσεται. εἰ δὲ ἄμφω ἐν τῷ κινουμενω καὶ πάσχοντι, καὶ ἡ ποίησις καὶ ἡ πάθησις, καὶ ἡ δίδαξις καὶ ἡ μάθησις, δύο οὖσαι ἐν τῷ μανθάνοντι, πρῶτον μὲν ἡ ἐνέργεια ἡ ἑκάστου, οὐκ ἐν ἑκάστω ὑπάρξει, εἶτα ἄτοπον τὰς δύο κινήσεις ἅμα κινεῖσθαι. τίνὲς γὰρ ἔσονται ἀλλοιώσεις δύο τοῦ ἑνὸς, καὶ εἰς ἓν εἶδος, ἀλλ' ἀδύνατον.*

89

Plate from fol. 200^r. Canon *παρακλητικός* composed of theotokia from odes some of which are printed in *Μηναῖα* (Rome, 1888-1901), VI. 321, 182, 468. *Μ(ητ)ὴρ θ(εο)ῦ ὡς παρρησί(αν) ἔχουσα πρ(ὸς) τ(ὸν) τεχθέντα ἐκ σοῦ· μονογενῆ λόγ(ον). κ(αὶ) π(ατ)ρὶ συνάναρχ(ον)· δυσώπε παναμῶμητε· τὴν ψ[υ]χήν μου ῥυσθῆναι· δαιμόν(ων) πάσης κακῶσε(ως) καὶ πυρ(ὸς) κ(αὶ) πάσ(ις) κολασεως: ὠδ[ή] γ̅: Σὺ εἶ τὸ στερέωμα τ(ῶν) Ὅλην μου τὴν ἔφεσιν· πρ(ὸς) σὲ κινῶ ἁγνὴ δέσποινα· τ(ῶν) σαρκικῶν ἐπιθυμιῶν μου. διὰ τάχους ἀπάλλαξον: Λαμψον μετανοί(ας) μοι· τὰς καθαρὰς αὐγὰς δέσποινα· πύλη φωτ(ὸς) τ(ῶν) ἁμαρτι ... ἱλάσθη τι μοι σ(ωτ)ήρ. πολλαὶ : Μαρια τὸ καθαρ(ὸν) τοῦ βασιλέ(ως) παλάτιον τοῦ πάντ(ων) δϊμηουργοῦ, ψυχῆς καθαρτήριον· παράσχου μοι δάκρυον (καὶ) μελλούσ(ης) δίκ(ις) κ(αὶ) κολάσε(ως) ἐξ ἅρπασ(ον); Ἡ πύλη ἡ τοῦ θ(εο)ῦ, εἰσόδους θείας ὑπόδειξον. τῇ ταπεινῆ μου ψυχῆ. ἐν αἷς εισελευσομαι· ἐξομολογούμ[εν](ος)· κ(αὶ) κακῶν τὴν λύσιν· θ(εοτο)κέ ἀπολήψομαι; Πελάγι ἁμαρτιῶν κ(αὶ) κύμ(α)τα ἀπογνώσεως χειμάζουσί μου τ(ὸν) νοῦν σπλαγχνίσθητι δεσποινα· καὶ χείρα μοι ἔκτει*

90

Plate from fol. 87^v. End of office for 30 June, ed. *Τυπικόν* (Venice, 1603), fol. νδ'. *ἀνοίξω τὸ στόμα μου. ἔπειτα τῶν ιβ'. ἱστῶμ(εν) (δὲ), στιχ[ηρα] ἕξ· εἰς τ(οὺς) αἴν(ους), στιχ[ηρα] τῶν ιβ'. δό[ξα] ἦχ(ος) π[λαγιος] δ'· ἣν διήλθετε κτῖσ(ιν) φωτΐσαντες· (καὶ) ν[ῦν] θ[εοτοκίον]· δοξολογ[ία] μεγ[ά]λ[η] (καὶ) ἀπόλυ[σ](ις)· εἰς τ(ὴν) λειτ[ουρ]γ[ίαν], τυπ[ικ]ὰ. (καὶ) ἐκ τοῦ κα[νόν](ος) των ιβ' ὠδ[ή] γ' (καὶ) ϛ'. προκ[είμενον] ἦχ(ος) πλ[αγιος] δ'. εἰς πᾶσ(αν) τ(ὴν) γῆν. στΐχ[ος] οἱ οὐ(ρα)νοὶ διηγοῦνται. ὁ ἀπ(όσ)[τολος] πρ[ὸς], κορινθΐ(ους) α'. ἀδε[λφ]οὶ. ὁ θ(εό)ς ἡμ(ᾶς) τοὺς ἀποστ[ό]λ(ους). ζήτ[ει] κυ[ριακ]ῇ ϊ'. ἀλλη[λούια] ἦχ(ος) α'. Οἱ οὐ(ρα)νοὶ διηγοῦντ(αι). στιχ[ος] ἡμέρ[α] τῆ ἡμέρ[α]· εὐα[γγέλιον] κ[α]τ[ὰ] λοῦκ[αν] τῷ και[ρῷ] ἐκείν[ω] ἔστη ὁ ἰ(ησοὺς)ς π(αρὰ) τ(ὴν) λΐμνην: κοινωνοικ(όν), εἰς πᾶσ(αν) τ(ὴν) γῆν:-*

91

Plate from fol. 13^r. *History of Greece* I.23, ed. H. G. Reichard (Leipzig, 1770), pp. 49, line 11 - 50, line 11. *πόλιν. ἣν ἔκτισε μ(ὲν) μίνως ἐκεῖνος ὁ κρητῶν βασιλεὺς. ὅτε ἐς σικελίαν κατὰ δαιδάλου ζήτησιν ἀφιγμένος, κωκάλω τῷ σικανῶν βασιλεῖ ἐπεξενώθη. τότε δὲ καρχηδονίοις ὑπήκουε, καίπερ τῆς ἀκραγαντίνης πρότερον οὖσα μοίρας. δΐωνι δὲ φίλος ὢν, ὁ ταύτης τῆς πόλεως ἐπιστάτης, σΰναλος τοὔνομα, ἐδέξατό τε προθύμως. καὶ δεηθέντι, πανοπλί(ας) πεντακϊσχιλί(ας) ἃς ἐπὶ τοῖν πλοίοιν ἦγε, πρὸς τὰς σΰρρακούσας ἁμάξαις συμπαρακομίσαι οἱ, ὑπήκουσ(εν). αὐτὸς δὲ δΐων τ(οὺς) μισθοφόρους*

92
Plate from fol. 26^{v}. Commentary on *Nicomachean Ethics* I. 3, ed. in *Eustratii ... in Ethica Nicomachea commentaria*, ed. G. Heylbut (Commentaria in Aristotelem Graeca XX, Berlin, 1892), p. 38, lines 8-15. *βίους δὲ ὀνομάζει 'πάντως, τοὺς τρόπους τῆς μετὰ σώματος κατὰ τὴν ἀν(θρώπ)ου διϊαγωγῆς· βουλόμ[εν]ος δ' ἤδη κ(αὶ) περὶ τοῦ θεωρητικοῦ λέγει ὅπ(ως) ἔχει καταλλήλως ἑαυτῷ περὶ τῆς δόσεως τῶν ἀγαθ(ῶν), ἐπεὶ ἡ περὶ τούτου διϊδασκαλία πλείονος ἐδεῖτο λόγου, νῦν μέν, ταύτην* ***ἀφίησϊ· παραπέμπει δὲ εἰς τοὺς ἑξῆς λόγους, ὡς ἐν*** *ἐκείνοις εὐκαιρότερον ἐρῶν περὶ αὐτοῦ· τοσοῦτον μόνον ἐν τούτοις εἰπών: τρίτος δ' ἐστὶν ὁ θεωρητϊκὸς περὶ οὗ τὴν ἐπίσκεψιν ἐν τοῖς ἑπομένοις ποιησόμεθα· ἐν γὰρ τῷ*

93
Plate from fol. 6^{r}. *Anthologia Palatina* IX. 240, 243, 265, 339 (= Anth. Plan. I^{a} 21. 5-8). *κάπρ(ος) δ' ἡράκλειος ἀπορρήξας ἀπὸ δεσμῶν, ἐς νηδὺν κριοῦ πᾶσαν ἔβαψε γένυν· ζωὴν νηπιάχω δὲ χαρῖσσατο· ἆρ' ἀπὸ ἥρης ἡρακλέης βρεφέων ᾤκτϊσεν ἡλικῖην:- Γήθησαν περὶ παιδὸς ἀριστῖπποιο τοκῆες· καὶ κλαῦσαν· μοίρης δ' ἦμαρ ἓν ἀμφοτέρης εὖτε γ(ὰρ) αἰθόμενον δόμον ἔκφυγεν, ἰθὺ κεραυνοῦ ζεὺς κατά οἱ κεφαλῆς ἄσπετον ἧκε σέλας. τοῦτο δ' ἔπ(ος) τότ' ἔλεξαν ὅσοι νέκυν ὠδύροντο· ὦ πυρὶ* ***δαιμονίω τλῆμον ὀφειλόμενε:- Ἰοτυπὴς διὸς ὄρνις ἐτῖσα-*** *το κρῆτα φαρέτρης οὐ(ρα)νόθεν τόξω τόξον ἀμυνόμενος· κεῖνον δ' εὐθὺς ἄκοντϊ παλινδρομέοντι κατέκτα· ἱερόθ(εν) πῖπτων δ' ἔκταν(εν) ὡς ἔθαν(εν)· μηκέτ' ἐφ' ὑμετέροις ἀψευδέσι κρῆτες ὀϊστοῖς αὐχεῖθ'· ὑμνείσθω καὶ διὸς εὐστοχῖη:- Ἔν ποτε παμφαίνοντϊ μελάντερ(ος) αἰθέρι νωμῶν σκορπίον ἐκ γαίης εἶδε* ***θορόντα κόραξ· δν μάρψων ὦρουσεν· δδ' ἀΐξαντος ἐπ' οὖδας οὐ βραδὺς, εὐκέντρῳ πέζαν ἔτυψε βέλει·***

94
Plate from fol. 120^{v}. Prolegomena to Hermogenes *περὶ ἰδεῶν*, ed. in *Prolegomenon sylloge*, ed. H. Rabe (Rhetores Graeci XIV. Leipzig, 1931), p. 390, lines 7-18. *τέχνης· δι' ἧς ὀρθῶς ἂν καὶ τοὺς ἀρχαίους ζηλώσωμ(εν). ὅτϊ περὶ καθολϊκῆς ἰδέ(ας) γέγραπται τὸ σύγγραμμα. οὐ περὶ δημοσθενϊκῆς ἢ πλατωνϊκ(ῆς). ὅτϊ διὰ τ(ων) δημοσθενϊ-κ(ῶν) λόγ(ων), περὶ πάσης ἰδέας διϊδάσκει· οὗτος γ(ὰρ) ποικίλ(ος) μάλϊστα ὁ ῥήτωρ· ὅτϊ δϋσχερὲς τὴν μίξϊν τ(ων) ἰδεῶν εὑρ(εῖν). καὶ εὑρόντα φράσαι· ὅτϊ οὐδεὶς τ(ων) πρὸ αὐτ[οῦ] καθῆκ(εν) ἑαυτ(ὸν) εἰς τ(ὴν) περὶ* ***τ(ων) καθολϊκ(ῶν) ἰδεῶν πραγματείαν· ὅτϊ ἑπτὰ εἰσϊν ἰδέαι, τ(ὸν) δημοσθενϊκ(ὸν) ποιοῦσαι λόγον· ὧν αἱ μ(ὲν) γενϊκαί εἰσϊν· αἱ δὲ εἰδϊκαί· ἐξ ὧν ἅπας γίνετ[αι]***

95
Plate from fol. 150^{v}. Summary of Aquinas I^{a} II^{ae} 91.4, ed. cit. VI, pp. 107, line 35 - 108, line 8. *ἐχρῆν εἰς ἐκεῖνο τὸ τέλος. (καὶ) νόμω θεόθεν τεθέντι· δεύτερ(ον)· ὅτι διὰ τὸ ἀβέβαι(ον) τῆς ἀν(θρωπ)ίνης κρίσεως μάλιστα τῆς περὶ τὰ ἐνδεχόμενα (καὶ) μερικὰ, συμβαίν[ει] περὶ τῶν ἀν-(θρωπ)ίνων πράξεων διαφόρους εἶναι (καὶ) τὰς κρίσεις. ἐξ ὧν διάφοροι (καὶ) ἐναντίοι νόμοι προίασιν· ἵνα τοίνυν ὁ ἄν(θρωπ)ος ἄνευ πάσης ἀμφιβολί(ας), δύναιτο γινώσκ(ειν), τί δεῖ πράττειν κ(αὶ) τί φυλάττεσθαι, ἀναγκαῖον ἐν τ(αῖς) ἰδί(αις) ἐνεργείαις ἄγεσθαι νόμω θεόθεν δοθέντι. δν φανερὸν ὡς ἀδύνατον πλανηθῆναι· τρίτον,* ***ὅτι περὶ ἐκείνων ὁ ἄν(θρωπ)ος δύναται νομοθετ(εῖν), περὶ ὧν δύναται (καὶ) κρίνειν. τ(ὴν) δὲ τοῦ ἀν(θρώπ)ου κρίσιν ἀδυνάτον εἶναι περὶ τῶν ἔνδον κινήσεων (καὶ)*** *λανθανουσῶν. ἀλλα μόν(ον), περὶ τῶν ἔξωθεν καὶ φαινομέν(ων), (καὶ) ὅμως, πρὸς τὴν τῆς ἀρετῆς τελειότητα ζητεῖται, τὸ ἐν ἀμφοτέραις ταῖς ἐνεργεί(αις)*

96
Plate from fol. 179^{r}. Commentary on *Physics* III. 3, ed. in *Simplicii in Aristotelis physicorum libros ... commentaria*, ed. H. Diels (Commentaria in Aristotelem Graeca IX, Berlin, 1882), pp. 441, lines 28-33, 442, lines 12-17. *τὸ ἀμφοτέρας ἐν αὐτῷ τιθέναι, διὰ ταυτα μ(ὲν) οὖν παρῆκεν ἐκεῖνο τὸ τμῆμα τῆς διαιρέσε(ως), ὡς ἐν τοῖς πλείοσι γέγραπται τῶν ἀντιγράφων· ἔν τισι δὲ (καὶ* added*) τοῦτο πρόσκειται, τῆς γραφῆς ἐχούσης οὕτως· ἢ γὰρ ἄμφω ἐν τῷ πάσχοντι (καὶ) ποιουμένω, ἢ ἐν τῷ ποιοῦντι (καὶ) διατιθέντι· ἢ ἡ μὲν ποίησις ἐν τῷ ποιοῦντι, ἡ (δὲ)* ***πάθησις ἐν τῷ πά ... τῷ πάσχοντι, πρωτον ὑπαντᾶ, (καὶ)*** *λαβὼν, ὅτι κ[α]τ[ὰ] ταύτην τὴν ὑπόθεσιν, ὥσπερ ἐν τῷ κινουμένω ἐστὶν ἡ κίνησις ἡ οἰκεία, οὕτω καὶ ἐν τῷ κινοῦντι ἡ αὐτοῦ οἰκεία, ὁ γὰρ αὐτὸς λόγος ἐπ' ἀμφοῖν, ἐπάγει, ὅτι δυοῖν ἀτόποιν, θάτερον ἀνάγκη κ[α]τ[ὰ] ταύτην τὴν ὑπόθεσιν ὁμολογεῖν· ἢ γὰρ πᾶν τὸ κινοῦν (καὶ) κινήσεται, εἴπερ τὸ κινοῦν ἔχει κίνησιν, τὸ δὲ ἔχον*

97
Plate from fol. 53^{r}. *Protrepticus* XI. 115.4 - 116.1, ed. U. Treu (Berlin, 1972), pp. 81, line 23 - 82, line 1. *τειλάτωσαν· τὸν ἐγκεκρυμμένον ἔνδον ἐκφαίνουσαι, (καὶ) ἀποστίλβουσαι ἀν(θρωπ)ον· τὸν μαθητὴν τοῦ φωτός· τὸν χ(ριστο)υ γνώριμόν τε καὶ συγκληρονόμον· μάλιστα. ἐπειδ' ἂν τὸ τιμιώτατον, καὶ σεβασμιώτατον, εὐσεβεῖ, τε καὶ ἀγαθωι παιδί. ἀγαθοῦ π(ατ)ρ(ος) ὄνομα, εἰς γνῶσιν ἀφίκηται προστάττοντος ἤπια καὶ τῶι παιδὶ ἐγκελευομένου τὰ σωτήρια· ὁ δὲ πειθόμενος αὐτῶι. κατὰ πάντα δὴ πλεονεκτεῖ· ἕπεται τῶι θ(ε)ωι· πείθεται τῶι π(ατ)ρι· ἔγνω πλανώμενος αὐτόν· ἠγάπησε τὸν θ(εο)ν· ἠγάπησε τὸν πλησίον· ἐπλήρωσε τὴν ἐντολήν· τὸ ἆθλον ἐπιζητεῖ. τὴν ἐπαγγελίαν ἀπαιτεῖ· πρόκειται δὲ ἀεὶ τῶι θ(ε)ωι. τὴν ἀν(θρωπ)ων ἀγέλην σώιζειν· ταύτηι καὶ τὸν ἀγαθὸν ποιμένα. ὁ ἀγαθὸς ἀπέστειλεν θ(εο)ς· ἁπλώσας δὲ ὁ λόγος τὴν ἀλήθειαν. ἔδειξε τοῖς αν(θρωπ)οις, τὸ ὕψος τῆς σ(ωτη)ριας· ὅπως, ἢ μετανοήσαντες. σωθῶσιν. ἢ μὴ*

98
Plate from fol. 74^{v}. Hierocles, Commentary on Pythagorean *Carmen aureum* XI, 17-20, ed. in *Fragmenta philosophorum Graecorum*, ed. F.W.A. Mullach (Paris, 1860-81), I, p. 441, col. 1, lines 10-23. *τ(ας) τ(ης) κρίσεως ἀρχ(ας). κυριωτάτ(ας) ἀποδεχόμεθα· τ(ην) ἀγαθότητα τοῦ θ(εο)υ· τ(ον) ἀπὸ ταύτ(ης) νόμον. τ(ον) ἐν ἡμῖν παρανομούμεν(ον) ὀρθὸν λόγον. (καὶ) (ὥσ)π[έρ] τινα ἔνοικον θ(εο)ν πλημμελούμεν(ον). ἀπὸ τέλεσμα δὲ τ(ης) κρίσε(ως). τ(ὰ) ἄλγεα (ὡς) φη[σι] ταῦτα, ὅσα τραχύτερον ἡμῖν ποιεῖ τ(ον) βίον. ταῖς περι σῶμά τε (καὶ) τὰ ἐκτὸς λύμαις· ἃ δὴ πράως φέρει(ν). ὁ παρὼν εἰσηγεῖτ(αι) λόγ(ος)· ἐνθυμουμέν(ους) τ(ας) αἰτίας αὐτ(ων)· κ(αὶ) ὅσον οἷόν τε π(ερι)κόπτοντ(ας). κ(αὶ) μετατιθ(έν)τ(ας) εἰς ὠφέλειαν τὰ δοκ(οῦν)τα βλαβερά· μάλιστα μ(ὲν), τ(ων) θείων ἀγαθ(αν), ἑαυτ(οὺς) ἀξι(ους) παρέχ(εσ)θ(αι)· δ(ια) τ(ης) ἀκροτάτ(ης) ἀρετ(ης). εἰ δέ τωι τ(οῦ)το, οὔπω ἐν ὀρέξει· τ(ων) γ' (οὖν) πολιτικ(ων) ἀγαθ(ων), δ(ια) τ(ης) μέσ(ης) ἀρετ(ης) τυγχανέτω· τοῦτο γ(ὰρ) ἦν, ὃ (πρὸς) τὸ πάσχειν κ(α)λ(ῶς), τὰ ἀλγεινὰ, καὶ*

99

Plate from fol. 101^{r}. *Thesaurus* XXI ed. *PG.* 75 361 D. 2 - 364 A. 5. *ἐν ἀρχῆι· πολλῶι δὲ ὕστερον χρόνωι, γέγονεν ὑπὲρ ἡμῶν ἀρχιερεὺς· ὥσπέρ τινα ποδήρη τὸν ἐκ γυναικὸς ἄν(θρωπ)ον ἤτοι παθητὸν ἀναλαβὼν, ἵνα τῶι ἰδίωι αἵματι καθαρίσῃ τὸν λαὸν ἑαυτὸν προσενεγκὼν ὡς ἀμνὸν ἄμωμον τῶι θ(ε)ῶι· οὐ γὰρ ἐποίησεν ἁμαρτίαν, οὐδὲ εὑρέθη δόλος ἐν τῶι στόματι αὐτοῦ :- Β̄ Τί σημαίνειν βούλεται τὸ πιστὸν, ἢ ὅτι ἀληθινὸς καὶ ἀναλλοίωτος:- Πιστὸς ὁ σ(ωτ)ὴρ καλεῖται δικαίως μίαν ὑπὲρ πάντων θυσίαν προσενεγκὼν, τὴν αὐτὴν ἀεὶ καὶ οὐκ ἀλλαττομένην· ἅπαξ γὰρ ἀποθανῶν ὑπὲρ ἡμῶν, οὐκ ὄψεται θάνατον ἐκ δευτέρου· καὶ πάλ(ιν) ὁ ἀπόστολος ἐπιστέλλων τισὶ, λέγει· πιστὸς ὁ θ(εὸ)ς δι' οὗ ἐκλήθητε εἰς ἀποστολὴν τοῦ υἱοῦ αὐτοῦ· ὁ πέτρος ὁμοίως· ὥστε καὶ οἱ πάσ*

100

Plate from fol. 190^{v}. Platonic theology V.34, ed. A. Portus (Hamburg, 1618), pp. 321 line 47 - 322, line 5. *μὴ μόνον ἐν τούτ(οις) τ(οὺς) δύο τούτ(ους) π(ατέ)ρας τῆς φρουρητϊκῆς ταύτης μετέχ(ειν) τάξε(ως), ἀλλὰ καὶ τὴν μέσην αὐτῶν θεὸν τὴν ζωογόνον, τὴν σύστοιχον αὐτ[οῦ] μονάδα τῶν ἀτρέπτων εἰληχέν[αι] θεῶν, ἀνάγκη δὴ που καὶ τὴν τῶν ἀχρ(άν)των ἡγεμόνων πρωτίστην ἐν τοῖς νοεροῖς π(ατ)ράσϊ τρϊαδϊκὴν εἶναι· καὶ τοῖς τρϊσὶ νοεροῖς θε(οῖς), τὸν αὐτ(ὸν) ἔχειν τέλειον ἀριθμ(ὸν)· καὶ τὸν μ(ὲν) πρῶτον, τῷ πρώτῳ μονίμως ἡνῶσθαι· τὸν δὲ δεύτερ(ον), δϊακρίνεσθαί πως ἐκ τοῦ δευτέρου, μετὰ τῆς πρ(ὸς) αὐτ(ὸν) ἑνώσεως· τὸν δὲ τρίτον ἤδη, δϊακεκρίσθαι τοῦ τρίτου· καὶ οὕτω δὴ κατὰ τὴν τάξϊν τὴν π(ατ)ρικ(ὴν), καὶ τὴν ἄχραντον αὐτοῖς σύμπρο*

101

Plate from fol. 59^{v}. *Hecuba* 885-8 with scholion on 886 ed. in *Scholia in Euripidem*, ed. E. Schwartz (Berlin, 1887-91), 1, pp. 69, line 28-70, line 4.

λίαν ψέγω·
Ἀγαμ[έμνω]ν. δεινὸν, τὸ μέντοι θῆλϋ μέμφομαι γένος·
κ(αὶ) ἐφόνευσαν·
Ἑκ[άβ]η. τί δ' οὐ γϋναῖκες εἷλον αἰγύπτου τέκνα.

ἀπὸ τῆς λήμνου· κ(αὶ) ὁμοῦ· κ(αὶ) ἐστέρησαν·
καὶ λῆμνον ἄρδην ἀρσένων ἐξώκϊσαν

κ(αὶ) ὅπως κ(αὶ) κατάλειψαι.
ἀλλ' ὥς γενέσθαι τόνδε μ(ὲν) μέθες λόγ(ον)· τοῖς ὑϊοῖς αὐτοῦ· ἑτοίμ(ως) (δὲ) κ(αὶ) ἐπηγγειλάμ[εν]ος τῶ αἰγύπτω, σϋνεβούλευσε ταῖς θϋγατράσ(ιν) ὁ δανα(ὸς) ὥστε ἀνελ(εῖν) νύκτωρ τ(οὺς) ἑαυτ(ῶν) ἄνδρας πρὸ τ(ῆς) μίξεως τῆς πρ(ὸς) ἑαυτοὺς· θάνατον ἐπαπειλήσας ταῖς μὴ τοῦτο ποιησάσαις· αἱ μ(ὲν) οὖν πᾶσ(ιν) ἔχουσαι τὰ ἐκ π(ατ)ρ(ὸ)ς προστάγματα, ἀνεῖλον τ(οὺς) ἄνδρας. μία (δὲ) μόνη τούτου ἐφείσατο τοῦ λϋγγέ(ως), ἀπὸ τῆς μίξε(ως). ὡς δϊάθεσ(ιν) ἔχουσα πρ(ὸς) αὐτ(ὸν)· οὗτος (δὲ) σωθεὶς, ἐξεδίκησε τ(οὺς) ἑαυτοῦ ἀδελφ(οὺς)· ἐφόνευσε γὰρ τὰς

102

Plate from fol. 12^{r}. Epigram ed. in *Iani Lascaris rhyndaceni epigrammata* (Paris, 1544), fol. 5^{r}, line 27 - 5^{v}, line 14. *ἑρμοῦ λελογχὼς κλῆσϊν· εἰκῆ δ' οὐχ ὅλως εἴρων μ(ὲν) οὐ· κλέπτων δὲ τ(ῶν) σοφ(ῶν) πόν(ους)· πωλῶν τ' ἀναιδῶς ὡς ἔλε(ον) ἔμπορος ἑρμ(ῆς) διαστρόφοισϊ γλήναις εἰκόνα ψϋχῆς φέρων. μούσαισϊν ἔχθϊστ(ον) κάρα· μίτρην ἐπισκόποιο πρώην ἐλπίσας μάστευσε φλῶραν· σχῶν μ(ὲν) αὐτῆμαρ σκοπ(ὸν) ἑλ(εῖν) ἀμοχθὶ κ(αὶ) τϋχεῖν τῆς ἐλπίδος· σκοποῦ δ' ἁμαρτ(ῶν) ἔκπεσε παντὸς σκοποῦ σκοπεῖ δ' ὅπως γένοιτο πρηστῆρος σκοπ(ὸς)· ἔχεις χόλ(ον) ζεῦ· μάρτϋς ἡλίου γόνος· τϋροῦς πατὴρ φέριστ(ος)· ἡρώων τ' ὄχλος· τούτ(οις) ἄναξ κάρχαρ(ον) ἅρμοσον κῦνα· μῦσους δ' ἀπόσχοις μηδὲν οἷα κνωδάλου σὸς παῖς ἀχϊλλεὺς ἕκτορα κτεῖν(εν) μέγαν. παῦσάν τε χειρὸς ἐκ μιᾶς αἶσχ(ος) θρασύ:*

103

Plate from fol. 494^{r}. *Trachiniae* 1046-68. *ὦ πολλὰ δὴ καὶ θερμὰ καὶ λόγῳ κακὰ καὶ χερσὶ καὶ νώτοισι μοχθήσας ἐγὼ κ οὔπω τοιοῦτον οὔτ' ἄκοιτϊς ἡ διὸς προὔθηκεν, οὐδ' ὁ στϋγνὸς εὐρυσθεὺς ἐμοί. οἷον τόδ' ἡ δολῶπις οἰνέ(ως) κόρη καθῆψεν ὤμοις τοῖς ἐμοῖς ἐρινύων ὑφαντὸν ἀμφίβληστρον ὧ δϊόλλυμαι. πλευραῖσϊ γὰρ προσμαχθὲν, ἐκ μὲν ἐσχάτας βέβρωκε σάρκας πλεύμονός τ' ἀρτηρΐας ῥοφεῖ ξυνοικοῦν· ἐκ δὲ χλωρὸν αἷμά μου πέπωκεν ἤδη καὶ διέφθαρμαι δέμας τὸ πᾶν, ἀφράστω τῆδε χειρωθεὶς πέδη κ' ου ταῦτα λόγχη πεδιὰς. οὐθ' ὁ γηγενὴς στρατὸς γϊγάντων, οὔτε θήριος βΐα, οὐθ' ἑλλὰς, οὔτ' ἄγλωσσος, οὐθ' ὅσην ἐγὼ γαῖαν καθαίρων ἱκόμην· ἔδρασέ πω γϋνὴ (δὲ) θῆλυς οὖσα κ' ουκ ἀνδρὸς φύσϊν, μόνη με δὴ καθεῖλε. φασγάνου δΐχα. ὦ παῖ γενοῦ μοι παῖς ἐτήτυμος γεγὼς κ(αὶ) μὴ τὸ μητρὸς ὄνομα πρεσβεύσης πλέον δός μοι χεροῖν σαῖν· αὐτὸς ἐξ οἴκου λαβὼν ἐς χεῖρα τὴν τεκοῦσαν. ὡς εἰδῶ σάφα εἰ τ' οὐμὸν ἀλγεῖς μᾶλλον, ἢ κείνης ὁρῶν*

104

Plate from Oxford MS., fol. 139^{r}. Nicias 7.5-7, ed. in *Plutarchi Vitae parallelae*, ed. C. Lindskog and K. Ziegler (Leipzig, 1969-), I.2, p.94, lines 14-27. *πρῶτον, ἀνεδύετο· μὴ προσδοκῆσαι τοῦτο θορϋβούμενος· ἐγκελευομ[έν](ων) δὲ ταῦτα ... ἀθηναίων καὶ τοῦ νϊκίου καταβοῶντος, ἐξαρθεὶς (καὶ) ἀναφλεχθεὶς τὸ φιλό ... ὑπεδέξατό τε τὴν στρατηγίαν· καὶ προσδϊωρίσατο πλεύσας ἐντὸς ἡμερῶν εἴ ... ἢ κατακτενεῖν ἐκεῖ τοὺς ἄνδρας, ἢ ζῶντας ἄξειν ἀθήναζε· τοῖς ἀθηναίοις ἐπῆ ... ελάσαι μέγα μᾶλλον, ἢ πίστεῦσαι· καὶ γὰρ ἄλλως εἰώθεισ(αν) αὐτοῦ τὴν κουφότ ... (καὶ) μανίαν φέρειν μετὰ παιδϊᾶς οὐκ ἀηδῶς· λέγεται γὰρ ἐκκλησΐας ποτὲ ού ... τὸν μ(ὲν) δῆμον καθήμενον ἄνω, περϊμένειν πολῦν χρόνον· ὀψὲ δ' εἰσελθεῖν ἐκεῖ ... ἐστεφανωμένον· καὶ παρακαλεῖν ὑπερθέσθαι τὴν ἐκκλησΐαν εἰσαύριον· ἀσχ ... γὰρ ἔφη σήμερον, ἑστϊᾶν μέλλων ξένους καὶ τεθϋκ(ὼς) τοῖς θεοῖς· τοὺς δ' ἀθην*

105

Plate from fol. 22^{v}. *History* I.60.5-9, ed. in *Polybii Historiae*, ed. T. Büttner-Wobst (Leipzig, 1962-) I, p.84, lines 4-21. *εἰς τὴν αὔριον ναυμαχΐας· ὑπὸ δὲ τὴν ἑωθινὴν ἤδη τῆς ἡμέρ(ας) ὑποφαινούσης, ὁρῶν τοῖς μὲν ἐναντΐοις φορὸν ἄνεμον καταρρέοντα (καὶ) λαμπρ(ὸν)· σφΐσὶ δὲ δϋσχερῆ γϊνόμενον τὸν ἀνάπλουν προσαντΐον τὸ πνεῦμα, κοίλ(ης) (καὶ) τραχεί(ας) οὔσης τῆς θαλάττης, τὸ μὲν πρῶτον διηπόρει τί δεῖ χρῆσθαι τοῖς παροῦσι· σύλλογϊζόμενος δ' ὡς ἐὰν μὲν παραβάλληται, χειμῶνος ὄντος, [Π]ρὸς ἄννωνα ποιήσεται τὸν ἀγῶνα (καὶ) πρὸς αὐτὰς τὰς ναυτικὰς δϋνάμεις· καὶ πρὸς ἔτι γέμοντα τὰ σκάφη· ἐὰν δὲ τηρῶν εὐδΐαν (καὶ) καταμελῶν ἐάσῃ διάραι (καὶ) σύμμϊξαι τοῖς στρατοπέδοις τοὺς πολεμΐους, πρός τε τ(ὰς) ναῦς εὐκινήτους καὶ κεκουφισμένας ἀγωνϊεῖται. πρός τε τοὺς ἀρίστους ἄνδρ(ας) τῶν ἐκ τοῦ πεζοῦ στρατευμάτων· τὸ δὲ μέγιστον, πρὸς τὴν ἀμίλκου τόλμ(αν)· ἧς οὐδὲν ἦν τότε φοβερώτερον· διόπερ ἔκρϊνε, μὴ παρεῖναι τ(ὸν) ἐνεστῶτα καιρ(όν).*

106

Plate from fol. 157^{r}. Consolation to Jacopo Antonio Marcello on the death of his son, lines 73-83. *ἡ δ' ἀρετὴ μούνη καὶ θοῦσιον εὐσεβὲς ἄμφω ἡμᾶς ἡμετέροις παισὶ συνάψαι ἔχοι· τοῦτο δὲ ποιοῦντες, κατὰ πᾶν κράτος ἕξομεν ἄκρον οἶκον ἐν οὐρανίᾳ ὦ ἰάκωβε πόλει· σῷ παρὰ οὐαλερίῳ σὺ μὲν, ἀλλ' ἐγὼ αὐτὸς ὀλύμπῳ υἱῷ ἐμῷ· ἄμφω ἐσσόμεθ' ὡς μάκαρες· πένθος ἄρα στυγερὸν καὶ ανάξιον ἔνθεν ἀφέντες πάντα γόον, λάβομεν μείζονα ἔργα φίλε· Σῶμα βροτοῖς θνητὸν φύσις ἡμῖν δῶκε βαρεῖα· ἀλλὰ θεὸς ψυχὴν ἔγχεεν ἀθάνατον· λήψεται ἡμέτερον δέμας ἡ γῆ καίπερ ἀκόντων*

107

Plate from fol. 55^{r}. *Anthology* III.17.44, ed. C. Wachsmuth, and O. Hense (Berlin, 1884-1912), III, p. 510, lines 5-17. *(καὶ) πολλάκις αἰσθανομένους τῶν ἀγαθῶν τε καὶ τῶν κακῶν, ἐκπλήξασα ποιεῖν τὸ χεῖρον ἀντὶ τοῦ βελτίονος αἱρεῖσθαι; γίνεται τοῦτο ἔφη: σωφροσύνην δὲ ὦ εὐθύδημε, τίνι ἂν φαίημεν ἧττον, ἢ τῷ ἀκρατεῖ προσήκειν· αὐτὰ γὰρ δήπου τὰ ἐναντία, σωφροσύνης καὶ ἀκρασίας ἔργα ἐστὶν; ὁμολογῶ κ(αὶ) τοῦτο ἔφη: τοῦ δ' ἐπιμελεῖσθαι ὧν προσήκει, οἴει τὶ κωλυτικώτερον ἀκρασίας εἶναι; οὔκουν ἔγωγέ φημι: τοῦ δὲ ἀντὶ τῶν ὠφελούντων τὰ βλάπτοντα προαιρεῖσθαι ποιοῦντος, καὶ τούτων μὲν ἐπιμελεῖσθαι, ἐκείνων δὲ ἀμελεῖν πείθοντος, καὶ τοῖς σωφρονοῦσι τὰ ἐναντία ποιεῖν ἀναγκάζοντος, οἴει τὶ ἀνθρώπῳ κάκιον εἶναι; οὐδὲν ἔφη: οὐκοῦν τὴν ἐγ-*

108

Plate from fol. 63^{r}. Homily 12 on Genesis, ed. *PG* 53 104, 1-11. *τάξει δεσποίνης ὀφείλουσαν προκαθῆσθαι καὶ ἐπιτάττειν καταβιβάσαντες ἀπὸ τοῦ θρόνου, (καὶ) ὑπακούειν ταῖς τ(ῆς) σαρκὸς ἡδοναῖς καταναγκάζομεν, ἀγνοοῦντες αὐτῆς τὴν εὐγένειαν, καὶ ὅση ταύτης ἡ προεδρία τυγχάνει. ἐννόησον γάρ μοι τὴν τάξιν τ(ῆς) διαπλάσεως, (καὶ) λογίζου πρὸ τοῦ ἐμφυσήματος τοῦ δεσπότου. ὅπερ αὐτῷ γέγονεν, εἰς πνοὴν ζωῆς. (καὶ) ἐγένετο εἰς ψυχὴν ζῶσαν. τί ἦν ὁ πλασθείς, ἁπλῆ εἰκὸν ἄψυχος καὶ ἀνενέργητος, (καὶ) εἰς οὐδὲν χρήσιμος. ὥστε τὸ πᾶν καὶ τὸ εἰς τοσαύτην τιμὴν αὐτὸν ἀγαγὼν, ἐκεῖνό ἐστι τὸ παρὰ τοῦ θεοῦ γεγονὸς εἰς αὐ-*

109

Plate from fol. 127^{v}. *De vita in Christo* VI ed. *PG* 150 653 B.6 - 11. *κ(αὶ) πικρῷ τινι μεταμέλῳ τὴν καρδίαν πιέζειν, ὡς οὐκ ὂν βιωτὸν τηλικούτοις κακοῖς τοιοῖσδε περιπεσοῦσι· ταύτην δὲ τὴν λύπην, ἀποτρέπεσθαι δεῖ, θανάτου μ(ητέ)ρα φανερῶς οὖσαν, κ(αὶ) πρὸς ᾅδην ἄγουσαν· τὴν μὲν γ(ὰρ) ἀλαζονεία, κ(αὶ) τὸ πολλοῦ τινος ἡμᾶς αὐτοὺς ἀξιοῦν· τὴν ἑτέραν δὲ, τὸ περὶ τὸν δεσπότην ἐγείρει φίλτρον, κ(αὶ) τὸ σα-*

110

Plate from p. 1025. Homily 11 on Philippians, ed. *PG* 62 268, 45-52. *τρίαν γῆν· ὁ καταναλώσας πᾶσαν τὴν πατρικὴν οὐσίαν καὶ ἐν λιμῷ ζῶν· ἔχομεν οὖν πατρικὴν οὐσίαν καὶ ἡμεῖς, ποίαν δὴ ταύτην; ἀπήλλαξεν ἡμᾶς τῶν ἁμαρτημάτων· ἐχαρίσατο ἡμῖν δύναμιν· ἰσχὺν πρὸς τὴν τῆς ἀρετῆς ἐργασίαν· ἐχαρίσατο ἡμῖν προθυμίαν. ὑπομονήν· ἐχαρίσατο ἡμῖν ἐν τῷ βαπτίσματι πν(εῦμ)α ἅγιον. ἂν ταῦτα καταναλώσωμεν,*

INDEXES

No expressions of uncertainty are admitted in the indexes.

I. MANUSCRIPTS

illustrated (italicized) or mentioned

(A number in brackets, with no other indication, is that under which the manuscript is to be found in a published catalogue.)

Athens, National Library
gr. 263 53
suppl. gr. 641 20
Athos
Dionysiou
8 (3542) 67
Esphigmenou
25 (2038) 25
55-7 (2068-70) 31
58 (2071) *31*
Iveron
46 (4166) 62
353 (4473) 109
archives (Dölger neg. N. 92) 71
(Dölger neg. N. 107) 73
Laura
A 19 (19) 53
B 64 (184) 49
Γ 131 (371) 53
Δ 70 (446) 53
Δ 75 (451) *53*
Protaton
archives (Dölger neg. N. 7) 73
Vatopedi
949 (949) 49
Bologna, Biblioteca universitaria
2302 107
Cambridge, Trinity College
R.9.22 (823) 92
Cambridge (Mass.), Harvard University Library
Typ. 18 60
Dublin, Trinity College
K.3.8 (925) 92
Escorial, Real Biblioteca
Σ II.10 (90) 16
X III.6 (384) *30*
Ω I.16 (517) *56*
Florence, Biblioteca Medicea Laurenziana
11.9 *33*
31.14 60
31.17 101
32.6 60
32.9 73
32.15 73
59.2-3 77
59.32 49
60.3 6, 37
69.2 20
70.3 61
74.7 20
81.7 60
81.11 15
Ashburnham 64 *66*
conv. soppr. 103 100
206 20
Grottaferrata, Badia greca
A γ II 89
A δ VI 68
B α IV *7*
B α XIX 38
B α XX *38*
B β I 38
Δ α II *44*
Δ α IV 68
Δ γ XXXV 68
Heidelberg, Universitätsbibliothek
Palat. gr. 23 98
252 15
398 18
Jerusalem, Patriarchal Library
Holy Cross 43 *51*
Mar Ibrahim 18 (*olim* Anastasis 9) *34*
Patriarchate (Holy Sepulchre) 21 *79*
36 72
54 *75*
524 109
S. Saba 229 *36*
Leiden, Universiteits-Bibliotheek
BPG 60 A 73
Vulcan. 62 I 109
Leningrad
Bibliotcka Akademii Nauk SSSR
76 (*olim* Athos, Simopetra 34 (1302)) 56

Gosudarstvennaya Publichnaya Biblioteka
gr. 219 (71) *12, 13*
311 (448) 56
355 (521) *31*
359 (314) *51*
431 (545) *36*
789 (311) (*olim* Russkogo Archeologicheskogo Obshchestva MS.1) *64*
London, British Museum[1]
Add. 11727 99
11728 *105*
17210 1
22506 *70*
28817 *65*
36751 *62*
Burney 86 50
Harl. 5598 *3*
5600 60
5658 60
5672 60
5694 6, 97
6322 60
6325 60
Madrid, Biblioteca nacional
N. 71 5
Messina, Biblioteca universitaria
gr. 24 *46*
Meteora, Metamorphosis
591 *14*
Milan, Biblioteca Ambrosiana
D. 538 inf. (gr. 1000) *104*
F. 100 sup. (gr. 354) *85*
L. 93 sup. (gr. 490) 15
Biblioteca Trivulziana
873 (Santoro 351) 106
Modena, Archivio di Stato
letteratura greca B[a] 1.I.1 49
Moscow
Gosudarstvennii Istoricheskii Muzei
62 (75 / LXXVI) 62
101 (104 / CV) 53
108 (100 / CI) 53
121 (29 / XXIX) *9*
231 (394 / t.II XXXII fol.) 6, *26*
272 (456 / t.II LII qu.) *90*
380 (162 / CLXIII) 62
381 (15 / XV) 62
Nauchnaya Biblioteka im Gor'kogo Gosudarstvennogo Universiteta 2 *43*

[1] A library's change of name cannot alter the name its manuscripts have borne in the publications of 200 years.

Munich, Bayerische Staatsbibliothek
gr. 451 104
Naples, Biblioteca nazionale
III E. 3 (gr. 325) 60
New York, Metropolitan Museum of Art
Accession no. 24.2.4 *11*
Oxford
Bodleian Library
Auct. D.5.2 (Misc. 9, *SC.* 1864) 92
E.2.7 (Misc. 35, *SC.* 3090) *108*
E.2.12 (Misc. 40, *SC.* 3092) *20*
E.3.7 (Misc. 51[7], *SC.* 2780) *110*
T.2.2 (Misc. 202, *SC.* 20588) *50*
T.4.10 (Misc. 248, *SC.* 20528) *101*
Barocci 50 (*SC.* 50) 98
134 (*SC.* 134) *19*
Canon. Gr. 7 (*SC.* 18460) 60
52 (*SC.* 18505) *109*
93 (*SC.* 18546) *104*
102 (*SC.* 18555) *80*
108 (*SC.* 18561) *60*
E.D. Clarke 15 (*SC.* 18377) *10*
39 (*SC.* 18400) 6, *37*
D'Orville 301 (*SC.* 17179) *6, 18*
Gr. class. e. 96 (*SC.* 36205) 92
Holkham Gr. 6 *63*
85 107
Laud Gr. 13 (*SC.* 713*) 106
18 (*SC.* 704) *100*
55 (*SC.* 719) 88
Rawl.G. 199 (Misc. 178, *SC.* 14916) *52*
Roe 7 (*SC.* 253) *83*
Seld. supra 19 (Seld. 18, *SC.* 3407) 92
29 (Seld. 54, *SC.* 3417) 92
Auct. P.2.2 (printed book) *103*
Christ Church
Gr. 6 *58*, 76
70 *22*
Corpus Christi College
23-4 92
77 92
100 107
106 *92*
108 13
109 92
Lincoln College
Gr. 18 92
35 *84*
New College
68 92
230 107
236 107
240-1 92
254 92
258 *94*
260 107
270 *107*
297 107

Palermo, Museo nazionale
pergamena greca of 1105 86
P. Berol. 10677 *8*
P. Lond. inv. 729 8
1552 *4*
PSI 1302 8
Paris
Bibliothèque nationale
grec 11 *82*
384 *81*
438 *27*
451 6, *97*
510 *5*
529 62, *72*
891 *24*
922 *55*
973 *74*
1085 *54*
1116 *86*
1470 *16*
1476 16
1570 *67*
1741 71, 98
1807 18
1906 88, 96
1908 *88, 96*
1909 88
1919 88
1957 50
1962 18
1983 49
2061 102
2202 107
2352 60
2389 5
2702 77
2713 106
2811 107
2823 107
2854 107
2891 102
2934 16
2935 13
2951 6, 37
Coislin 248 *99*
265 *28*
suppl. gr. 384 98
469^{A} *73*
Musée du Louvre
Ivoires A.53 *87*
Patmos, S. John
33 *17*
138 73
Ravenna, Biblioteca Classense
137.4^{A} (inv. 429) 49
Rome
Biblioteca nazionale
gr. 6 5
Biblioteca Vallicelliana
E. 36 (70) 107
F. 10 (79) 6
Vatican
Barberin. gr. 541 (V.37) 89
Chigi R.V. 29 (23) *59*
Ottob. gr. 422 62
Palat. gr. 13 *47*
173 71
Regin. gr. 63 *69*
Urbin. gr. 35 6, *61*
Vat. gr. 1 13
65 *78*
90 *71*
124 49
204 13
218 97
284 41
342 58, *76*
433 *95*
463 *57*
770 *68*
1070 *89*
1164 49
1221 *35*
1291 *2*
1335 73
1412 *102*
1413-14 102
1594 18
1646 *23*
1650 *29*
1660 *15*
1669 15
1671 15
1973 *32*
1992 40
2002 *21*
2020 39
2021 40
2050 *40*
2138 *39*
2155 *41*
2197 18
2290 *25*
Vat. lat. 1790 *106*
Venice, Biblioteca Marciana
gr. 94 (colloc.no. 427) *42*
101 428 50
200 327 60
201 780 *49*
246 756 18
258 668 18
384 1046 60
388 333 60
395 921 61
406 791 *91*
447 820 37

Venice, Bibl. Marc. (cont.)

gr. 453	**colloc. no.** 821	**57**
454	822	**73**
460	330	***77***
481	863	***93***
538	540	**20**
IV.1	542	**49**
IV.3	1186	**60**

Vienna, Österreichische Nationalbiblio-. thek

Med. gr. 1	***1***
Phil. gr. 314	***98***
Theol. gr. 19	***48***
89	***45***

II. DATES

c. 513/14	**1**
6th cent.	**4**
697	**11**
713	**8**
813-20	**2**
835	**12, 13**
862/3	**14**
879-83	**5**
888	**18**
888-	**6**
888-901	**61**
890	**16**
895	**37**
913/14	**97**
916	**15**
925	**98**
c. 925-45	**71**
932	**26**
941	**17**
947/8	**19**
953	**20**
954	**49**
964/5	**38**
981	**41**
986	**53, 73**
-991	**7**
991	**39**
992	**27**
995	**3**
999/1000	**54**
1008	**62**
1013-21	**72**
1020/1	**33**
1036/7	**28**
1037	**29**
1044/5	**74**
1050-2	**63**
1052	**21**
1056	**75**
1059-60	**55**
1062	**57**
1062/3	**42**
1063	**78**
1065	**99**
1067	**50**
1072	**43**
c. 1077/8	**10**
1079	**79**
1081	**58**
1086	**9**
c. 1087/8	**76**
1104	**22**
1105	**40**
1106	**64**
1107	**30**
1112	**44**
1112/13	**85**
1118	**23**
1118-23	**81**
1122	**51**
1123/4	**86**
1127	**67**
1129	**45**
1131	**46**
1136	**24**
c. 1140-95/6	**77**
1141	**52**
1153	**34**
1154	**35**
1167	**47**
1185	**65**
1186	**82**
1196	**48**
1197	**25**
1259/60	**69**
1278/9	**83**
1279/80	**68**
1288/9	**66**
1291	**89**
1292	**56**
1297	**90**
1299	**93**
1304/5	**70**
1308	**94**
1316	**31**
1357/8	**100**
1362	**104**
1373	**32**

1383 **80**
1394 **59**
1397 **84**

c. 1400-52 **91**
1405 **36**
1408 **87**
1416 **105**
1438 **101**
1441 **88, 96**
1461 **106**
1464-5 **95**
1471 **60**
1491-2 **102**
-1493 **103**
1495 **92**

1523 **107**
1564 **108**

1600 **109**
1610 **110**

III. PLACES

connected with scribes or patrons

Alexandria **8, 109**
Antioch **42, 63**
Aphrodito **4**
Athens **45**
Athos
  Esphigmenou **31**
  Iveron **62**
  Laura **53**
  S. Auxentios **90**
  S. Demetrios or *τοῦ Ποριανήτος* **22**
  Vatopedi **64, 90**
Bovalino (Calabria) **25**
Caesarea (Cappadocia) **26, 97**
Capua **39**
Chalce
  monastery of SS. Akepsima, Ioseph, and Aeithala **19**
Constantinople **1, 5, 6, 18, 20, 37, 55, 61, 77, 92, 95, 100, 108,**
  church of S. Sophia **80, 84**
  monastery *τῶν Ἀβραμιτῶν* **41**
  — of Christ *ἀκατάληπτος* **93**
  — — — *πανοικτίρμων* **58, 76**
  — *τῶν Γαλακρινῶν* **57**
  — *τοῦ παντεπόπτου σωτῆρος* **46**
  — of Prodromos in Petra **24, 67, 105**
  — of Stoudion **12, 13, 15**
  — of Theotokos or S. Aberkios in patriarchate **9**
  — — — *τῆς βεβαίας ἐλπίδος* **84**
  — — — *εὐεργέτης* **50, 99**
  — — — *κεχαριτωμένη* **81**
  — — — *τῶν ὁδηγῶν* **59**
  — — — *ἡ περίβλεπτος* **48**
Crete **45, 47, 60, 107, 108**
Cyprus **70, 110**
Egypt **54, 109**
Fiesole **103**
Florence **88**
Galesion (near Ephesus) **69**
Grottaferrata **44, 66, 68**
Italy, southern **38**
Jerusalem **36, 79**
  church of Anastasis **51**
Kios (Bithynia)
  monastery of S. Anna **14**
Larissa **71**
Mercourion (Calabria)
  monastery of S. Zacharias **7**
Messina
  monastery of S. Salvatore **52, 68**
Milan **106**
Miletos (near)
  monastery of *Ξηροχωράφιον* (Hiera) **74**
Mistra **91, 104**
Nicaea **71**
Nymphaion **82**
Padua **88, 96**
Paris
  monastery of S. Denys **87**
Patrae **6, 18, 37**
Phile **86**
Rametta (Sicily) **38**
Reading (Berkshire) **92**
Reggio Calabria **17, 23, 29, 52**
Rhodes **56**
Rome **60, 107**
Rossano
  monastery of S. Maria del Patire **40, 89**
  metochion of S. Sisinnios **89**
S. Benedetto Ullano (Calabria) **89**
S. Cristina (Calabria) **32**
S. Filippo di Fragala (Sicily) **30**
S. Giovanni a Piro (Campania) **33**
S. Maria delle Cerrate (Puglia) **35**
Sicily **29**
Taverna (Calabria) **21**
Thebes (Egypt) **11**
Thessalonica **77**
Tiberias
  church of Theotokos **34**
Vatican **110**
Zagora **65**

IV. SCRIBES

Alexander bp. of Nicaea (925-45) 71
Anastasios (890) 16
Anthes *ἱερεύς* (1106) 64
Antonios *ἱερεύς* (1373-4) 32
Arethas of Patrae (888) 6
Argyropoulos, Ioannes (1441) 96
Arsenios *μοναχός* (1136) 24
Athanasios *ἀρχιμανδρίτης* (1297) 90
Athanasios *ἱερομόναχος* (1197) 25
Baanes νοτάριος (913/14) 97
Balsamon, Demetrios *διάκονος, σκευοφύλαξ* of S. Sophia (1397) 84
Barlaam μοναχός (1259/60) 69
Bartholomaios *μοναχός* (1105) 40
—— (1131) 46
—— (1141) 52
Basileios *ἀναγνώστης* (1122) 51
Charases, Konstantinos *ῥεφερενδάριος ἱερεὺς καὶ κληρικός* of S. Sophia 80
Choumnos, Stelianos (1358) 100
Chrysoloras, Manuel (1408) 87
Daniel (941) 17
Dionysios *μοναχός* (981) 41
Dioskoros of Aphrodito (6th cent.) 4
Ephraim *μοναχός* (954) 49
Esaias (1020/1) 33
Eustathios abp. of Thessalonica (-1175) 77
Eustathios *μοναχός* (862) 14
Filelfo, Francesco (1461) 106
Gabalas, Leon bp. of Nymphaion (1186) 82
Galaction *μοναχός* (1278/9) 83
Georgios *ἱερεύς* (1153) 34
Gerasimos *μοναχός* (1104) 22
Gregorios *μοναχὸς καὶ πρεσβύτερος* (1067) 50
Gregorios ὑποδιάκονος (888-901) 61
Iakobos (1405) 36
Iakobos metropolitan of Larissa (925-45) 71
Ioannes (1438) 101
Ioannes *γραμματικός* (925) 98
Ioannes *καλλιγράφος* (895) 37
Ioannes *μοναχός* (916) 15
—— (986) 53
—— (1036/7) 28
Ioannes *μοναχὸς καὶ πρεσβύτερος* (1086) 9
Ioasaph (1394) 59
Kalliandres, Symeon, *ἱερεὺς, νομικὸς καὶ πρωτέκδικος* of Rhodes (1292) 56
Kallierges, Zacharias (1523) 107
Kamarenos, Georgios (1167) 47
Konstantinos *πρεσβύτερος* (995) 3
Konstantinos *πρωτοπαπᾶς* (1052) 21
Kosmas *μοναχός* (1185) 65
Kyriakos *μοναχὸς πρεσβύτερος* (991) 39
Kyrillos *μοναχός* (947/8) 19
Laskaris, Ianos (1491-2) 102
Laurentios *μονότροπος καὶ δομέστικος* (1106) 64
Leon *κληρικός* (1000) 54
Leon *νοτάριος* (1056) 75
Leontios *μοναχὸς καὶ πρεσβύτερος* (1107) 30
Loukas abbot of S. Zacharias, Mercourion (991) 7
Makarios *μοναχός* (1279/80) 68
Markos *ἱερομόναχος* (1316) 31
Maximos *ἀρχιδιάκονος* of Alexandria (1600) 109
Michael *μοναχός* (1081) 58
Michael *μοναχός* abbot of monastery of Christ πανοικτίρμων, Constantinople (1087/8) 76
Neilos *ἱερομόναχος* (1112) 44
Neilos *μοναχός* (964/5) 38
Neophytos *ἱεροδιάκονος καὶ μοναχός* (1304/5) 70
Nikolaos (1118) 23
Nikolaos *γραμματικός* (1079) 79
Nikolaos *μοναχός* (835) 12, 13
—— (941) 17
Panerges, Michael βασιλικὸς νοτάριος (1072) 43
Paul (1196) 48
Planudes, Maximos (1301) 93
Plethon, Georgios Gemistos (1400-52) 91
Poliziano, Angelo (1493) 103
Rhosos, Ioannes *ἱερεύς* of Crete (1471) 60
Romanos abbot of monastery τοῦ ἁγίου Βενεδίκτου Οὐλλάνου (1291) 89
Sanctamauras, Ioannes (1610) 110
Scholarios, Georgios (1464-5) 95
Serbopoulos, Ioannes (1495) 92
Skalidros, Basileios νοτάριος (1123/4) 86
Stephanos ἱερομόναχος καὶ σκευοφύλαξ of monastery of Prodromos in Petra, Constantinople (1416) 105
Stephanos *κληρικός* (888) 18
Strozzi, Palla (1441) 88
Stylianos *διάκονος* (932) 26
Symeon *ἱερομόναχος* (1288/9) 66
Symeon *μοναχός* (1062) 57
Symeon *νοτάριος* (1154) 35
Tarsites, Konstantinos of Athens (1129) 45
Theodoros *κληρικός* (1037) 29
— *ὕπατος καὶ βασιλικὸς νοτάριος* (1063) 78
Theodosios *μοναχός* (1065) 99
Theoktistos (1127) 67
Theophanes *μοναχός* (1020) 93
— — *καὶ ἱερεύς* (1008) 62
Theophylactos *κουβουκλείσιος καὶ δομέστικος* (1050-52) 63
Tourrianos, Nikolaos (1564) 108
Triklinios, Demetrios (1308) 94
Tzykandyles, Manuel (1362) 104

V. CONTENTS

Ammonius of Egypt 33
Anastasius of Sinai 54
Anonyma, miscellanea
- ascetica 22, 33
- hagiographica 33
- philosophica 98
- polemica 26
- theologica 45, 55

Anthology 93
Aphthonius 94
Apophthegmata patrum 85
Apostolic fathers 75
Aristotle 49, 61, 88
Astronomical tables 2
Basil 9, 20, 40, 46, 60
Basilicorum synopsis 47
Bible
- Psalms 10, 76, 89
- Wisdom books 82
- Prophetologion 68
- Gospels 13, 21, 25, 70
- Gospel lectionary 3, 34, 39, 62, 65
- Acts and Epistles 29, 43, 59
- Epistle to Hebrews 32, 51
- Apocalypse 30

Cabasilas, Nicolas 109
Canon *παρακλητικός* 89
Chrysoloras, Manuel 87
Chrysostom 14, 41, 42, 45, 53, 108, 110
Clement of Alexandria 97
Climacus 19, 28, 30, 79
Creeds 63, 76
Cyril of Alexandria 99
Damascus, John of 86
Didache 75
ps.-Dionysius the Areopagite 27, 87
Dioscorides 1
Dioskoros of Aphrodito 4
Dorotheus abbas 38
Euclid 6, 18
Euripides 101
Eustathius of Thessalonica 77
Eustratius of Nicaea 92
Euthymius Zigabenus 83
Filelfo, Francesco 106
Firman of dux Thebaidos 11
Gregory of Nazianzus 5, 17, 57, 58, 72
Hermogenes 94
Hierocles 98
Isocrates 78
Kontakarion 66
Lascaris, Janus 102
Liturgy of S. Chrysostom 32
Lucian 71
ps.-Macarius the Egyptian 74
Maximus confessor 7, 23
Menaion 31, 36, 44, 67, 69
Menologion 15, 16
Nicephorus Ouranus 52
Nonnus abbas 57, 73
Obits of Stoudion abbots 12
Oppian 1
Palladius 22
Paschal letter 8
Pentekostarion 59, 80
Plato 37
Pletho 91
Plutarch 104
Polybius 105
Proclus 100
Scholarius, Georgius 95
Simplicius 88, 96
Sophocles 103
Sticherarion 64
Stobaeus 107
Synodikon 63
Theodore of Studium 24
Theodoret 50
Theophylact 35, 48, 56
Timotheus Constantinopolitanus 26
Typikon of monastery 51, 81, 84, 90